# DOS ¦ UNIX SYSTEMS
# becoming a super user

MARTIN D. SEYER
WILLIAM J. MILLS

PRENTICE-HALL, Englewood Cliffs, New Jersey 07632

*Library of Congress Cataloging-in-Publication Data*

Seyer, Martin D.
  DOS/UNIX systems.

  Includes index.
  1. MS-DOS (Computer operating system) 2. UNIX
(Computer operating system)  I. Mills, William J.
(William Joseph), 1949–      II. Title.
QA76.76.0′63S49 1986      055.4′46      85-25725
ISBN  0-13-218645-4

Editorial/production supervision: LISA SCHULZ
Cover design: LUNDGREN GRAPHICS, LTD.
Manufacturing buyer: GORDON OSBOURNE

© 1986 by Prentice-Hall
A Division of Simon & Schuster, Inc.
Englewood Cliffs, New Jersey 07632

MS-DOS is a trademark of Microsoft.
UNIX™ is a trademark of AT&T Technologies.

Martin D. Seyer, Leo J. Scanlon, *The AT&T PC 6300 Made Easy,* © 1985, pp. 128, 130–131.
Reprinted by permission of Prentice-Hall, Englewood Cliffs, N.J.

Martin D. Seyer, *The IBM PC/XT: Making the Right Connections,* © 1985, pp. 180, 253–254,
256–267, 270–275. Reprinted by permission of Prentice-Hall, Englewood Cliffs, N.J.

The authors and publisher of this book have used their best efforts in preparing this
book. These efforts include the development, research, and testing of the theories
and programs to determine their effectiveness. The author and publisher make no
warranty of any kind, expressed or implied, with regard to these programs or the
documentation contained in this book. The author and publisher shall not be liable
in any event for incidental or consequential damages in connection with, or arising
out of, the furnishing, performance or use of these programs.

Printed in the United States of America

10  9  8  7  6  5  4  3  2  1


ISBN  0-13-218645-4  025


PRENTICE-HALL INTERNATIONAL (UK) LIMITED, *London*
PRENTICE-HALL OF AUSTRALIA PTY. LIMITED, *Sydney*
EDITORA PRENTICE-HALL DO BRASIL, LTDA., *Rio de Janeiro*
PRENTICE-HALL CANADA INC., *Toronto*
PRENTICE-HALL HISPANOAMERICANA, S.A., *Mexico*
PRENTICE-HALL OF INDIA PRIVATE LIMIED, *New Delhi*
PRENTICE-HALL OF JAPAN, INC., *Tokyo*
PRENTICE-HALL OF SOUTHEAST ASIA PTE. LTD., *Singapore*
WHITEHALL BOOKS LIMITED, *Wellington, New Zealand*

# contents

# foreword

There are over 150,000 UNIX-based computers in the hands of endusers today, creating an overwhelming need for information about the UNIX operating system. As personal computer users become more sophisticated, increasing power is required for their applications. *DOS:UNIX Systems becoming a super user* provides the personal computer, MS-DOS user a smooth bridge to the powerful UNIX system.

Microcomputer users are looking for more powerful and flexible systems. Having successfully conquered the mysteries of MS-DOS, users are ready for more; in looking around the computer industry for possible candidates for expansion, we see expensive minicomputers, dedicated word processing equipment, but little that addresses the need for multiuser and multitasking computer power on a desk. The efforts of many universities, computer vendors, and AT&T have introduced large numbers of users to the UNIX operating system. Today, over 150,000 UNIX systems are in use, from micro to mainframe. A wide range of UNIX computer products and application software are available today, and more is on the way. AT&T's continuing dedication to improve UNIX has increased personal computer users' interest in UNIX.

MS-DOS users who turn to UNIX-based departmental supermicro and minicomputers for more complex applications receive the best of both worlds. By using MS-DOS based PCs for simple applications and accessing UNIX systems for multiuser applications, databases, and complex projects, users bridge the gap from the PC to the departmental computer. The need for departmental computing is growing rapidly, and is well served by UNIX products.

This book adds substantially to the information that personal computer users need to use UNIX. Its practical focus and down-to-earth language make it an ideal tool for the beginning UNIX user, while the more sophisticated UNIX user will find it informative as well. Welcome to the world of UNIX computing. May you have many happy logins!

*Jean L. Yates*
*Vice President*
*International Data Corporation*
*Palo Alto, CA*

# preface

A user of a computer system has a basic operational knowledge of the hardware and software that comprise his/her system. The typical user has an applications view of the system. They, for example, know how to load and run LOTUS® 1-2-3® or Microsoft's Multiplan™. The user has a reasonable knowledge of the operating system and its command set. His/her need to know is based solely on the problem at hand, which in the MS-DOS single-user environment is a perfectly acceptable approach. However, as the microcomputer industry moves toward small distributed multi-user UNIX-based machines, the typical DOS user will develop a need to enhance his/her understanding of the operating system environment.

Computer vendors will attempt to ease transitional pain by creating friendly front-end interfaces that shield the user from the operating system. This approach is certainly a benefit to the end user and will probably solve most problems, but regretfully will not solve all.

A super user is an individual who takes advantage of the features the system provides to accomplish things in a "super easy" way. A super user knows about print spoolers, RAM buffers, I/O redirection, pipes, filters; but more important than understanding, he/she uses these features to make his/her job easier.

While DOS has some 75 commands, UNIX has well over 250. It takes time to learn which commands are commonplace and which are rarely used. The following chapters provide a path for you—the DOS user—to bridge your existing knowledge over the world of UNIX. For those UNIX users requiring knowledge of MS-DOS environments, the reverse is provided. This approach will allow you to prepare for the future while maximizing the system you use every day.

The bridge between DOS and UNIX system is fast becoming a reality. Recent announcements from AT&T have made significant inroad in this area. The PC 6300 PLUS is a new PC product that allows DOS to run as task under UNIX System V. We cover the PC 6300 PLUS in Appendix K.

The DOS-73 System is an add-on board for the AT&T UNIX PC that allows DOS to run on a window to UNIX System V. We cover the DOS-73 System in Appendix L.

The opinions expressed in this text are those of the authors, based on facts available at time of printing, not those of AT&T Information System, with which we are both affiliated.

*Martin D. Seyer*
*William J. Mills*

# introduction

**1**

## EVOLUTION OF MS-DOS

MS-DOS is the operating system offered by Microsoft of Bellevue, Washington. Bill Gates formed the company several years ago to meet the needs of the up-and-coming personal computer hardware vendors.

The birth of MS-DOS stemmed from a requirement of a company, Seattle Computer Products, who designed and built 8086-based personal computer products. SCP had a desire to create an operating system that went beyond the available capabilities of CP/M, the then dominant operating system for personal computers. The system was to be fine tuned for the 808X series of microprocessors. The core operating system was developed by SCP. Microsoft acquired the rights to the operating system, enhanced it, and sold rights of use to IBM for their soon-to-be announced IBM Personal Computer. Originally occupying only 12,000 bytes of memory, MS-DOS or PC-DOS version 1 became an industry standard for personal computers. This environment was easy for CP/M software houses to port their existing applications.

Version 1 of the operating system was available with every personal computer sold, of which there were many. Because of the PC's widespread use, the operating system could not help but become the standard. However, application software developers needed certain abilities beyond those that the current operating system offered. The ability to add device drivers for different add-on hardware devices was absent. Furthermore, hard disk technology and price/performance were at the point that they could be cost justified in a personal computer. Enter MS-DOS 2.X. MS-DOS 2.0 was an enhanced version offering these two capabilities. Now hardware developers could customize the environment to capitalize on their hardware features through the use of installable device drivers. IBM introduced the XT model of the personal computer which supported 2.0. It was this version of operating system that first began resembling the UNIX operating system as we know it today.

With the rapid growth and deployment of personal computers, the need to share information has become an opportunity for many hardware and software vendors. As multiple computers were installed in a building, a convenient method of sharing data had to be developed. Hand carrying floppies simply wouldn't suffice. Many vendors began offering communication capabilities for uploading and downloading of files. Networks began appearing, allowing computers to access files not residing on the computer's own disk system. These local area networks offered resource optimization through file servers and printer servers. No longer was it necessary to have hard disks and printers with every computer. However, MS-DOS 2.X did not offer a network interface to allow for standardization of these networks and software. Enter MS-DOS 3.X. The latest version of Microsoft's operating system was developed to allow personal computer networking. It retained the UNIX-system features of the earlier version.

Although the goal may not be to force MS-DOS and UNIX systems to merge, the years of evolving have produced a product with similar features. Chapter 7 discusses how close these operating systems actually are. Why UNIX operating system? Why the convergence? The next sections will highlight why this is occurring.

## EVOLUTION OF UNIX

UNIX operating system was developed by AT&T Bell Labs and is now emerging as the premier operating system of the 1980s. It is available for systems ranging from micros to mainframes. The office automation industry seems to have adopted the UNIX system as the base operating system for networked work stations and information-based systems. IBM is using it in some of its products; in fact, the IBM PC/AT will run XENIX, a version of the UNIX system, as its multi-user-based operating system. What makes it so popular? The UNIX operating system has become a major force in the computer industry for some very important reasons: UNIX software is one of the first operating systems to allow software developers to write their code without fear of machine dependence. Once written, a program can be moved (ported) to another computer with a minimum of effort. This is possible because it is mostly written in a high-level language called C. Since C language is portable across many different systems, the operating system can be made available with a minimum of effort. Furthermore, most application software can be moved from UNIX machine to UNIX machine without any major changes in code. These benefit both the software developer and the end user. The developer can now offer nis product on many different systems with minimal effort. This results in reduced programming and conversion costs. The end user, on the other hand, can purchase a UNIX-based application without fear of hardware obsolescence.

In addition, because the UNIX operating system was developed by programmers for programmers, it provides an environment conducive to software development. Many of the utilities that programmers need to write code have already been included. The power is in its primary philosophy that a collection of utilities each designed to do one thing very well will provide a flexible yet powerful environment for both the programmer and the end user. This philosophy has contributed to the concepts of "tools" and "workbenches" as programmer aids.

The UNIX system, just as any operating system, controls the operation of the computer it is running on. The operating system serves a role as a "resource manager," allocating disk drives, tapes, files, printers, and memory as needed to the users it serves. The user therefore need not be concerned with many of the low-level functions of the computer. While all operating systems provide these basic functions, some have a very rigid, limited set of rules that a programmer must know and understand to control the execution of his/her program. Because it is both powerful and flexible, the UNIX system can be thought of as an operating system that does not get in the way. The system does not require you to know all about the specific hardware of the computer, yet the power to access the low-level system calls is available to the more experienced user.

Despite these advantages, the UNIX environment is only now becoming popular, some 15 years after it was first developed at AT&T Bell Laboratories. This is quite unusual in an industry where last year's products are considered potential museum pieces. Why? Has AT&T kept it a secret all these years? Or does the popularity have ties to the recent breakup of the Bell System? Perhaps we may learn the answers to these questions by examining the history of the development of the UNIX system.

## HISTORY

The development of the UNIX operating system is attributed to Ken Thompson, Dennis Ritchie, and their colleagues at Bell Laboratories. In 1968 and 1969 Thompson and Ritchie worked on a project called MULTICS. In addition to AT&T, this joint development project included MIT and General Electric. Development did not move along as expected; as a result, Bell Labs withdrew from the project. Bell Labs' management, still quite uneasy about the demise of the MULTICS project, was not enthusiastic about searching for another operating system. The Bell Labs development community, on the other hand, never stopped searching for an operating system that would provide an environment for programmers and also a system around which they could form a fellowship of other programmers.

Meanwhile, Thompson and Ritchie were growing tired of a version of a popular game they played called Space Travel. The version they were currently using was developed under an operating system called GECOS and performed poorly. It was Thompson and Ritchie's desire to find a better operating system under which to run this game that led to the early development of the ''new'' operating system.

Thompson and Ritchie first attempted to write their new version of Space Travel on a Digital Equipment Corp PDP-7 computer. The PDP-7, however, allowed only one user to use the system at a time, and most functions were crude and rudimentary. During the next rewrite the idea for a command interpreter (shell) was first conceived. In early 1970 Brian Kernighan, a fellow programmer, coined the name UNIX, a takeoff on the name MULTICS.

DEC had just introduced a new machine, the PDP-11, and Thompson and Ritchie thought that it would be a better machine on which to develop and run UNIX code. Still under strict orders not to write an operating system, they decided to build a text-processing system to disguise the UNIX project. The text-processing system was a success, and the patent department became the first users of the UNIX system.

Work continued throughout the early 1970s and gathered a following within Bell Labs. The First Edition system was documented in a manual authored by Thompson and Ritchie in November 1971.

This paper described all the major ideas found in today's version with the exception of pipes. In 1972 the Second Edition appeared; it included pipes and filters. In 1973 the kernel and the input/output system were written in C language, which was developed at Bell Labs for use in the UNIX text-processing project. In 1975 the Sixth Edition became the first commercially available version of the UNIX system. For a nominal fee many universities obtained copies for educational use.

Work continued, and in 1979 the Seventh Edition UNIX was released for general use. The year 1980 saw acceptance by other computer vendors, and it began to appear on 16-bit microcomputers. In addition, the first port to a mainframe was completed in early 1981. AT&T introduced UNIX System III in late 1980. This act became the first step in recognizing the UNIX system as a product.

At the January 1983 Unicom, System V was announced; AT&T for the first time provided support to UNIX licensees. This began AT&T's endeavor to promote UNIX System V as the standard for the UNIX operating system and UNIXlike operating systems.

Since its inception it has had the interest of the programming community and has gained quite a following. Many of the universities that received UNIX source for an extremely modest fee in the mid 1970s were producing ardent advocates of the UNIX system. It has been estimated that some 1300 universities use some version in their computer science programs. The UNIX operating system has grown in leaps and bounds, and today it runs on systems from micros to mainframes. Even IBM runs a version on its PC.

## AT&T UNIX Releases

| Year | Internal Release | External Release |
|------|------------------|------------------|
| 1972 | Version 2 | |
| 1973 | Version 3 | |
| | Version 4 | UNIX V4 |
| 1974 | Version 5 | |
| 1975 | Version 6 | UNIX V6 |
| 1977 | Version 7 | UNIX V7 |
| 1980 | Release 3.0 | UNIX System III |
| 1981 | Release 4.0 | |
| 1982 | Release 5.0 | |
| 1983 | | UNIX System V |
| 1984 | | UNIX V release 2 UNIX System V |
| | (Release 2.0) | |

For their outstanding efforts, Thompson and Ritchie received the 1982 Electronics Achievement Award, the first time the award had been presented to members of the software community. Thompson and Ritchie were again recognized in 1983 when they received the Association for Computing Machinery Turing Award and the new Software System Award for their development of generic operating systems theory and specifically the UNIX operating system.

## AT&T AND COMPUTERS

AT&T is a very large user of computers; the company probably possesses one of every popular computer made, from mainframe to micro. AT&T first developed computers to be used in the telecommunications network. Various special-purpose computers, such as the  5ESS and the Dimension PBX, were developed to switch and manage calls. As an outgrowth and in response to demand for faster computers, the 3B line of computers was born. These computers were utilized in the switching network and internal office automation projects. Prevented from selling computers for general use, AT&T's primary focus remained telephony.

As a result of deregulation and the breakup of the Bell System, AT&T began to offer general-purpose computers through its Information Systems Division in 1984. Upon its entrance into the computer industry, AT&T signed joint ventures with companies such as Olivetti and Convergent Technologies for the primary purpose of developing new computers for the low end of its line. The result of these ventures produced the AT&T PC 6300 and the AT&T UNIX PC model 7300, respectively. AT&T also introduced an internally developed new super-micro called the 3B2 computer. The 3B2, running UNIX System V, employed new technology and began to set the pace for AT&T to produce other UNIX-based products.

In 1984 AT&T Information Systems announced a personal computer, the PC 6300, an IBM-compatible micro made by Olivetti. Along with the announcement of the 3B2, 3B5, and 3B20 computers, AT&T announced a new release of UNIX System V, coined "UNIX System V Release 2." This new release included many improvements over its predecessor, Release 1.

AT&T's strategy to promote its computers began to unfold as it courted many software vendors to produce and port code to UNIX System V. Numerous contracts were signed with companies such as Microsoft, Ashton-Tate, Ryan McFarland, Locus Computing, Handle Corporation, and others for the purpose of producing application software for UNIX. An extensive advertising campaign began to promote UNIX System V as a standard. AT&T began with System V to include many of the features of the Berkeley releases, such as shared memory, vi editor, more commands, termcap database, flex filenames, and so on. Thus, AT&T has worked very hard to include in System V features that users have deemed desirable.


## FOCUS OF THIS BOOK

The focus of this book is on the features and functions of both DOS and UNIX operating systems. Our examples will feature the IBM PC/XT, AT&T PC 6300, UNIX PC Model 7300, and the 3B2 computers. We will explore the UNIX system from the DOS user's view and get a preview of things to come.

Our approach is a practical "how to" view of each product, with the objective to allowing you to maximize the features that each has to offer. In addition, we include tips, shortcuts, and special techniques that we have learned through our work at AT&T and elsewhere.

Many of the issues discussed and examples can be applied to other MS-DOS/UNIX products. We urge the reader to scan the appendices, as we feel that they contain information not readily available elsewhere.


## THE MERGER OF DOS AND UNIX
## OPERATING SYSTEMS

In late January 1985, at UNIFORUM in Dallas, AT&T and Microsoft announced that future releases of MS-DOS will be feature/function compatible with UNIX System V. This is a major step in the eventual convergence of MS-DOS and UNIX systems.

MS-DOS, the most popular operating system running on 16-bit micros, retains its popularity for one reason: its association with the market leader, IBM. Users did not choose MS-DOS/PC-DOS; it was supplied with the system, and until recently there weren't many alternatives. The fundamental design behind MS-DOS/ PC-DOS was a single-user operating system that exploited the power of the IBM PC. It remained, therefore, fairly easy to use but lacked the power of larger full-scale operating systems. In the early days of 1982 memory was a cherished commodity, with the average system consisting of 64K. The tradeoff of power versus economy seemed a wise decision.

Since 1982 there have been some significant changes: Memory is relatively inexpensive, and today most systems have a minimum of 256K; the demand for more functions, such as windows, has been limited somewhat by the design of MS-DOS; multitasking and multiprocessing capability is becoming necessary to allow multiple active windows; small, local area networks with disk servers and communications servers are starting to appear. The issue at hand, then, is how to revamp DOS, a single-user operating system, to provide more functions while protecting the plethora of existing software available for the PC.

The UNIX operating system, on the other hand, has a reputation for being programmer friendly, which does not necessarily equal to user friendly. Remember it was developed for one purpose: to be a hospitable environment for programmers who would know how to exploit its power and avoid its weaknesses. Therefore the system became known as "user hostile." While MS-DOS users had thousands of application programs to choose from, the UNIX community until recently had a somewhat more limited set to choose from. The problem: how to become more user friendly and stimulate the availability of application software for UNIX systems. In addition, there must be a clear standard for UNIX systems.

As MS-DOS becomes more powerful and the UNIX system becomes more user friendly, their paths are destined to collide. Software developers are becoming more interested due to its machine independence. Many are writing their code in the C language so that it does not tie them into one machine's architecture. Many of the application programs currently running under MS-DOS are now running under UNIX System V. Examples of this are Multiplan, Microsoft Word, and dBASE III.

Yet in all this unsettling activity one question remains unanswered: What about you and me, the end users? Many of us who own IBM PCs or their clones feel comfortable with MS-DOS and are reluctant to buy any system that does not offer both power and simplicity. Will we have to choose MS-DOS or XENIX for the IBM PC/AT? Will we run both? How are we going to learn UNIX commands, which seem much more complicated and prone to wizardry, in order to perform some tasks? Can it be made to appear more DOSlike? Will DOS continue to be more UNIXlike? Will we be able to have both available on a single desk-top machine that is within the financial reach of most users?

MS-DOS is not going to go away, and although the UNIX operating system is coming on fast, there will be a time when peaceful coexistence will reign and you will be able to master both environments.

# 2

# planning your system

If you have ever purchased a computer, you know that the analysis done before the actual purchase is well worth the effort. If you have never purchased a computer, take heed: Every ounce of planning is worth ten pounds of complaining. Today, the potential buyer is faced with the problem of choosing a system from the myriad of ever-changing products and manufacturers that exist in the current marketplace. How do you know if you have made the "right" decision? The bottom line is that if the computer you buy does exactly what you want, then you have made a wise decision.

What questions should I ask the salesman? How can I separate reality from sales hype? How can I be sure the computer will provide enough power for my application or that the programs I need will actually run on the system? What about the peripherals, such as printers and modems? Will they work correctly? How about the cabling required to connect these devices? Does the salesman really know what he/she is talking about? What growth can be supported by the system? Is service readily available? Will the manufacturer still be in business a year from now? What the heck does "state of the art" have to do with this anyway?

These are all difficult questions that many of us who own computers have pondered before making our purchase decision. Unfortunately, some of us know a lot more now than we did before taking that big step. If you have not purchased your first system or are planning to purchase a new system, this is the chapter for you. In this chapter we will learn how to develop a step-by-step approach to apply our buying criteria and make a sound purchase decision.

Many of us are interested in purchasing single-user systems, while others may be considering multi-user systems. The multi-user system adds levels of complexity far beyond the single-user environment, so we will deal with these two areas separately.

## PLANNING YOUR SINGLE-USER SYSTEM

The single-user computer industry is dominated by MS-DOS-based machines offering various levels of compatibility and additional built-in features and functions. The rule here is to return to basics. Don't be misguided by the packaged software, the promise of future add-on boards or upgrades. Let's view the system in its basic system components.

### Microprocessor

What type is it? The popular IBM PC uses an INTEL 8088 microprocessor; most compatibles use the same INTEL 8088 or a sister from the 80XX family. The AT&T PC 6300 uses the 8086 microprocessor, which is code compatible with the 8088 chip but runs almost twice as fast. Type is important because it may affect compatibility.

Speed is important because it affects the amount of time it will take to perform a function. If you were to recalculate a 100-by-100-cell spreadsheet on the AT&T PC 6300, you would find that it is 40 to 50 percent faster than the IBM PC because of its increased speed. The 8088 in the IBM runs at 4.77 MHz and the 8086 in the AT&T PC 6300 runs at 8 MHz. Most IBM PC look-alikes will run either the 8088 or the 8086, and some will differ in the speed that they are running. Refer to the tech specs for the product for this information.

### Memory

How much memory can the system support? Most IBM compatibles will allow the ability to address the full 640K bytes of memory just as the IBM PC does. How is the memory supplied? How much memory is included on the motherboard? Is it removable? How is additional memory added? Can you add the memory yourself? Are the chips readily available? Can the additional memory be used to emulate a floppy disk (RAM disk)? In what increment is the memory supplied—16K, 32K, and so on? How fast is the memory access time?

### Peripheral Compatibility

Quite often an unsuspecting user buys a computer and a printer, only to find that they do not work together. Upon returning to the store, the buyer is surprised to find that the salesman not only does not know how to remedy the problem, but quite often refuses to get involved, leaving the buyer to resolve the problems with the manufacturers of the equipment. The frustration of this situation can only be appreciated through experience. In order to avoid this unpleasant situation we can employ a little prevention.

Test the computer with the peripherals you wish to purchase before you leave the store. This simple rule will help uncover many future problems. If you are buying a printer, test the ability to print from your application, such as Lotus 1-2-3 or WordStar; also test the SHIFT PRTSC function to dump the screen contents to the printer. What about the cable? Will it be supplied? Is it specially made or is it a standard cable? Test the printer at various speeds. Does the print look acceptable? Test the graphics print if it supports such a feature. If you are purchasing a modem, try a test call to a bulletin board or another computer. Can you transmit properly? Try a file transfer to/from the target system. Can the modem be put in any slot?

If you intend to connect more than one RS232C device, such as a modem and a serial printer or two serial printers, you must check to see if the address of the device can be optioned for COM1: or COM 2:. If not, some devices could occupy the same address and be mutually exclusive. You should check with the vendor to see if either address can be used and that there is an option switch or software means of performing this change.

### Applications Compatibility

Will the programs that you intend to use run on the system? A strong suggestion here—Try it before you buy it! Run the program(s) in the store on the intended system. Does it operate properly? Can you perform the functions in the tutorial without the system hanging? Can you print to the printer? Are drivers included in the software for the printer you have chosen? If you don't know or the salesman doesn't know, have him call the software company. How much memory does it take? Is it more or less than the documentation states? Will the application program read the system clock/calendar if it is included? If you are buying a system with a hard disk, can the programs be loaded and run from the hard disk?

### Growth

How many expansion slots are provided? Are they full slots or are some ''short'' slots that will not receive a full-length add-on board? Can the system power supply support a full complement of add-on boards? Can you add on an expansion box? What about adding on another vendor's external hard disk? If you add graphics capability, will it require another board? Does the system include an RS232C port and a parallel port or will these require add-on boards? Is a clock/calendar provided?

# PLANNING YOUR MULTI-USER SYSTEM

Planning a multi-user system requires the same thoughtful approach as is needed to plan and buy a single-user system. The complexity of the multi-user configuration adds a few additional wrinkles to the process.

The UNIX operating system is beginning to dominate the multi-user environment. Along with its derivatives and look-alikes, the UNIX operating system presents a world of new terminology and acronyms that are unfamiliar to the DOS user. In this section we will uncover the important issues and disclose a commonsense approach to buying a multi-user UNIX-based system.

As the name multi-user suggests, more than one user can use the system at any time. Since this is probably why you purchased it in the first place, you should be aware that this environment is totally different from the single-user configuration. The system must share its resources among users on the system; therefore, performance is of paramount concern when buying a multi-user system. If the users on the system are not getting the performance they expect, you might as well have purchased multiple single-user machines rather than be the recipient of their criticism.

### Microprocessor

What is its size? Microprocessors are rated by their bus width in bits. This is sometimes expressed as 16/32 or 32/32, which equates to the size of the *data bus* and *address bus*. The size of the data bus determines how much data can be handled in a single operation. Thus, a 32/32 microprocessor can handle twice as much data as a 16/32-bit processor.

The size of the address bus determines how much memory, real or virtual, can be addressed by the processor. The smaller the bus, the less memory it can handle. For example, the WE32000 microprocessor used in the AT&T 3B2 computer is a "full" 32-bit processor, thus it is a 32/32-bit configuration. The address bus being 32 bits wide can address $2^{32}$ bytes of memory or just over 4 million bytes of memory.

How fast is it? This measurement can be expressed many ways. One measurement is its clock rate in MHz (megahertz). This is the raw rating of how fast the microprocessor can operate. Generally, the higher the clock rate, the better the performance. Another measurement is given in MIPS, which stands for Million Instructions Per Second. This is less important and can usually not be substantiated by the vendor, since there is no standard way to perform this measurement.

### Memory

Memory is even more important in a multi-user system than in a single-user system, because it's one of the most precious resources managed by the operating system. The overall performance of the system can sometimes depend on the amount of available memory and how memory is managed by the system. Multi-user multitasking systems allow multiple applications to be resident in memory simultaneously; the microprocessor gives each a slice of time to run. This time is usually measured in microseconds (thousandths of a second), creating the illusion that the applications are running at the same time.

As a result of this "time slice," allocation programs or portions of programs can be swapped in and out of memory to make room for other programs needing time to run. For example, in a four-user system it is possible to have one user running Multiplan, another dBase III, a third compiling a C program, and a fourth sending or receiving electronic mail. As a general rule, there are two memory-related issues that will affect the overall performance the users will receive. First is the amount of memory available. The rule here is "The more the better." Because some portion of the operating system is always resident in memory, the amount of available memory is the amount of physical memory minus the operating system overhead. In some systems the maximum size of any program is determined by the amount of available memory; therefore, purchase the most memory you can afford.

The second factor that affects performance is how memory is managed by the system. Most UNIX-based systems employ one of the following two methods of memory management.

## Swapping

The name *swapping* implies that programs/processes are interchanged to allow them to execute. In practical terms, a process or program is loaded into memory from secondary storage, usually hard disk, and is given some time to execute. At or about the same time, other programs can be read into memory. When the first program, program A, has completed its allotted time and there is not enough internal memory to store the entire program, it is written back out to the hard disk. Program B is then allowed some time to run and then may be written out to disk. Program A can then be read into memory and allotted a second time slot to run. This entire process is known as swapping. Swapping does impose some limitations. First, the largest program you are able to run is determined by the size of available memory. For example, if the total physical memory is two megabytes and the operating system consumed one megabyte, the largest program you could run is one megabyte. This could become a serious limitation if you are running or plan to run very large programs. Second, because the entire program must be swapped out to hard disk, and I/O can be a slow process, overall performance can be negatively affected.

## Demand Paging

An alternative to swapping is *paging*. With paging, programs are broken up into small pieces, usually one kbyte, called pages. The analogy to the literary world is appropriate if we can consider the program to be the entire book and portions of the program to be the pages. The paging system then allows portions of the program to be swapped in and out. This process is called paging. A system that keeps track of currently active pages and swaps out the inactive pages is called a *demand paged* system.

Paging systems allow for the use of *virtual memory*. Virtual memory provides the user with the illusion that there is more internal memory than is actually present. In order to create this illusion, portions of the hard disk are used as memory. This area on the hard disk plus the actual internal memory is known as the virtual address space. For example, the AT&T UNIX PC can have as little as 512 kbytes, but allows a virtual memory space of four megabytes. Thus, 3.5 megabytes are provided on the hard disk for paging programs in/out.

Paging does have some limitations. First, it is an entirely more complex system than swapping. As a result, the system overhead is increased. More tables have to be kept as to the status and location of the active and inactive pages. When a page is moved from real memory to disk memory, this is known as a "page fault"; the overhead required to keep track of these faults is quite complex. The paging system overhead increases with the number of page faults and can actually reach a point where all that the system is doing is paging. This condition is known as *thrashing*. When thrashing occurs, the system effectively is so caught up in page allocation and deallocation that it ceases to provide decent response time or can shut down altogether. Second, the system normally requires additional hardware to assist in overall page management; this can translate into increased cost.

## Paging versus Swapping

Which is best? The answer to this really depends on the applications that will be running on the system and the amount of memory available. If a large amount of memory is available and the size of the typical program is relatively small, then swapping in some cases could provide superior results. If, on the other hand, you intend to run very large programs with a limited memory space, demand paging is preferred. The following table summarizes the benefits and limitations of both techniques.

| Issue | Swapping | Paging |
|---|---|---|
| able to execute larger programs than you have internal memory | | X |
| less overhead | X | |
| more complicated hardware | | X |
| less efficient use of memory | X | |

## I/O Ports

Another factor to consider before purchasing a multi-user system is the number of I/O ports the system can support. This number should be broken down by type of port—RS-232C or parallel, for example—and also by practical limitations.

Even though a system can physically support 18 RS-232C ports does not necessarily mean that if all 18 ports were active they would receive adequate response time. Most vendors can provide the number of practical users a system can support for a much application mix. This number is usually much lower than the physical ports supported.

You should also consider the speed at which the port is able to run in bits per second (bps). Most RS-232C ports should be able to run at up to 9600 bps as a minimum. Do the ports conform to existing standards? Are cables generally available? One place to check for this is the Black Box Corporation Catalog, 412-746-5500. This source provides many cables for the mini and micro market.

Incremental cost per user is another consideration. Some systems allow ports to be added in multiples of some number. For example, the AT&T 3B2 computer has the ability to support four I/O cards, each having four RS 232C ports and a centronics parallel interface. Thus, the incremental cost would be the price of the I/O card divided by four.

## Terminal Support

The UNIX system provides two types of utilities to support terminals. One utility is called termcap and was supplied with System V Release 1. The termcap utility contained a list of all the terminal control sequences for approximately 200-plus terminals. This utility was originally developed by the people at the University of California at Berkeley who produce versions called 4.1 BSD and 4.2 BSD (the BSD suffix means Berkeley Software Distribution).

Another utility developed at Berkeley is called curses/terminfo. Curses is a terminal handler and terminfo is a database containing terminal specifics.

So what? Well, some applications software is dependent on termcap and others on curses/terminfo in order to operate properly. The ideal solution would be to have both. That is exactly what is provided with UNIX System V Release 2. If a system does not come with both utilities you may be able to port the other from another system. Again, check with the vendor of the applications software to find out the dependencies on either utility.

## Floating-Point Operation

Floating-point numbers are numbers that represent digits after a decimal point. For example, 999,988. 4444445 is a floating-point number. All systems support floating point; the issue is how—software or hardware. The routines to handle and optimize floating-point operation can be implemented either way. The use of additional hardware such as coprocessors or accelerator units can improve performance to ten times that of a comparable software implementation. If your applications require heavy statistical or mathematical manipulation, then hardware floating point could be required.

## Backup

All current multi-user systems include a hard disk or disks. Some require the user to back up the contents of the hard disk using floppy diskettes. This can be quite a task. For example, to back up the IBM PC/XT can take as many as 30 floppy disks. The time to perform the backup then can be so objectionable that the process is not performed regularly. Thus, in the event of a crash, data can be lost forever.

A better way to provide backup is with streaming tape. This device provides a high-speed tape cartridge that can provide storage capacities in the 23-megabyte range and beyond. Thus, with this device the time to back up can be greatly reduced. Most systems will usually include the streaming tape device or allow the user to purchase it as an option. Don't despair if the vendor does not provide the streaming tape unit, because many add-on companies specialize in just these devices.

The process of backing up your data files and programs is extremely important, and a routine should be established to allow returning to the previous day's state, minimizing the loss of data in the event of a crash to a single day. In some cases even this loss of data could be intolerable and backup duplicate "mirror" systems should be considered.

Most UNIX systems provide options to back up the total system, certain file systems, or only files that have been modified since the last backup was done. The last method of backup checks the modification date in the i-node of the file against the last backup date.

Determine how and when backup should be done and who will perform this function. Next, approximate how much data in bytes will be backed up at each stage (full system, modified, or certain file system only). Then apply this to the time required to back up in bytes to determine total time required for backup. For example, if your system includes a 23-megabyte streaming tape unit and it takes 23 minutes to back up 23 megabytes of hard disk data. We therefore can determine that it takes approximately one minute to back up 1 megabyte of data. Thus, if we had a 70-megabyte system it would take 70 minutes. You should also consider the time it takes to change tape cartridges for a more accurate result.

The cost to purchase additional tape cartridges should also be considered. In addition, any tape device can wear out or malfunction, so give some thought to rotating tapes to minimize your exposure. For example, let's assume that it takes two tapes to perform backup and that the backup is done daily on a five-day week. We could establish five sets of tapes, called sets A through E. In the first week A would correspond to Monday, B to Tuesday, C to Wednesday, and so on. A schedule could be established to rotate the sets to minimize data loss in the event of a physical tape malfunction. Consider the following as an example of a schedule:

|           | Mon | Tues | Wed | Thur | Fri |
|-----------|-----|------|-----|------|-----|
| Week #1   | A   | B    | C   | D    | E   |
| Week #2   | D   | C    | B   | A    | E   |
| Week #3   | A   | B    | C   | D    | E   |

This type of schedule allows the user to return to the previous day's state if the restore process fails as a result of a bad tape. For example, if we were to use a single set of tapes and we had a crash on Monday and the tapes were physically damaged, then we would be out of luck. With our sample schedule we could always revert to the previous day's state; if that too failed, we could go back to the prior day. This schedule should only serve as a sample, as more elaborate schemes could be constructed. The process you choose should be dependent on the type of data, its sensitivity, and the loss that can be tolerated. The same process can be used if you are employing floppy diskettes as a backup medium.

## FILE AND RECORD LOCKING

A *file* is a collection of related data. A *record* is a portion of a file. For example, a file could be a list of clients and billing information. A record within this file would be the XYZ Corporation of Frostbite Falls, Minn. *Locking* is a term that describes a process that once a file or record is accessed, the file/record is not available to another user. This feature is necessary due to the multi-user environment.

Consider the following scenario: User A accesses the record for XYZ Corporation and checks the company's credit balance, to find that $5,000 is available for additional purchases. While user A is entering the new order for 1000 widgets at $5 each, another user, user B, also reads in XYZ Corporation and deducts $3000 for an outstanding purchase, rendering the new credit balance $2000. Now when user A completes the order, instead of having $0 as a balance we end up with a $-$2000 balance, creating havoc for our collections department. Locking is the feature that prevents this from happening. Once a file/record is accessed, all other users would be prevented from modifying this data until the record is released.

Some systems provide locking as a mandatory feature, others as an advisory feature. Advisory file/record locking means that the application must specifically lock and unlock the file/record. The technique used is incorporated in the operating system and is usually not easily changed. However, applications can indeed provide their own means of locking files and/or records.

This feature is certainly desirable and in some cases absolutely necessary. The nature of your application as well as the number of concurrent users running under the same applications program will determine whether this feature is required.

Check with the vendor of the hardware to see which method is employed. Also check with the software to see if the program supports this technique on the hardware chosen.

## SHELL

The shell is a command interpreter that acts as an intermediary between the user and the operating system. The shell is what you see when you log in to the system. There are two major types of shells: the Bourne shell, supplied with all AT&T UNIX System V computers, and the C shell, supplied with all systems running Berkeley versions. Some users prefer one to the other, and the debate within the UNIX community rages on.

Specialized shells that provide increased levels of user friendliness are becoming more popular. This so-called "friendly front end" allows the naive user to operate without any in-depth knowledge of UNIX code or the shell. An example of this is the user agent supplied with the AT&T UNIX PC. The user agent presents a window environment coupled with icons metaphors and extensive help files. With the mouse, the user can perform many powerful functions without any knowledge of the UNIX operating system. For more sophisticated users, the standard Bourne shell is also included. The trend will be to move to this and other specialized shells to help move the UNIX system into the office environment. The use of such specialized shells should be considered, as they can greatly reduce the amount of user training required and ease the pain of converting from an existing system.

## EDITORS

The UNIX operating system provides two major editors: the line editor ed and a screen-oriented editor called vi. The vi editor is definitely preferred over ed, mainly due to its relative ease of use. The vi editor is a feature that was included with the Berkeley releases of UNIX and is now also included in UNIX System V. The ease of use of each of these editors is debatable in comparison to some of the mainframe editors; however, it is possible to purchase specialized editors from other vendors and load them on your system.

## COMMUNICATIONS: cu/uucp

The UNIX system provides extensive communications features for communicating with other systems. The cu command is used to call another system and emulate a terminal. The cu stands for call unix, but can be used to call other non-UNIX systems.

The uucp command, which stands for UNIX-to-UNIX copy program, is used to transfer files to and from UNIX-based computers. The built-in electronic mail function uses this program to send mail among UNIX machines. In addition to the basic file transfer function, uucp also provides notification upon reception of the transmitted file and the ability to create subnetworks of UNIX machines to forward mail and files to other locations. Any good UNIX computer will include uucp bundled with system software or as an option.

The authors recommend that you do not purchase a UNIX system without cu and uucp. The combination of cu and uucp provides the flexibility to communicate with many other systems, and all communication software depends on the existence of these two commands. We will discuss how to use these two commands in Chapter 3.

## ENCRYPTION, DECRYPTION, AND RESTRICTED SHELL

Encryption, decryption, and restricted shell all relate to the security aspects of the UNIX system. The encrypt/decrypt commands allow the user to create files that are unreadable by other users without the proper key. The key is chosen by the user when the file is encrypted and must be used to decrypt the file. These features give the user the ability to send information over telephone lines and then decrypt at the receiving end.

The restricted shell, called rsh, allows the system administrator to set up logins that will limit the user to access files within his/her own directory. The restricted shell should be used to prevent users from rummaging around the system and will add another level of security to prevent hackers from vandalizing your system.

## PROGRAM DEVELOPMENT LANGUAGES

Many UNIX systems have the option of adding language compilers such as C, Fortran, Cobol, Pascal, and BASIC. Compilers convert high-level code such as Fortran into machine-language code that is executed by the computer. The benefit over interpreters such as GWBASIC or BASICA on IBM and compatibles is that with compilers the translated code, called object code, is in the language that the computer's microprocessor understands. The result is much better performance than with interpreters that must translate the code each time the program is run.

Because language offerings differ from vendor to vendor, you should take note of the language and version that are offered. If you plan to develop a lot of programs on your system, you should test the compiler for accuracy and for speed. This can be done by bringing in a sample program and measuring its results. If the vendor can make documentation available on a loan basis, take advantage of this offer to disclose any hidden abnormalities.

## PLANNING CHECKLISTS

In order to help gather data for analysis, we have included two checklists: one for single-user systems and one for multi-user UNIX systems. We suggest that you either fill out these sheets based on available information or have the vendor fill them out and return them to you.

These sheets are only a data-gathering aid; the ultimate buying criteria are up to you. We have used these sheets and have found them extremely useful in setting up a database and assigning point values to specific areas. We hope that they can assist you in this effort as well.

### How to Use the Checklists

We have already discussed most of the items in the checklists, with the exception of benchmarks. A *benchmark* is a program that is run to measure the performance of a system. Many of the computer magazines provide benchmarks for DOS systems. *Byte* magazine is an example of one such publication. The UNIX community is so much involved in benchmarking systems that there are entire companies that provide this service. One such company is Aim Technology, located in Santa Clara, California. This company provides extensive performance data on most UNIX-based machines available in the marketplace.

We suggest that you select a benchmark that makes sense to you. For example, how long does it take to recalculate a 100-by-100 spreadsheet, how long to sort a 10,000-item list, how long to compile a Fortran program, and so on. The application you intend to run should dictate the benchmark chosen.

To use the checklists, choose the application packages that will be in your top five or top ten category. Fill out the checklist for each vendor and model offered. Analyze the data as it pertains to your particular situation. Consider growth and compatibility. Narrow the list to three or four models. Test the software you intend to run on the machine. If you are considering a multi-user system, bring one of the users with you for unbiased input, then make your decision.

**Single-User Checklist**

| | |
|---|---|
| Name of manuf./model: _____ | Price: _____ |
| Operating System: _____ | Processor: _____ |
| | Clock (mhz): _____ |

Memory

| | |
|---|---|
| Minimum memory: _____ | Maximum memory: _____ |
| Increment of: _____ | Installable by user: _____ |

Floppy Disk

| | |
|---|---|
| Capacity (bytes): _____ | No. of tracks: _____ |
| | Sectors per track: _____ |

#### Hard Disk

Capacity (bytes): _____          Integral to the unit: _____
Optional
external hard disks: _____

#### Clock/Calendar

Included: _____          Price to add if not with
system: _____

#### I/O Ports

RS-232 port included: _____          Price to add: _____
Parallel port included: _____          Price to add: _____
No. of slots for boards: _____          No. of short slots: _____

#### Display

Monochrome: _____     Price: _____     Resolution: _____
Color (RGB): _____     Price: _____     Resolution: _____
No. of colors: _____

#### Special Features

#### Benchmark Results

#### Compatibility with Top Five Programs

#### Maintenance Available

Price: _____          Quality: _____

#### Features Least Liked

#### UNIX Multi-User Checklist

Name of manuf./model: _____          Price: _____
Operating system: _____          Version: _____
Support for oper. sys.: _____

#### Bus

Address bus size: _____          Data bus size: _____
Maximum addressable memory: _____

#### Processor

Microprocessor: _____          Clock rate (mhz): _____
MIP rate: _____

## Memory

| | |
|---|---|
| Minimum memory: _____ | Maximum memory: _____ |
| Increment of: _____ | Installable by user: _____ |
| Amt. of memory dedicated to the operating system: _____ | |

## Memory Management

| | |
|---|---|
| Swapping or demand paging: _____ | Size of largest process: _____ |
| Virtual memory space: _____ | Page size: _____ |
| File/record locking: _____ | Mandatory: _____ |

## Floating-Point Operation

Hardware or software
implementation: _____

MFLOPS (million floating-point operations per
second): _____

## User Support

| | |
|---|---|
| Maximum no. of users: _____ | Practical no. of users: _____ |
| Maximum no. of RS-232C ports: _____ | Parallel ports: _____ |
| Incremental cost per user: _____ | Special ports: _____ |

## Disk Capacities

| | |
|---|---|
| Floppy disk capacity: _____ | Hard disk capacities: _____ |
| | Maximum no. of drives: _____ |
| | Total hard disk storage: _____ |

## Backup Medium

| | |
|---|---|
| Floppy diskette: _____ | No. of floppys for backup: _____ |
| Streaming tape: _____ | Capacity of tape (mbytes): _____ |
| | Additional cost: _____ |
| Estimated time to back up using | |
|   Floppy disk: _____ | Streaming tape: _____ |

## Growth

| | |
|---|---|
| No. of I/O slots included: _____ | Add-on box available: _____ |
| | No. of slots: _____ |
| | Additional disks: _____ |

## Peripheral Support

| | |
|---|---|
| Termcap provided: _____ | Terminfo/curses provided: _____ |
| Printers supported: _____ | |
| cu/uucp provided: _____ | Ethernet interface available: _____ |
| Modems supported for communication: _____ | |
| Graphics terminals supported: _____ | |

### UNIX Features

Shell (Bourne or C): _____          Specialized shell: _____

Editors supplied: _____

Crypt/decrypt: _____          Restricted shell: _____

TCPIP: _____

### Program Development

Languages compilers available: _____

Debugging tools provided: _____

### Benchmark Results

### Compatibility with Top Ten Programs

### Special Features

### Features Liked Least

# 3

# setting up systems

In Chapter 2 we learned some of the issues we must deal with before purchasing a system. In this chapter we will learn what to do once you get the system home. The primary goal of this chapter is to provide an understanding that will aid in the initial setup and configuration of both MS-DOS and UNIX computers. References made to PCs are applicable to supermicros and minicomputers as well. This chapter will be followed by discussions of the AT&T PC 6300, UNIX PC, and 3B2 computer specifics.

## COMPUTER ACQUISITION

So you finally decided to take the plunge! After all those trips to computer stores, many sleepless nights, a loan or two, or possibly a healthy budget allocation, your computer is a reality. You arrive home or at the office proudly carrying the boxes that will make up your system. Hurriedly, you unpack it. Nestled between pieces of cardboard and styrofoam lies the magic box of plastic, metal, and wires. Excitement has caused you to ignore your peers, your wife, your boss, your secretary, your job, and your children while you begin to assemble your systems. As you examine the contents, you are relieved to find no visible broken parts; quickly, you locate the manuals that come with the computer.

Because you are anxious to begin and being the technocrat that you are, or assume you are, you debate whether or not to read the instructions. Maybe you will employ the technocrat's credo, "When all else fails, read the instructions." After coming to your senses and letting your pocketbook override your ego, you read the step-by-step procedure for device assembly. The instructions are outlined in a procedure similar to the following:

1. Pop the top.
2. Scrape off the tape.
3. Guard the cards.
4. Put what you got in the slot.
5. Attach the cord to the motherboard.
6. Label the cable.
7. Make sure the drive is alive.
8. Don't be sloppy with the floppy.
9. Switch the switch.
10. Load the code.

Not all systems are that easy to bring up, nor are all instructions that explicit. The actual process may differ in the specific steps performed, but on a generic basis you must first

1. Install the hardware system, memory boards, interfaces, and so on.
2. Load in the operating system code.
3. Attach the system monitor or display.
4. Run the system diagnostics.
5. For multi-user systems, install the log-ins for other users.
6. Connect the peripherals such as printers and modems.
7. Install the applications software.
8. Install terminals for multi-user configurations.
9. Test the complete system.
10. Congratulate yourself!

To successfully install and maintain computer systems, whether they are single- or multi-user environments, the user/administrator should possess knowledge of the diffferent aspects of a system. This includes familiarity with disk systems, printers, spoolers, modems, communication, electronic mail, system boot procedures, system backup, and security issues. Each one of these topics will be covered, including a generic overview, followed by specifics of both MS-DOS and UNIX operating systems environments.

## DISK SYSTEMS

Humans have "permanent" memory. Once you fully learn skills or facts, such as how to read and write or in what year Columbus discovered America, they are embedded in your brain. They are not lost like a telephone number you dialed once or yesterday's news headlines. By contrast, a computer develops amnesia the instant you switch off the power. That is, its memory is erased completely, and it forgets everything it ever knew. Hence, if you (or a gremlin in the power line) switch off the power or pull the plug, all your current work will be lost. For this reason, computer users need a way to store data and programs so that this information can be loaded back later into the computer's memory. We refer to the units that let users to this as *mass storage devices*. They are available in a variety of sizes, capacities, and formats. Both MS-DOS and UNIX systems offer floppy and hard disk systems. A look at the different offerings yields a better understanding of their use and benefits.

### Floppy Disks

Floppy disk drives offer the user an inexpensive mechanism for saving data that would otherwise be lost once the computer system lost power. The floppy disk units are small rectangular objects with a slot in the front. Disk drives act much like record players except that they play thin, flexible disks called *floppy disks* (or sometimes just *disks* or *diskettes*). The most popular size in use today is the 5¼-inch floppy. However, a new standard size of 3½ inches is gaining in popularity. This is largely due to the advent of the lap-size portable computer systems. With as much, if not more, storage space as the larger disks, these will become more prominent as time goes by.

### Heights

The heights of floppy and hard disk drives have been decreasing since the first days of personal computers. The first 5¼-inch drives were approximately 3½ inches tall. These became the standard-size floppy drives found on microcomputer and minicomputer systems. However, recent reductions in component sizes have allowed a half-height floppy unit. As you would surmise, it is half the height of a standard-size floppy drive. Consequently, two drives now occupy the space that an older drive once did.

### Capacities

The technique used to format these drives dictates the capacity of the floppy disks. Each disk has an outer protective cover encompassing a floppy medium, which looks like a flexible 45 rpm record. It has a magnetic coating which allows

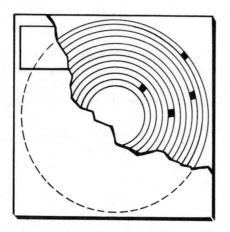

**Figure 3-1** Track and sectors on disks (Courtesy of AT&T Information Systems, Inc.)

data, ones and zeros, to be magnetically stored on the surface. Prior to actual data storage, the medium must be formatted. Refer to the section on formatting to actually perform this operation on your system. The concept to understand here is that the formatting lays out a pattern on the disk surface for orderly storage and retrieval of information. This is accomplished using tracks and sectors as pictured in Figure 3-1. The number of tracks and sectors determines the ultimate capacity of the disk surface. Typical quantities are 360,000 bytes, or 360 kbytes, of information for MS-DOS systems. However, the capacity of floppies is growing, as AT&T's 3B2 Super Micro's floppy offers a capacity of 760 kbytes of information. In today's computers, both sides of the floppy are used. To make sure maximum capacity is possible, use disks capable of storing on both sides. They are usually labelled as single-sided (ss) or double-sided (ds), with the latter type being the ones to use.

### Formatting Disks

A major operating procedure you must learn involves working with floppy disks. Most operating systems require the floppy disks to be formatted according to their own specifications. These specifications dictate the amount of space available on the disks. To get this space available for use, the user must perform a function known as *formatting the disks*. You can think of formatting as "breaking in" the disk.

Formatting allows the user to store programs and data files on the disks. Both MS-DOS and UNIX operating systems encourage the use of double-sided disks. However, MS-DOS allows the user to format a single or both sides of the disk. Generally speaking, the single-sided disks are less expensive, but only hold half the amount of data as double-sided disks. The next chapters explain the procedures for formatting floppy disks for particular types of systems.

## Hard Disks

In contrast with removable floppy disks, hard disks are available for both MS-DOS and UNIX operating systems. These disks are termed "hard" because of the platters that are inside the housing. Whereas a floppy disk has a flexible medium inside the cover, hard disks have rigid platters similar to record albums bought in most stores. More than a single platter may be contained in these units to yield different storage capacities.

Hard disk systems are available in the same sizes as floppies: full and half height. As before, two half-height drives can be used in the place normally occupied by a full-height drive. A key difference exists in that the greater the capacity, the less chance of the unit being available in a half-height system. Because of today's rapidly changing technology, this is generally a short-term problem. Disk drive manufacturers are continually decreasing the size of the drives while increasing the amount of data that can be stored. For example, the first 10-megabyte drives available in MS-DOS machines were full-height systems. Now the user will find both 10- and 20-megabyte systems available in half-height disk drives.

### Formatting Hard Disks

Both operating systems include facilities for formatting hard disks. Different commands are used, but the concept and operation are the same. This operation is generally only performed once unless new versions of operating systems are to be used. Because this operation destroys all data on a hard disk, as with the floppies, cautiously use these commands.

### RAM Disks

For those systems where only floppy disk drives are available, a function exists for providing the user with the speed of access found in hard disk systems. Known as RAM disks, this concept evolved due to the relatively slow floppy disk access time. The input and output associated with an MS-DOS system tends to be the slowest operation in the system. The I/O can cause a serious bottleneck. If you find your PC "I/O-bound," as it is termed, consider a RAM disk. The electronic disk is as fast as a hard disk would be. Because large quantities of memory are available at relatively inexpensive rates, vendors have capitalized on this. Software was written to allocate a portion of the total memory available to emulate a hard disk, hence the term *RAM disk*. Once memory is allocated for the disk emulator, a drive ID is assigned to the emulated disk. Files from a floppy disk may then be copied to the emulated disk for high-speed access. This copy routine may be part of the AUTOEXEC. BAT file, explained later, which contains commands to be processed upon system reset or startup. Because all UNIX systems discussed in this text include hard disk systems, RAM disks are not used.

## Clocks

Most computer systems, both MS-DOS and UNIX based, are equipped with a clock as a standard feature. Software is generally provided to read the date and time automatically from the clock, thus relieving the user of having to set the clock manually. Battery backup is used to maintain the clock when the computer system is powered off intentionally or accidentally loses power.

A clock can be used to provide systems administration features such as appending the filename with an extension identifying the date and time the files were last written to. Furthermore, certain applications are enhanced when the time and date are available automatically. Communication packages can capitalize on this feature by displaying the time that has expired during a session with another computer. Vertical application packages can time transactions to determine costs for given functions.

## PRINTERS

Not too many computer system environments exist without the capability of obtaining a hardcopy of certain information from a computer. *Hardcopy* is the term used to describe the output generated by a printer.

### Print Quality

Before a printer is purchased, the user should determine the quality level(s) required for their installation, as many printers are available offering a multitude of features. One of the first decisions to be made involves the quality of print necessary. The possible output includes data processing, draft, correspondence, near-letter, and letter-quality appearance. Different printers offer varying qualities of print, with some offering more than one type. For example, the NEC Spinwriter 3500 series offers letter-quality printing. The Okidata Pacemark 2410 offers three printing modes: correspondence, draft, and data processing qualities. Refer to Figure 3-2 for a comparison. The data processing quality output is of minimal quality for people who truly do not care what the output looks like. This descriptor arose from data processing shops, where massive amounts of output were generated, of which little was actually read. Draft quality is a step above data processing quality, but significantly more readable. A single pass of a dot matrix printhead, to be covered later, generates draft-quality print. Next in quality is correspondence printing. This is generally decent enough to send to someone in an office environment, but the reader will be able to distinguish the letter from one generated on a typewriter. If

```
THIS IS DATA PROCESSING MODE PRINT
so is this but in small letters.

THIS IS DRAFT MODE PRINT
so is this but in small letters.

THIS IS CORRESPONDENCE QUALITY PRINT
so is this but in small letters.
```

**Figure 3-2** Different print qualities, printed on the Okidata Pacemark 2410 printer

you desire to fool the reader into thinking that the letter is true typewriter letter quality, demand near-letter-quality printing capability. This is the next best thing to the top output, letter quality. Letter-quality printing is accomplished in the same manner as a typewritten letter. Fully formed characters are generated by typewriterlike balls, daisywheels, or thimbles. The output is indistinguishable from typeset print. The choice as to quality of print will generally be inversely proportional to the speed of the printer for most PC printers. Laser printers may be an exception, but are generally out of the price range of the average PC user. Many of these qualities may be acceptable to you or the recipients of your output. One of the safest ways of judging the quality is to compare samples of the paperwork currently used in your environment with the output of various printers before making your decision.

## Impact Printers

To achieve the different qualities of print, a variety of technologies is used. Generally, printers are divided into two categories, impact versus nonimpact. Impact printers utilize some sort of typing element with a letter or piece of a letter which is hammered against a ribbon onto the paper. The two types of impact printers discussed here include full-character impact and dot matrix impact printers. The *full-character* uses the same principle as a typewriter. A ribbon sits between the fully formed character of an element and the paper. A hammering device causes the image on standard types of paper. The noise of these letter-quality printers is similar to that of a typewriter. However, cabinets are available to enclose these printers, reducing the noise. These devices use daisywheels, thimbles, or balls like the IBM Selectrics, allowing multiple copies to be printed. Different elements, easily installed, are available to accommodate different printing requirements. Examples of full-impact printers include the AT&T 450 series, the NEC Spinwriter series, the Qume Sprint series, and Diablo Systems 600 series letter-quality printers. Impact printers offer speeds ranging from 10 to 75 characters per second and are constantly being improved.

The other type of impact printer is the *dot matrix*. On these machines the let-

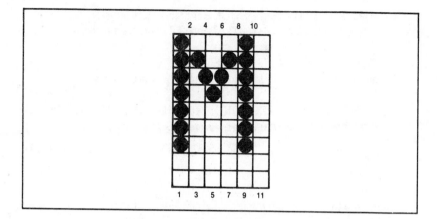

**Figure 3-3** Dot matrix printing technique

ters are generated using tiny dots that approximate the shape of a character instead of forming them fully. The term *matrix* is used due to the grid, array, or matrix of dots or pins available for hammering against the ribbon and ultimately the paper. The size of the matrix and the number of dots determine the legibility of the characters. Printheads generally have seven or more pins in a vertical column. As the printhead moves across the paper, the hammers hit the pins as necessary to form the characters (see Figure 3-3). The AT&T 473 printer is an example of this type of printer. The characters being printed on this machine can be shrunk, compressed, italicized, or double-struck, all under control of the PC. Descenders, which are the parts of the letters g, j, p, q, and y that descend below the print line, are printed. Typical speeds of dot matrix printers are between 100 and 200 characters per second. These types of printers are very popular with personal computer owners. Specific vendor offerings are described later in this chapter.

## Nonimpact Printers

Nonimpact printers do not strike the paper at all. Hammers are not used to get the print on the pulp. A thermal printer, a good example of this type, requires special heat-sensitive paper. Although these printers are less expensive than their impact counterparts, the paper is more expensive and potentially more difficult to obtain than is standard paper. Other technologies in this category involve electrosensitive, photographic, and light techniques. Ink jet printers are becoming increasingly popular. They contain nozzles used to spray dots of ink onto the paper. Laser printers use the same principles as a photocopying machine, offering speeds significantly faster than those of impact printers. Laser printers' output is generally paced according to the number of pages of print per minute, with a range of 20 to 50 ppm. At the current pace of technological improvement in printer technology, ink jet and laser printers could soon be affordable by the average PC owner.

The features offered by a printer may be the determining factor in purchasing a particular output device. These features can be categorized as follows:

1. Performance
2. Interfaces available
3. Add-on options
4. Printing characteristics
5. Graphics capabilities
6. Media-supported
7. Format controls
8. Proven reliability

## Printer Performance

A printer may offer a variety of print speeds, depending on the printing method enabled. For example, if the data-processing-quality mode is invoked in a printer offering different modes, the output rate may be very high. For example, the Okidata Pacemark 2410 is capable of printing 350 characters per second (cps) in the data processing mode. This printer also offers a correspondence-quality print at a rate of 85 cps. To achieve these high throughput rates, bidirectional printing is used as well as logic-seeking functions. *Logic-seeking functions* are optimizing routines that force the printer to take shortcuts to increase throughput. If a short line is printed, there is no need to print spaces filling the remainder of the line. The printing of spaces is generally done to position the printhead at the end of a line for printing the next line right to left. Logic seeking allows a carriage return line feed to be performed, saving valuable time and consequently improving print speed.

## Interfaces

Generally, two interfaces are used for connecting printers to the AT&T PC 6300 and other systems: serial and parallel. RS-232 and Centronics parallel interfacing are available, but here we will say only that it is important to determine which is to be acquired in the printer. Furthermore, consideration should be given to future expansion. If a parallel interface is standard on the printer, is a serial interface option available for easy installation later? For example, the Epson FX-80 printer comes standard with a Centronics parallel connector. Practical Peripherals, Inc., offers a user-installable serial interface in the printer. These interfaces are mutually exclusive but offer extreme flexibility as a system expands and evolves.

## Add-On Options

Add-on options are available with many printers. As the printer is generally the slowest device in the PC configuration, a means of making the PC available while the printer is chugging along is desirable. Buffers of different sizes are available for most printers. Generally, (2K) 2000 bytes or 4K increments are possible in the printer itself. The computer than quickly dumps the data to the buffer and may proceed to another task. The buffer feeds the data at the printer's operational speed. This feature is inherent in UNIX multi-tasking systems, but is an option in MS-DOS. Often, multicolor ribbon support is available. If single sheets of paper are to be used, sheet feeders may be a required option for the printer. Single- and dual-bin-cut sheet feeders are generally the two options. A dual-bin feeder allows both plain paper and letterhead paper to be loaded into the printer automatically. If the printer is using single sheets of paper, *friction feed* is the technique used to roll the paper around the platen. Often, a *tractor-feed* option is available. Also known as *pin feed* or *sprocket feed*, mechanisms allow for paper with holes on the sides to be used. This paper is generally continuous, with perforations between sheets for easy separation. Tractor-feed operation may either be an option or come standard with the printer. If tractor feed is used on the printer, insure that the printer supports variable-width paper. This means that the sprockets are adjustable to support different-size papers.

## Printing Techniques

The actual printing characteristics vary from printer to printer. The matrix size may vary depending on the quality and size of print. One of the most popular features of a printer is *condensed* or *compressed printing*. This is the ability of a printer to alter the size of the characters being printed. The standard output is 10 characters per inch (cpi) horizontally. With compressed/condensed print, up to 17 characters may be squeezed into an inch of space. In this mode a printer can squeeze 132 characters into the space normally available in 80-column printers. Refer to the sample printout in Figure 3-4—with 132 columns available, or 13 inches, over 220 characters are possible. This allows for large spreadsheets to be printed. It may be desirable to do the opposite and reduce the number of characters per line by *expanding* the print. This is useful for headings on documents. If an item needs to stand out in text, *double-striking* and/or emphasized printing is available to print bold lettering. Superscripts and subscripts may also be desirable. *Proportional spacing* as used by typesetters is also available on many printers. Most if not all of these features are operable under computer control. Commands in the form of control or escape sequences are used to set up the different modes of printing. These characters are received and acted upon but not printed. Many programs, such as VisiCalc, offer printer setup sequences. The control and escape sequence may be entered for desired printing results. Consult Appendix C for a list of popular printers and their

## Normal Print:

- Superscripts and Subscripts QWERTYUIOP[]ASDFGHJKL;'~<>,.?/\|!@#$%^&*()_-+=1234567890
- Condensed Font (16.7 cpi) - ABCDEFGHIJKLMNOPQRSTUVWXYZ1234567890abcdefghijklmnopqr
- COMPRESSED FONT (12.5 CPI) - ABCDEFGHIJKLMNOPQRSTUVWXYZ123456
- Standard Font (10 cpi) - ABCDEFGHIJKLMNOPQRSTUVW
- Correspondence Font (10 cpi) - ABCDEFGHIJKLMNOPQ
- Elongated Font (10 cpi) - ABCDEFGHIJKLMNOPQRSTUV
  - Expanded Font (5 cpi) -
  - Expanded, Normal, superscripts and subscrip
- ELONGATED AND EXPANDED

## Bold (Double-strike) Print:

- Superscripts and Subscripts QWERTYUIOP[]ASDFGHJKL;'~<>,.?/\|!@#$%^&*()_-+=1234567890
- Condensed Font (16.7 cpi) - ABCDEFGHIJKLMNOPQRSTUVWXYZ1234567890abcdefghijklmnopqr
- COMPRESSED FONT (12.5 CPI) - ABCDEFGHIJKLMNOPQRSTUVWXYZ123456
- Standard Font (10 cpi) - ABCDEFGHIJKLMNOPQRSTUVW
- Correspondence Font (10 cpi) - ABCDEFGHIJKLMNOPQ
- Elongated Font (10 cpi) - ABCDEFGHIJKLMNOPQRSTUV
  - Expanded Font (5 cpi) -
  - Expanded, Normal, superscripts and subscrip
- ELONGATED AND EXPANDED

## Emphasized (Shadow) Print:

- COMPRESSED FONT (12.5 CPI) - ABCDEFGHIJKLMNOPQRSTUVWXYZ123456
- Standard Font (10 cpi) - ABCDEFGHIJKLMNOPQRSTUVW
- Correspondence Font (10 cpi) - ABCDEFGHIJKLMNOPQ
- Elongated Font (10 cpi) - ABCDEFGHIJKLMNOPQRSTUV
  - Expanded Font (5 cpi) -
  - Expanded, Normal, superscripts and subscrip
- ELONGATED AND EXPANDED

**Figure 3-4** Different print pitches, printed on the Printronix MVP 150B printer

control commands with respective functions. Should these printing modes always be desired, switches may be set to enable them permanently.

One final printing characteristic is printer *emulation*. Because of the widespread use of some printers, such as Texas Instruments 800 series, Printronix, Qume Sprint series, and Epson printers, support for their control codes is inherent in certain applications. Other printers offer emulation modes allowing them to be used in these environments and perform just as the emulated devices would. Some printers go a step further by offering the ability to download a character set to the printer from the PC, allowing for personalized applications development.

### Graphics

Graphics is another desirable feature for dumping images from the computer to a printer. Either block-mode or bit-mapped graphics may be supported. *Block-mode graphics* offers simple horizontal and vertical lines as well as shapes such as squares, circles, and rectangles to draw pictures. If better resolution for pictures is desired, *bit-mapped graphics* is the choice. Generally, the printer vendor will publish the number of points that are addressable in the form of dots per inch. The greater the density, possible the better the picture. Figure 3-5 offers sample graphics available on dot matrix printers.

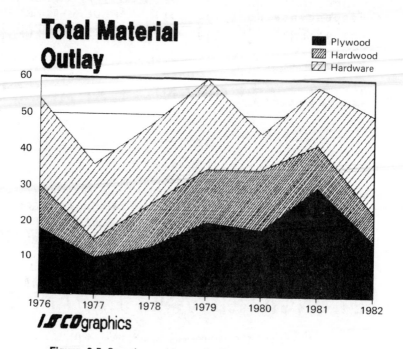

**Figure 3-5** Sample graphics on the Printronix MVP 150B printer

The medium supported by the printer determines whether pin-feed paper or single-feed paper is usable. Furthermore, multiple copies may be allowed. If single sheets are fed by a sheet feeder, forms control should be an option. This allows for the top of the form to be set and automatically aligned for subsequent sheets if the form length is properly set. *Horizontal and vertical tabbing* are also desirable format controls, as they can reduce actual printing time and may ensure compatibility with software packages that rely on them.

### Reliability

The final feature to consider, but perhaps the most important, is the reliability of the printer. Because it is largely a mechanical device, a printer is subject to breakdowns because of the moving parts. Vendors generally set forth rigid requirements for printer testing, as they realize the importance of uptime for these systems. The measurement for reliability is generally expressed as MTBF, *mean time between failures*. This is the amount of time between successive failures on a printer. Furthermore, downtime should be considered as how long it takes to repair the machine. This is expressed as MTTR, *mean time to repair*. These should be prime considerations if the printer will be used heavily.

### Printer Interfaces

Various interfaces are available on computers. The two most prevalent are *serial* and *parallel*. Printers with a serial interface conform to the RS-232 standard. For a complete understanding of the interfacing of devices using this interface, the reader is encouraged to consult *RS-232 Made Easy* by Martin D. Seyer. This will explain the physical connectivity issues.

The parallel interface is becoming increasingly prevalent among personal computers and multi-user systems. It is the recommended printer interface on the PC 6300, UNIX PC, and 3B2 computers. All these systems will support printers with serial interfaces, but parallel-type printers are widely used.

### Print Spoolers

Earlier in the chapter the problem of a computer becoming I/O-bound was discussed. This is a situation when a lot of input and/or output is to be performed. The attached peripheral, in this case a printer, is much slower than the computer's processing capability. Because the printer has mechanical in addition to electrical components, there is no way it can keep up with the computer that is dumping information to it. This tends to decrease overall system throughput, as the computer is tied up while waiting for the printer to catch up. To overcome this degradation, a concept known as print spooling was developed.

*Print spooling* is a technique used to allow the computer to dump information destined for the slower device to an interim entity for later printing. Typically, this interim entity is RAM controlled by software. The spooling software intercepts the output and saves it either in RAM or in a file on the disk. The data is later fed to the printer without tying up the computer. The computer can move on to other tasks.

Spooling software comes in many varieties. Some packages merely feed the data to the printer as soon as it can print it. These packages output data at the transmission rate of the interface. It is the responsibility of the printer to indicate to the computer that it needs to halt output. There could be many reasons for this, including the need to catch up, out-of-paper condition, or another error condition. Once the condition clears, the printer would indicate that it is ready to receive more data. The spooling software monitors the interface for these types of signals and behaves accordingly.

In addition to the basic spooling operations, others allow multiple requests for printing to be queued and printed as possible. In both single- and multiple-user computer environments, many printer requests are made. These spooling packages accept many simultaneous requests and feed them to the printer as fast as the printer can handle them. Because multiple jobs are being queued, facilities are generally included to allow the user to check on the status of his/her printing jobs (a job is a printing request). The spooling software keeps a log of all requests along with their status of either having been printed or in line to be printed. Each of these jobs has a print number. Using this number, the job may be cancelled at the user's option.

Still others allow timed printing and multiple copies. A user may request that a job be printed at a certain time. As you would imagine, the spooling software uses the computer's clock to schedule these jobs. If multiple copies of a document are required, the spooling software will allow the user to make a single request yet still receive multiple copies.

Because the spooling software is printing jobs from possible multiple users, a means of separating each one must be arranged. To allow for this delineation, header and trailer pages are used to surround a given job. These pages usually list the user who requested the task, along with the date and time of the printing. This type of flagging allows multiple users to separate their output from all others performed on the same printer.

## COMMUNICATION ENVIRONMENTS

This next section deals with those computer systems where communications will be used. This may be as simple as accessing a computer service such as The Source, or as complex as uploading and downloading files between computer systems. We will discuss asynchronous communication systems, as these are the most prevalent with MS-DOS and UNIX systems. The IBM PC/XT and AT&T PC 6300 will be used as references for the following discussions on communication. For information regarding specific computers, refer to the chapters on those systems.

## Asynchronous Environments

In what areas would an asynchronous dial-up environment be appropriate? A dial-up connection is normally used, for example, to access a database service, such as The Source. The information available from The Source, such as commodity and stock quotes, is to be shared by a large terminal or computer population. Typically, access to the service is for short periods of time. For example, a PC user may desire a small report once each day from the service. Over a dial-up facility, the user connects to a port, retrieves the information, logs off, and then disconnects from the port. The port is now available for other users to access. Dial-up facilities fit nicely where there are low traffic volumes per user. Many different dial-up facilities, such as Telenet and Tymnet, are available for accessing the different services. Charges for these access services generally are based on a minute of use. The cost of these facilities in conjunction with traffic volumes determines when dial-up lines are more economical to use than other facilities, such as private lines. These two major factors influence the use of asynchronous dial-up connections in the following types of service offerings:

1. Public databases
2. Service bureaus
3. Message services
4. Computer-to-computer data exchanges

Although but a few of the many areas in which the PC will use asynchronous communications, these are the ones highlighted in this chapter in our discussion of modems and, communication ports.

## Intelligent Modems

What features are necessary in a modem for it to be considered intelligent? Asynchronous modems of the past possessed very few features beyond the basic transmission requirements of modulating and demodulating. Prevalent features were items such as auto-answer, loopback tests, and lamps. Until the incorporation of microprocessors into modems, users accepted these capabilities and configured their systems accordingly. By adding the power of a computer, modem capabilities are enhanced considerably. These enhancements center around the user's interface to the modem for establishing communication links with other machines. By definition, an intelligent modem contains a microprocessor, memory, and offers enhanced dialing capabilities such as auto-dialing, keyboard dialing, mnemonic dialing, and the storage of frequently used numbers. The enhanced dialing features warrant discussion, as they offer a user-friendly interface for an otherwise complex modem. Prior to the arrival of intelligent modems, the establishment of a communication link was accomplished by lifting the handset on the phone associated with a modem, such as an AT&T 212A. The number was dialed on the rotary or Touch-Tone pad of the phone. Once the far end answered, the calling party would push a button, known as the *exclusion key,* to complete the connection. This was termed "going to data" because it would place the modem in the on-line data mode. The intelligent modem did away with the requirement for a separate handset for dialing. Dialing is accomplished by the PC operator entering the desired number directly on the keyboard. This became known as *keyboard dialing.*

Typically, a PC user with communication requirements will access the same remote computers repeatedly. Intelligent modems offer the capability of storing these frequently used numbers for ease of dialing. To use one of the stored numbers, only a single keystroke is required. The modem recognizes this and translates this digit into the desired number stored in the modem's memory. Battery backup in the modem allows the numbers to be retained even if the modem loses power or is unplugged. The tables that contain the numbers are becoming more elaborate, allowing for descriptions of the computers accessed by the numbers stored. Also, mnemonic selection of telephone numbers is appearing. This feature allows a name instead of a number to be typed for dialing. For example, the word DALLAS might be set up in the modem to be translated into the number of the computer in that city. This eliminates the need for the user to memorize a lengthy phone number. Rather, the word DALLAS is all that is needed by the modem to establish the connection. Once the computer at the far end answers the call, the modem automatically goes into the on-line mode.

The intelligent modem can redial the last number with a single keystroke. Furthermore, the modem can be set up for repeat dialing. This feature causes the modem, in response to an unanswered call, to continue to dial a number forever or for a preset number of times. There are instances when the user does not want the modem to continue dialing an unanswered call. For example, if a user dials a computer that has more than one access number and receives a busy signal or no answer, it is desirable for the alternate number(s) to be dialed. Number linking is a feature that allows for multiple numbers to be chained together and dialed sequentially until a connection is established. If the last number in the chain is linked to the beginning of the list, continuous dialing is possible.

Another feature offered by many modems is the ability to dial a number using either TouchTone or rotary dialing. The telephone company determines which is the valid method for dialing. Normally, the user must option the modem to match the environment. This is accomplished either through the setting of switches or by a keyboard command. As the level of intelligence increases within modems, the ability to switch between pulse and TouchTone dialing can be done automatically. This feature's value is generally realized when a user has to dial several numbers to reach a computer. The use of different phone companies' services increases this possibility.

Not only must the modem deal with the different dial options, but there is also a need to detect multiple dial tones before dialing subsequent numbers. To access discount long-distance services, a subscriber must dial a number to access the service, followed by a password, and finally the desired number. Each entry requires a separate dial tone. Modems that can detect secondary dial tones allow the user the advantage of discount rates with minimal dialing aggravation. Often this can be accomplished with a single keystroke.

There are areas of the country where all dial tones are not created equal. This is evident when the customer's equipment is providing the dial tone, such as with a *private branch exchange* (PBX). A PBX is a customer's version of a telephone system. The PBX, or switch, provides a dial tone, processes calls, and connects users to the regular telephone network. Because different vendors provide these switches, dial tones from PBXs vary. Intelligent modems are used with a variety of PBXs. Consequently, the modems may not be able to detect all dial tones. Modems overcome this dilemma by providing what is known as *blind dialing*. Blind dialing allows the intelligent modem to dial a number even when no dial tone is detected.

### Board-Level Modems

Before being able to determine the proper address setting, the user must develop an understanding of modems and communication boards. Two types of modems are available to a computer owner. One is of the nature just discussed, a board-level modem. For our purposes, we will assume that the modem offers a significant amount of intelligence. A board-level or expansion board modem is one that contains all the components on a single board, as depicted in Figure 3-6. This

**Figure 3-6** Hayes Microcomputer Products' Smartmodem 1200B (Courtesy Hayes Microcomputer Products Inc.)

board plugs directly into one of the PC's expansion slots, or directly on the motherboard. An expansion board modem offers a number of benefits over a stand-alone modem. Because the modem plugs directly into a slot, no space outside the PC unit is needed for storage. This factor alone may convince you to purchase this type of modem if space is limited. Furthermore, because the modem resides within the PC, whenever you move the computer the modem is automatically carried along.

Another benefit of a board-level modem is that no special serial port is needed. Because no port is required, no RS-232 cable is required. Furthermore, no additional power outlets are needed. The modem draws its power from the slot within which it is placed. The only cable requirement is one of a modular cord to connect the modem to the telephone outlet. Since the modem is internally housed in the PC system unit, the board is not readily accessible for hardware switch op-tioning. Most of the options are set via software-controlled commands, which is considered a major benefit.

Although an expansion board modem offers a variety of benefits over the stand-alone version, there are a few other considerations. An expansion board modem requires a dedicated slot. This implies that the modem conforms to the ex-pansion slots. If for some reason the user outgrows or upgrades to a different sys-tem, the modem cannot be used. The chances that the new computer system will support the expansion board could be slim. A new modem might have to be pur-chased for the system. The only way to circumvent this is for the vendor to offer a housing that can be used with an expansion board modem. If this is available, the board-level modem can be converted into a stand-alone modem with this acquisi-tion. The housing will provide an inexpensive slot equivalent to the one in the com-puter. The lack of a housing accommodation is one reason the board-level modem is cheaper than stand-alones. Should this feature become available, the user must then supply an RS-232 interface as required by any stand-alone modem. This reduces the risks associated with purchasing a plug-in modem.

Also, use of a board-level modem does not allow for the optimization derived from sharing the modem between multiple computer types. Because an expansion-level modem is physically plugged into a computer, no other computer can use the modem except by moving it from one machine to another. The modem is dedicated to the PC that contains it unless some sort of local area network that offers device sharing is used.

### Stand-Alone Modems

Should the risks of purchasing a board-level modem be of major concern, a stand-alone modem is the alternative. A stand-alone modem offers the same trans-mission capabilities as an expansion board modem but is housed separate from the PC. This type of modem has been used with computer systems long before the PC came into existence. Because of this, some modems do not yet incorporate microprocessors to offer the features of an intelligent modem. Nonetheless, they can be used with the PC. The ability of keyboard dialing is not present, so an external telephone set must be used for dialing a number. Once the computer answers, the operator must enter the data mode. There are a significant number of such modems around. For example, the AT&T 212A can be used with the PC 6300. This unit requires a telephone together with an RS-232 port on the PC. The number is dialed on the phone associated with the 212A modem and placed on-line by depressing the exclusion key. The exclusion key places the modem in the data mode.

Within the past few years, stand-alone modem vendors have incorporated microprocessors into their units as in expansion board modems. This does provide the intelligent modem features of the board-level modems. Keyboard dialing and keyboard commands are equivalent to those of board modems. Many vendors offer these modems, including those that offer board-level modems. Examples of these include the Hayes Smartmodem 1200, Ven-Tel 1200 Plus, AT&T's 2212A and 4000 series, and U.S. Robotics Passport modems. Because of the installed base of Hayes modems, most vendors now offer a Hayes-compatible mode. This mode allows the modem to accept commands normally issued to a Hayes. This is known as *emulation*. For example, the Rixon PC212A offers a Hayes emulation mode.

Modems of the type just described offer benefits over their board-level competitors. A stand-alone modem has indicator lights on the front panel. These lights are used for modem testing as well as providing a visual indication of the status of the transmission. Indications for send and receive data, carrier detection, and data terminal ready are generally present.

The optioning of the modem is done by flipping switches. The switches are generally easily accessible because the modem housing design allows for this. If a modem reset is required, a switch is usually provided. If not, the modem can be powered down because it has its own power source. The heat generated by the modem does not add to that of other equipment inside the PC.

The two remaining benefits of stand-alone modems deal with flexibility. The pitfalls of expansion board modems, portability and shareability, are two of stand-alone modems' best features. Because a stand-alone modem is individually housed, it is not PC-specific. All that is required for connection to a PC is a serial port that conforms to the RS-232 interface. Because the modem connects to a standard interface, it may be used with other computers without concern. If the user outgrows the PC, the modem may be used with the new system. If a U.S. Robotics Passport modem was purchased for use with the IBM PC, it could also be used with the new system as long as a serial interface was provided. Many IBM PC plug-compatible computers are being offered today. The stand-alone modem is assured of working with these machines, whereas an expansion board modem is not guaranteed to work with these look-alikes. The portability of the stand-alone modem between different computers is a benefit to consider when faced with the acquisition of a modem.

Office environments are not necessarily limited to one PC. Often, multiple PCs as well as other types of computer systems are present. If the computers are not needed for constant communication with remote systems, a modem could be shared between two or more computer systems. The stand-alone modem lends itself to this environment. As long as the computer systems have serial interfaces, the modem can be shared. This feature allows for a substantial savings in equipment costs, as the user may reduce the total number of modems needed for multiple PC environments.

The RS-232 interface on a PC can also be shared. A single serial port may be used for multiple modems, printers, plotters, and a mouse. However, only one of these devices can be active at any given moment. The PC currently offers a means of addressing only two serial addresses, COM1 and COM 2. The ability to share a port is a means of overcoming this limitation. Recall that an expansion board modem required one of these addresses. Use of a stand-alone modem with a serial board allows for optimization of the COM1 and COM2 addresses.

If stand-alone modems allow for optimization of resources, what are the downside risks of such a purchase? Space is a consideration. A stand-alone modem requires storage space. The RS-232 distance limitation is 50 feet, so the unit must be placed somewhere near the computer. This could be of concern in an office environment where space is at a premium. Vendors are addressing this space factor by offering smaller modems that attach physically to the PC. For example, the U.S. Robotics Passport modem is three-fourths the size of normal modems. It also comes with a Velcro strip for mounting it on the side of the PC. Both of these features circumvent the space problem. If the modem is attached to the PC, when the PC is moved, so is the unit. Otherwise, the modem would have to be transported separately when moving the configuration.

Perhaps the biggest pitfall of stand-alone modems is that of the cable requirements. Because the modem is freestanding, a separate power source is required. The cable to the power outlet can be difficult to conceal. Furthermore, if the modem is not adjacent to the computer, an extension cord might be required. In addition to the power cord, an RS-232 cable is needed between the serial port and the modem. With this requirement comes consideration of the cable length and gender of the connectors. In most cases the PC serial port will have a male connector, while the modem has a female plug. The male is often referred to as a DB25P, where the "P" stands for pins or plug; the female is known as a DB25S, where the "S" stands for socket. The pins plug into the socket. If the cable provided is not long enough to reach the stand-alone modem, as is often the case, another RS-232 cable could be used as an extension. This cable is a cord with a male connector at one end and a female connector at the other. This is the same concept as that used in a standard extension cord used in the home. The only consideration is that the distance of all cabling should be less than 50 feet to conform to the standard.

If the cable distance between the port and the modem is greater than 50 feet, there are a couple of ways to complete the connection for error-free transmission. For one way to handle this, refer to the section on short-haul modems later in this chapter. However, if the distance is less than 500 feet, special cables are available to connect the two devices. They are referred to as *shielded cables* and are manufactured with special wrapping to extend the distance. Black Box Corporation is one company that offers such a cable. Their trade name for the product is Extended Distance Data Cables. These cables have been tested to 500 feet at speeds up to 9600 bits per second (bps). Generally, the cost of such cables is based on the number of RS-232 leads that are present. When connecting a PC to a modem, the author recommends that 12-conductor cables be used. This allows for both asynchronous and synchronous operation. There is also a charge for the connector at each end of the cable. These cables can be an effective way to connect a PC and modem with a significant distance between them.

## Communication Software

As you can see, there are many alternatives for communicating with remote computer systems using a PC. Our exploration of the various modems addressed the hardware requirements of communicating systems. What applications dictated the need for this communication? In other words, what software is to be used between the IBM PC or compatible and another PC or mainframe? Perhaps the PC is used to access remote databases on an IBM mainframe or Digital Equipment Corporation minicomputer or a UNIX system. Perhaps the PC will be used to connect to The Source for retrieval of news. This could involve the collection of information from these remote computer systems for local printing or perhaps storage on the PC's disk system. Collected and edited information may need to be transmitted back to the remote system for file updates. The programs that offer these and other services are referred to as *communication software, terminal emulator programs,* or *file transfer programs.* Specialized software packages are available for each of these services. However, the trend is toward incorporating these features into one program. Communication software extends a user-friendly interface to the computer operator for an otherwise complex system environment. Without the use of these software packages, the knowledge level of the average user would have to be upgraded. However, the user is now somewhat removed from the details of communication environments. This is made possible by menu-driven software that may already have setup procedures for communicating with popular information services such as Dow Jones/News Retrieval or The Source. Access to these types of services may require only one or two keystrokes, as shown in Figure 3-7.

The software that turns the IBM PC/XT into a terminal is often tied to specific modems. For example, Hayes offers a communication package, Smartcom II, which is written to work in conjunction with their Smartmodem series. PC-TALK III is a similar type of program offering similar features but designed to work with the bulk of the intelligent modems available. Regardless of the package being used, the common functions provided are transmission and reception of data. The communication software should transmit characters generated on the keyboard and display information received through the modem. This basic mode of transmission is referred to as *teletype transmission,* in which characters are transmitted and received at low speeds, typically 300 or 1200 bps. This transmission is the most popular of asynchronous modes involving 103- and 212-type modems. This minimum capability is common to all communication software. Enhancements beyond

```
Smartcom II                    Hayes Microcomputer Products, Inc.

1. Begin Communication   *. Receive File         7. Change Printer Status   (OFF)
2. Edit Set              *. Send File             *. Select Remote Access    (OFF)
3. Select File Command   6. Change Configuration  9. Display Disk Directory  (ON)
A,B,C - Change Drive                              0. End Communication/Program
                         Press F2 For Help
Enter Selection: 1       O(riginate, A(nswer: O
Enter Label: A           Phone Number: 1 555 1212

Communication Directory:

A - THE SOURCE Telenet      J - THE SOURCE Tymnet      S -
B - DJN/R Telenet           K - DJN/R Tymnet           T -
C - CompuServe              L - CompuServe Tymnet      U -
D - KNOWLEDGE INDEX TEL     M - KNOWLEDGE INDEX TYM    V -
E - Peoples Msg System      N -                        W -
F - Access (Phoenix)        O -                        X -
G - FORUM-80 (Kan City)     P -                        Y - Remote Access
H - ABBS (New York)         Q -                        Z - Standard Values
I - ABBS (Chicago)          R -

                                                ──────Smartmodem: UNAVAILABLE─

00:33:16                   Tuesday January 1, 1980                        CAPS
```

**Figure 3-7** Hayes Microcomputer Products' Smartcom II screen (Courtesy of Hayes Microcomputer Products, Inc.)

this are what separate the various communication packages. For example, the program can be as simple as that shown in Figure 3-8. Disk, monitor, printer, modem, and setup features are added to basic and enchanced transmission features to make these packages suitable for business applications in addition to home requirements. The next section will elaborate on the specifics of each feature.

One of the key features of communication software is its ease of use with standard and intelligent modems. Most packages will work with a standard modem such as AT&T's 212A modem. This modem has no auto-dial features or terminal prompting. Consequently, the user must manually dial the remote system with the associated phone, as mentioned previously. However, because the price of microprocessor-based modems is falling rapidly, you may decide later to upgrade to an intelligent modem. Should this occur, you will not want to purchase another software package. It is better to plan for support of both modem types than to purchase separate packages.

If you purchase an intelligent modem, the auto-dial feature should be used. The software package should capitalize on this feature. Auto-redial enables the user to redial the number accessed most recently. Continuous redial enables a user's PC or compatible to attempt continually to dial a number until a connection is estab-

```
 5 CLS
10 OPEN "com1:1200" AS #1 'sets up port 1
20 OPEN "scrn:" FOR OUTPUT AS #2      'sets up screen for displaying data
30 PRINT "make the call manually or by waking up the smart modem."
35 PRINT "hit a couple of returns"
40 B$=INKEY$      'gets input from the keyboard
50 PRINT #1,B$;      'displays characters gathered from line 40
60 IF EOF(1) THEN 40   'checks for end of file indication
70 A$=INPUT$(1,#1)   'gets characters from modem
80 PRINT #2,A$;      'displays characters gathered from line 70
90 GOTO 40           'repeats above procedure
```

**Figure 3-8** Dumb. Com Program

lished or until a preset number of attempts have been made. Both of these enhancements could require entry of the phone number. However, if the phone number is associated with a frequently accessed computer system, a directory of such numbers should be storable on the disk system. A directory of frequently accessed numbers allows for quick selection and connection with a remote system. The number of directory entries varies by package and is generally menu driven. Menus allow for each phone number to be assigned a letter, number, or symbolic name for quick reference. The user merely selects from the menu the system to be accessed, which will automatically set up the store options.

The aforementioned features are generally tied to the modem attached to the PC. The PC and the remote system often have characteristics that don't jibe very well. The various transmission features of communication software address this potential problem. Each of the two communicating systems may output data in a different fashion, having nothing to do with the associated modems. Rather, these characteristics relate to the format and characters transmitted. For example, a remote system may transmit only a carriage return character, indicating the end of a line. If the PC receiving the data attempts to display the data, all the information will be written on the same line, with overwriting occurring. The operator will not be able to read the data received. A line feed associated with every carriage return would solve this problem. Good communication software packages offer the ability to monitor the incoming or outgoing data stream and add or delete characters as needed. In this case a line feed could be added automatically by the software package whenever a carriage return was received. Another example of the monitoring capability is in the area of control characters. Reception of these characters may cause problems for the PC. For example, when receiving information from The Source, end-of-file (EOF) characters are intentionally embedded throughout the text being transmitted. The PC takes appropriate action when it receives the EOF character: It closes the file. To avoid this inadvertent action, a filtering function is offered. The communication software may be set up to monitor all incoming data and remove any EOF characters, thus allowing complete reception of the data. Along the same lines, certain mainframe computers may output different end-of-line (EOL) characters. Communication software allows for the substitution of the appropriate end-of-line character as needed.

In addition to the data-stream-handling capabilities offered by communication software, operational considerations must be addressed. Specifically, when communicating with remote computer systems, log-ins and passwords are required. Even when accessing discount communication services 'such as Telenet and Tymnet, multiple log-ins and passwords are required. The communication software should allow for storage of these strings of data. If stored, function keys may generally be used to recall them instead of entering them manually at each use. Persoft's SmarTerm/PC packages allow this, as shown in Figure 3-9. Furthermore, the package may be set to monitor the received data searching for the standard remote system prompts for this security-related data. Once received, the software would automatically transmit the log-in and password, freeing you of this repetitious task.

```
        TE100-FT SETUP PROGRAM - Version 2.1e
        (C) Copyright 1982, 1983 by PERSOFT, INC.
                    Configuration 1:
               SOFTKEY ASSIGNMENT UPDATE

Shift F1:   AT_____
Shift F2:   D 1 555 1212_____
Shift F3:   LOG ME ON PLEASE_____
Shift F4:   HERE IS MY PASSWORD_____
Shift F5:   _____
Shift F6:   _____
Shift F7:   _____
Shift F8:   _____
Shift F9:   _____
Shift F10:  _____
```

**Figure 3-9** Persoft's TE100-FT function key setup

## File Transfer

One other transmission-related feature deals with the transmission and reception of large quantities of data, specifically, too large a quantity for the computer to act on at any given moment. This problem generally surfaces when dealing with the disk-related feature of file transfer, also known as uploading and downloading of files. If a user is logged onto The Source and is receiving imporltant data that he or she wishes to save for later use, the software allows for the capturing of these data to disk. In order for the PC to write this information to a file on its disk system, it needs to halt temporarily transmission from the remote system. This dictates that the PC must be able to tell the remote computer when to stop the flow of data. This feature, termed *flow control,* is supported by most communication software packages. Flow control allows the PC to transmit a character, known as XOFF, to the remote system, ceasing transmission. The remote computer must recognize this character and interpret it accordingly. The PC will then have time to complete its write to the file. When ready to continue reception, the PC indicates this to the remote computer by transmitting an XON character. The computer then resumes transmission. Flow control reduces the risks of losing data because the PC is not ready to receive. With this the file transfer capability allows for the reception, or downloading, of large files from a remote computer. The same is true when the PC operator desires to transmit, or upload, a file to another PC or mainframe computer. The receiving device may have need to halt the transmitting PC temporarily, using flow control.

Specific file transfers require special attention. If non-ASCII files, known as *binary files,* are being downloaded to the PC, abnormal closing of the file could occur. Binary files are typically in assembly or machine language code. When received, some communication software may misinterpret bits for the EOF marker and inadvertently close the file. The communication software should allow for these specific types of file transfers without errors.

Capturing of files to disk is only one option for the data received. The data may be stored in memory for editing purposes. Once the changes are completed on the data in the PC's memory, the data may be retransmitted to the remote system.

This allows for prompt and easy updates to information without the need to reinput the data.

## Protocol

Not only is flow control necessary to avoid losing data, but a mechanism is often desired to insure accurate reception of data. Electrical noise is possible on communication facilities. If this occurs, errors are probably induced in the data. This may not be a major concern with files to be used on a word processing system. However, with transaction-type information such as that used in accounting, where many numbers are involved, such errors are significant. To avoid this, a method of detecting and correcting errors is needed. As discussed in the data communication overview, parity identifies bad data. No corrections are made. To allow for detection and correction of errors, a protocol is used. A *protocol* is an orderly means of accurately exchanging data between two communicating computers. A protocol has sophisticated error-checking algorithms, allowing for the identification of bad received data. The receiving computer, upon detection of incorrect data, asks for retransmission of the data. One of the most widely used protocols between communication software packages on the PC is the Ward Christensen XMODEM method. The XMODEM method must be used in pairs, meaning that the communication software on the PC and that on the remote system must both support it. The use of this protocol is prevalent in CP/M machines and the corresponding CP/M bulletin boards. By offering the XMODEM on PC communication packages, the user can be assured of error-free files.

## Printer Support

For backup reasons, hard copy of the data being received may be desired. If a printer is attached to the PC/XT, the communication software should allow for a print on-line function. This enables the operator to issue a command for the printer to print all the data as they are being received. As with the disk access, flow control may be required when a slow-speed printer is involved. The other printer-related feature of communication software requires the filter and substitution capabilities. Some systems, including the PC, often use tab characters instead of spaces in files. When printing on-line these tab characters may not be interpreted correctly. Conversion to an appropriate number of spaces may be required for proper printing or displaying of information. The communication software should be set up to monitor the data received and to substitute spaces as needed.

As one can see, communication software packages offer a significant number of options for the modem, transmission, disk, and printer features. If a user accesses the same system on a day-to-day basis, it is futile to rekey or manually set up the PC communication software with these options at each session. Ease of setup should be provided by allowing for the storage of all parameters related to a given configuration. As needed, the user would merely retrieve the saved communication

```
        ┌──────  CROSSTALK - XVI Status Screen  ──────┐        Off line

NAme     CROSSTALK default settings              LOaded    C:STD.XTK
NUmber   1 555 1212                              CApture   C:MARTY.

┌──────── Communications parameters ────────┐   ┌────── Filter settings ───────┐
 SPeed 1200    PArity Even    DUplex  Full     DEbug    Off    LFauto    Off
 DAta  7       STop   1       EMulate VT-100    TAbex    Off    BLankex   Off
 POrt  1                      MOde    Call      INfilter On     OUtfiltr  On

┌──────── Key settings ────────────────────┐   ┌────── SEnd control settings ──┐
 ATten  Esc              COmmand ETX (^C)      CWait    None
 SWitch Home             BReak   End           LWait    None

┌──────────────────── Available command files ─────────────────────────────┐

 1) NEWUSER       2) SET1200B      3) STD       4) TEST1


Command? _
```

**Figure 3-10** Crosstalk XVI by Microstuf

parameters for easy system setup. Once called up, editing will be easy for any minor changes between systems. Crosstalk XVI is one of many packages allowing this. Its setup screen is shown in Figure 3-10.

## Terminal Emulation

Software packages offering only the foregoing features generally turn the PC into a teletype-like device with smart terminal features. A teletype was a device that merely received data and printed the data on paper. Because no screen was used, the device was generally called a teleprinter. Examples of such devices include the Texas Instruments TI Silent 700 Printer, the General Electric Terminet 300, and the AT&T Model 43 Teleprinter. These devices have the capability to receive one character at a time, print it, and perform a carriage return and line feed at the end of each line in the same fashion as a typewriter acts. When CRTs arrived they also used this teletype mode of transmission. The data when received were displayed on the current line of the cursor. At the end of the line a carriage return and line feed were performed.

Teletype devices, also known as asynchronous ASCII terminals, sufficed for remote communications when mere transfer of data was involved. More sophisticated applications were eventually developed requiring specific types of asynchronous ASCII terminals or CRTs. Applications of this type were developed on minicomputers such as the Digital Equipment Corporation (DEC) PDP series processors and required DEC-manufactured terminals. For example, text processors were developed on DEC minicomputers to capitalize on specific features found only on the DEC VT52 terminal. Text processors were the predecessors to today's word processors. These applications required the manipulation of text on the VT52 screen. One way to achieve this was to retransmit the entire screen of data each time a change was made in the text. At 1200-bps operation over the communication line, retransmission of a full screen, 1920 characters, would take approximately 16 seconds (1200 divided by 10 bits per character into 1920 characters). If an access charge was associated with the use of the text processor, this was an unacceptable method of making changes to text. DEC resolved this by placing intelligence into the VT series terminals. The terminals allowed for direct cursor positioning anywhere on the screen. This feature alone saved transmission time by reducing the number of characters transmitted to make a text correction. The application positioned the cursor at the location of the incorrect data, allowing the user to correct the data directly. Function keys were added to the terminal for quick action using a single keystroke. The application would interpret the reception of a typed function key and take corresponding actions. The applications were programmed to issue command strings understood by the VT-type terminal.

Other applications were written to rely on specific features of terminals. Examples include menu-driven applications, accounting applications, and data forms packages. Menu-driven applications benefited by only having to send cursor positioning characters followed by the text instead of the full screen including spaces. Accounting software derived the same benefits. Forms entry packages capitalized on the cursor positioning features to paint a form on the screen. Furthermore, the cursor could be placed in the first blank field on the screen. Once the data were entered in this field, a carriage return would be typed. The forms package would receive this and position the cursor in the next field, either on the same line or on another line. These terminals also supported features such as underlining, highlighting of fields, protected fields, hidden fields, and a nonblinking cursor. All of these allowed for clearer presentation of information to a terminal operator.

If you have used a database management system such as dBASE or Microsoft's MultiWord word processing system on the PC, you have experienced the aforementioned features and may not have been aware of it. Applications such as these capitalize on the capabilities for direct cursor positioning, line deletion, underlining, and others. The commands used to perform these actions are specific to the PC, just as the VT series terminals responded to their own set of commands. The DEC was only one manufacturer of a terminal that understood a specific set of commands. Others include Hewlett-Packard's HP2621, IBM's 3101, Lear Siegler's ADM series, and Televideo's 900 series. Each of these had its own unique set of commands for the various screen functions. A function as simple as clearing the screen and placing the cursor in the home position of the CRT, line 1, column 1, varies among the terminals. For example, the IBM 3101 terminal requires an ESC H sequence to be sent by the remote computer system to home the cursor. The DEC VT100 terminal requires an ESC, left bracket, and H to perform the same function. The DOS 2.0 operating system has a command, CLS, which will clear the screen and place the cursor in the home position. The differences between this and other commands become obvious when using the IBM PC to access the text processor, menu-driven programs, and forms data entry applications of both mainframes and minicomputers. The commands sent by the applications are received by the PC but are not interpreted properly. Even if the PC is running the communication software discussed previously, these commands are processed improperly. A program is needed that will receive these terminal-specific commands and translate them into commands that the PC understands. Such programs are called terminal emulator packages. Vendors offer DEC VT100, IBM 3101, HP2621, Lear Siegler ADM 3A, Televideo 900, AT&T 4410, and other popular terminal emulator software. These packages receive the commands from the remote system, such as the home command, and issue equivalent commands that the PC understands. Use of terminal emulator packages on the PC allows the user to access a multitude of applications otherwise not available. Generally, 95 percent of all the features found in the terminals are offered in the software programs. The features not implemented may or may not be required for your installation. For example, most TE packages emulating the DEC VT100 do not support the 132-column mode found in the terminal, smooth scrolling, split screen, reverse video, and double-high and double-wide characters. The TE software brochures usually list the features not implemented. Insure that the remaining 5 percent of the features are not required within the applications accessed using the emulator software on the PC.

Terminal emulator software allows for more powerful replacement of old terminals with the IBM PC and compatibles. This benefit alone allows the PC to be flexible enough to access multiple systems. If different asynchronous terminals were used to access computers running terminal-dependent software, the PC is a single replacement for multiple terminals. The user merely selects terminal emulation software as needed, even if multiple packages are required. Businesses find this benefit a worthwhile investment in itself, as terminal costs may be reduced. The capabilities of terminal emulator packages offered today extend beyond basic emulation. The standard features found in a basic communication software package are also included. These features include file transfer uploading and downloading, filtering and substitution of characters, stored parameters, and functionality with both intelligent and nonintelligent modems. SmarTerm/PC is an example of a terminal emulation package offering TE and communication software capabilities. DEC VT100 or Data General Dasher emulation with programmable function keys is offered in addition to file transfer capabilities. Even the 132-column mode of the DEC VT100 is supported if a California Computer System SuperVision monitor board is used. PC/InterComm by Mark of the Unicorn offers similar features, with up to thirty function key assignments. Linkup by Information Technologies Inc. offers a communications support system offering asynchronous terminal emulation. See our earlier discussion of synchronous emulators, as this system offers communication hardware and software to include synchronous support in addition to asynchronous communication. Crosstalk XVI by Microstuf offers a long list of communication software niceties, including color capabilities (refer to Figure 3-10). Crosstalk allows the user to set the color of the characters, their background, and the status line. Furthermore, multiple terminals may be emulated with this software program, including the Televideo 900 series, IBM 3101, Adds Viewpoint, and the DEC VT series terminals.

The average user of the PC in the home who accesses services such as The Source or the Dow Jones/News Retrieval networks will not require the capability of emulating specific terminals. The features of a standard communication software package will generally suffice. However, business use of the PC/XT and compatibles will probably require the terminal emulation capability. An example of how the PC and a communication software package with terminal emulation software would be used is that of a minicomputer offering a word processing system. Normally accessed by a specific terminal with fancy editing capabilities, the PC could be used instead. Instead of the PC accessing the remote system and remaining connected while a document is created, the document could be created locally on the PC for later file transfer into the system's word processor. The PC operator could optionally insert results from a spreadsheet into the text prior to uploading. The use of the PC in this environment does not tie up the main computer system as would a standard terminal. Freeing up the communication ports on the remote system could save a business an investment in hardware that could be used for additional communication ports. Furthermore, the document could be stored locally on the PC. This could offload the minicomputer, especially in the case of an IBM XT and compatibles with its hearty 10 megabytes of storage. With file transfer, archiving is possible on the PC/XT. Consult Appendix B for attributes of popular asynchronous terminals. These are useful when writing software for the PC that is running the emulator software packages.

These communication factors will be explained in greater detail when they are discussed in a product-specific context in later chapters.

## AUTOEXECUTION

Many functions are provided by both UNIX and MS-DOS operating systems to allow the user to set and alter parameters that fine tune a configuration. These functions are either operating system commands or programs. A mechanism is provided within the software to perform these functions automatically when the system is booted.

Examples of such functions vary depending on whether the user is in an MS-DOS or UNIX environment. Within MS-DOS, a good example would be when a printer is connected to the serial port instead of the default parallel port. MS-DOS provides a command that allows all output to be redirected to the serial port. To initialize this, the user must key in a sequence using a MODE command. They must perform this every time the system is powered off and back on.

On the other hand, in a UNIX environment, a terminal's description must be known once a user logs in. This becomes important as applications are used that capitalize on terminal-specific capabilities (see discussion on termcap). Each time a user logs in, this definition must be set. If a DEC VT100 terminal is used, the UNIX system needs to know this. A UNIX command, TERM, is used to accomplish this.

Whether in an MS-DOS or UNIX environment, the user should not be required to set up these parameters each time he/she initializes the system or initiates a session. Autoexecution is a means of accomplishing this. Once set up, whenever a system is powered up or a user logs in, these functions are automatically executed. This saves the user from repetitious activities, as the computer will perform these without operator intervention. It is important for the user to understand what these are, as they are nice features of a system. For exact procedures on setting these up, refer to the chapters on the specific products, both MS-DOS and UNIX.

## EDITORS

The users of all systems are required to set up files in the computer system. How does one physically get text, data, or programs into the computer? Editors are provided with operating systems allowing the user to input information into the computer files. These are watered-down versions of word processors. Actually, they were predecessors to today's word processing system, providing the ability to input, alter, and delete information in a data file. Programmers use these to input their programs prior to compiling and executing them. The autoexecution functions may be set up using editors. In the absence of a word processor these may be used.

Some of these editors are very powerful. Features such as inserting, appending, and listing of data are common. However, the more powerful editors include the ability to search and replace text. Different versions are available, including line and full-screen editors. A line editor offers the ability to work on a line at a time, whereas a full-screen editor more closely resembles a word processing system by offering cursor-controlled editing. Once a user becomes familiar with a particular editor, they may be as proficient with it as they would be with a full-fledged word processing application program.

It is hoped that the above descriptions have offered users insights into terminology used in both MS-DOS and UNIX environments. To become a super user and properly set up a system, the reader must understand all these concepts and terms. Once these are understood, the reader is ready to proceed with the actual installation of a system.

# pc 6300 environment

# 4

In this next section a brief overview of the PC 6300 is given to establish a reference for describing DOS environments. Any reference to the PC 6300 is applicable to the IBM PC/XT. These configurations will be used to explain similarities and differences of operating system environments, command sequences, system administrations, and configuration setups.

## AT&T PC6300

The PC 6300 is one of AT&T Information System's personal computers. It is an MS-DOS based microcomputer that is operationally compatible with the IBM PC/XT computers. This means that users have immediate access to a very large number of existing programs, ranging from word processing, electronic spreadsheet, business graphics, and database management software that has been written for Microsoft's popular operating system. In addition to this capability, the PC 6300 can use the same peripherals used by the IBM PC/XT.

Two common configurations are possible with the PC 6300, a dual floppy disk and a hard disk system. Their configurations are outlined below:

| Floppy Disk (CPU2) | Hard Disk (CPU3) |
| --- | --- |
| keyboard | keyboard |
| 256 kilobyte RAM | 256K RAM |

| | |
|---|---|
| 8 MHz 8086-2 CPU | 8 MHz 8086-2 CPU |
| serial port | serial port |
| parallel port | parallel port |
| clock/calendar | clock/calendar |
| monochrome/color graphics | monochrome/color graphics |
| 7 expansion slots | 6 expansion slots |
| Two 5 1/4-inch floppies | One 5 1/4-inch floppy (half height) |
| | One 10 MB hard disk (half height) |

In addition to the above, numerous options are available. These include 128K chip sets, a 256K memory expansion board, monochrone or color monitors, a mouse, small expansion box with 10 MB of storage, and 3270 interfaces.

A CPU1 is also offered with only a single 5 ¼-inch floppy half-height drive. Often this is desired when local area networking or other communications are used. We will feature this in later chapters.

Depending on the configuration used, six or seven slots are available for expansion boards. Boards that may be used in these slots are standard IBM-compatible boards. This is possible because the expansion slots for the PC 6300 are designed to be bus-level compatible. This implies that the boards are 8-bit boards allowing 8 bits of information to be transferred at once. However, two of these slots can actually contain boards that are designed to transfer 16 bits of data at once. These boards improve system performance due to increased speed of data transfer. The 256K memory expansion board is an example of this.

The PC 6300 has a number of built-ins. An RS-232 compatible port is included with any of the configurations. This may be used for connection of a number of different peripherals. Should a modem be required for communications, it could be connected to the serial interface. With the use of terminal emulation or other communication software, the PC may connect to other computer systems or information services for on-line data activities. If the PC 6300 is to be directly connected to a computer, such as a UNIX system discussed later, the RS-232 port will be used. The fact that this serial port is built in frees up slots within the personal computer. As more boards are needed for a configuration, the benefits of this feature are realized.

Also, an IBM-compatible parallel port is provided. Although printers may be attached to the RS-232 port, most are connected to the system via a parallel interface. The connector looks much like the serial port but behaves differently. (For clarification, the reader is encouraged to read *The IBM PC/XT: Making the Right Connections,* by Martin D. Seyer.) Although most printers have a parallel port that is compatible with a default standard Centronics parallel interface, IBM has given us a different method of connecting the printer to the PC. Be aware that both the serial and parallel ports on personal computers are now similar in appearance but not function.

A clock is included on the motherboard. It is kept accurate with battery backup that is recharging when the unit is powered up. This feature eliminates the need to input the time and date each time MS-DOS is booted. Furthermore, many programs will read the clock to log activities.

Regardless of the system, graphics are supported with resolutions of up to 640 by 400. All of the IBM-compatible modes are supported, including color graphics with four colors. With the enhanced color graphics board, 16 colors may be displayed simultaneously in high-resolution graphics mode. Whether in IBM graphics mode or AT&T super resolution, the graphics are exciting. With the enhanced color graphics boards, the PC 6300 is actually capable of supporting two monitors simultaneously. This could be handy when a graphics drawing with text is needed. One monitor could be used for color graphics display of charts, diagrams, or other graphics, with another monitor displaying text that accompanies the graphics. Also, the authors of this text expect that by publication date there will be terminal emulation software that exists to capitalize on the extensive graphics capabilities. Several graphics terminals exist that are used in computer-aided design—CAD—systems. One such example is the Tektronix 4014 graphics terminal. Because of the super-resolution mode and speed of the PC 6300, emulation software can be written allowing the personal computer to function as a specialized graphics work station connected UNIX-based systems.

## MOUSE 6300

AT&T offers a two-button mouse for the PC 6300, as shown in Fig. 4-1. This mouse plugs directly into the back of the keyboard. This connection does not take up a slot in the computer or an RS-232 port as others do. Because of this type connection, the PC 6300 base unit may be placed to the side or under a desk without concern for having to cable the mouse back to the base unit. The user can hide the computer with only the keyboard, mouse, and monitor on the desk top.

The mouse is very adaptable, as it can be used in nonmouse-based applications such as Lotus 1-2-3 as well as in mouse-related programs such as Microsoft Word. The MOUSE 6300 uses a "quiet as a mouse" rubber ball (see Figure 4-2) requiring no special surface for operation. Only six inches of desk space are required for the mouse to operate.

The MOUSE 6300 option includes all items necessary to install the peripheral. The package includes a special ROM chip that dramatically increases the speed of operation. The cable and connector are standard for easy cabling to the keyboard. Also included is a disk comprised of software used to allow the mouse to work with

**Figure 4-1** Mouse 6300 (Courtesy of AT&T Information Systems, Inc.)

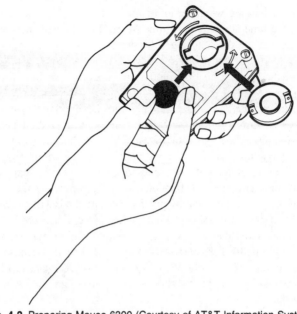

**Figure 4-2** Preparing Mouse 6300 (Courtesy of AT&T Information Systems, Inc.)

mouse-based software application. The list includes packages such as Microsoft Word and Multiplan, and Lotus's 1-2-3. For those software packages that do not support mouse operation, MOUSE 6300 may still be used, as the roller ball movement and buttons in the mouse may be user-defined. The following section outlines the procedures for setting up and using the mouse.

## MOUSE 6300 Installation

1. Turn the power off! I will repeat it—turn the power off!

2. Install the roller ball in the mouse.

3. Connect the cable from the mouse to the back of the keyboard as shown in Figure 4-3. Be sure to tighten the screws.

4. Install the MOUSE software onto the disk from which you boot the system.

   a. Format floppy—see section on formatting disks.

   b. Insert Mouse diskette in drive A, new formatted disk with operating system in drive B.

   c. At the A> prompt, type : copy a:*.*b: (This copies all of the files on disk in A to B. If a hard disk is used to boot the system, type: copy a:*.*c:)

   The mouse software is now loaded onto a disk that has the operating system on it.

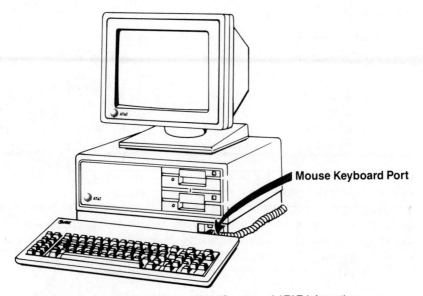

**Mouse Keyboard Port**

**Figure 4-3** Connection of Mouse 6300 (Courtesy of AT&T Information Systems, Inc.)

## Using the MOUSE 6300

Prior to actual use of the mouse with an application software package, the user needs to create a mouse setting. The procedure is similar for both mouse-based applications and standard keyboard-type applications, as in the following.

For keyboard-only software:

1. Type 'setmouse' followed by return (exclude quotation marks).
2. Use the mouse to point to KEYBASE.
3. Press the left button on the mouse to select this.
4. Define the buttons as well as the roller ball movement. Usually the defaults will work fine.
5. Use the mouse to point to SAVE and press the left button on the mouse. You are prompted for the filename that you want these settings saved in for later use.
6. Point to and select EXIT to exit from the setup software.
7. To actually use a setup file, type 'setmouse' followed by the filename from step 5. Keying in only the word 'setmouse' yields the default settings.

For mouse-based software:

1. Type 'setmouse' followed by a return.

2. Point to and select SETTINGS option.

3. Point to and select file from listing—for example, 'msword'.

4. Point to and select MOUSEBASE.

5. Point to and select EXIT.

6. Point to and select 'yes'.

The mouse will now be operational with the software, in this case Microsoft's Word. The above procedure could have been shortened by directly giving the filename initially with the 'setmouse' command. Using the above example, to set up for mouse use with Word, the user could type in 'setmouse msword'. The mouse will not be operational with the word processing program.

A program is included with the MOUSE 6300 for freehand drawing. The user, by typing 'setmouse dw', can draw line and block diagrams complete with supporting text and labels. This is similar to graph and drawing software normally purchased separately for hundreds of dollars. Once adjusted to, the mouse will be an invaluable partner to the PC 6300 personal computer system.

## PC 6300 FLOPPY DISKS

The PC 6300 offers three configurations: CPU1, CPU2, and CPU3. The CPU1 is a single floppy system incorporating a 5 ¼-inch floppy for data storage. The CPU2 offers two 5 ¼-inch drives, while the CPU3 contains both a floppy disk and a hard disk system. All of these drives, both floppy and hard, are half-height units. Because of this, two units can be placed in the same space as a single standard-size floppy drive. Approximately 180,000 bytes of information can be stored on each side of the disk. When both sides are utilized, over 360,000 characters can be saved.

## MOUNTING FILE SYSTEMS

Whether using MS-DOS or UNIX operating systems, a file system must be set up to be accessible prior to its use. This can be as simple as specifying a disk drive under MS-DOS. In UNIX systems, the user actually mounts a file system. Regardless of the system, the requirement is that the drive be active prior to accessing any files on the system.

### MS-DOS File System Mounting

Under MS-DOS, the user mounted the file system without actually knowing he/she did so. This was accomplished by denoting which disk drive was to be used. Under MS-DOS, the disk drive nomenclature was drive A:, B:, C:, and so on. When the user wanted to change drives to access different files, they merely typed in the drive name followed by a colon. See Figure 4-4 for the key sequence to accomplish this.

A) b:

B)

**Figure 4-4** Accessing files and drives

This MS-DOS command mounted the file system on drive B:. Whether the drive is a floppy or hard disk drive, the files are accessible. Mounting a file system was done on a frequent basis, as floppies are used to load and back up files.

FORMATTING MS-DOS DISKS: MS-DOS running on the PC 6300 allows for the formatting of floppy disks. The format command is used to break in floppy disks as in the following procedures.

Formatting a disk prepares it for use by the PC 6300. To format a disk, proceed as follows:

1. Insert the DOS disk in drive A (the bottom drive if you have two). Type

```
format b:
```

and press the Enter key.

2. You should see the following message on the screen:

```
Insert new diskette for drive B:
and strike any key when ready
```

If you have two drives, put a blank disk in drive B (the top drive); if you have only one drive, replace the DOS disk with a blank disk.

3. Press the space bar to tell DOS that you have inserted the new disk.

4. You should see the message

```
Formatting . .
```

followed shortly by

```
Formatting . . .Format complete
Format another (Y/N)?
```

5. If you do not want to format another disk, press the N key.

## PC 6300 HARD DISK

The PC 6300 offers a 10 megabyte half-height drive in one of its configurations, termed the CPU3. This allows room for a floppy drive in addition to the 10 megs in the same space normally occupied by a full-height 10 meg system.

The FDISK command is used to format the megabytes of disk space. Because of the large amount of space available, MS-DOS allows the hard disk to be split into different parts, known as partitions. These partitions may be used for storing different operating systems. You may also want to partition a fixed disk if several people will be using the same PC 6300. Once this is done, each user has his or her own storage area. The FDISK command presents the user with the following screen:

```
              Fixed Disk Setup Program

              FDISK Options

              Choose one of the following:

                 1 Create DOS Partition
                 2 Change Active Partition
                 3 Delete DOS Partition
                 4 Display Partition Data
```

Select item 1 to partition the surface of the hard disk. To actually format the hard disk, upon completion of the FDISK sequence the user should type the following with the DOS disk in drive A:

1. Type 'A:' return to return to drive A.

2. Type 'FORMAT C:/S return to actually format the disk.

3. Type 'COPY *.*c: return to copy all the system files onto the hard disk.

Now each time the system is powered up, or reset, and a floppy is not in drive A, the operating system will be loaded from drive C.

## COPYING PROGRAMS TO HARD DISK

To move application programs and data files from a floppy to a hard disk, the process is similar to the previous steps. With the floppy disk in drive A, issue a COPY command to move all or part of the files onto the hard disk. The following procedures may be used to accomplish this.

1. 'copy *.* c:' This copies all files of the active drive onto drive C.

2. 'copy data.txt c: This copies the file 'data.txt' to drive C stored under the same filename, data.txt.

3. 'copy data.txt c:qwert.txt This copies the file 'data.txt' to drive C stored under the filename 'qwert.txt'.

4. 'copy d* c: This copies all files beginning with 'd' to drive C.

5. 'copy *.txt' This copies all files with the suffix 'txt' to drive C.

These are a few possible combinations for copying files onto the hard disk so they will be directly accessible by the user without requiring have the floppy disk in use. Consult the MS-DOS User's Guide for all the options.

## RAM INSTALLATION

As of the publication date of this text, the CPU1 and CPU2 models of the PC 6300 come equipped with 128K of memory, whereas the CPU3 is shipped with 256K of memory. Please check your system documentation to be sure of the exact amount of RAM, as manufacturers change memory configurations depending on market requirements. For those environments where this is an insufficient amount of main memory, memory upgrades are available. In the case of the CPU 1 or 2, the memory on the motherboard must first be brought up to 256K using 64K chips. To install the memory, the user must gain access to the motherboard. An important feature of the PC 6300 is that the motherboard is physically turned upside down, as opposed to facing up as in other competitive products. Because of this, the unit may be turned on its side to actually gain access to the motherboard. To bring the system up to 256K of memory on the motherboard, proceed as follows.

1. Turn the power off! I'll repeat, turn it off!
2. Unscrew two screws, one on each side in the bottom back side of the system unit.
3. Turn the system unit on its side and slide the bottom plate forward, then out for removal of the plate.
4. Locate Bank 1 on the motherboard, the eighteen empty sockets.
5. Install RAM chips, insuring that pin 1 of the chip matches pin 1 of the socket.
6. Set the dips switches 1–4 of DIPSWO on the motherboard, found in the user documentation.
7. Replace the system module cover
8. Power system up.

To add memory beyond this amount, an optional memory expansion board is possible with up to 384K of memory for a total capacity of 640K. This board is placed in one of the slots found on top of the motherboard when the system is in its standard upright position. To install this board, proceed according to the following:

1. Turn the power off! I'll repeat, turn it off!
2. Remove the two screws in the top of the back side of the system unit.
3. Remove the cover by sliding the cover forward with the computer unit in its upright position. Next, lift up the back of the ivory colored top and pull it toward you.
4. Insert the memory expansion board in one of the two available slots with two

receptacle slots. These are full 16-bit slots, whereas the others are merely 8-bit slots compatible with all other PC boards.

5. Set the dip switches 1–4 in DIPSWO on the motherboard for the proper setting, depending on how much memory is now in the system.

6. Replace the system module cover.

7. Power up the unit.

For a more complete procedure, the reader is encouraged to consult the installation and user guides.

## RAM DISKS

For those systems where only floppy disk drives are available, a function exists for providing the user with the speed of access found in hard disk systems. Known as RAM disks, this concept evolved due to the relatively slow floppy disk access time. The input and output associated with an MS-DOS system tends to be the slowest operation in the system, and can cause a serious bottleneck. If you find your PC I/O-bound, as it is termed, consider a RAM disk. The electronic disk is as fast as a hard disk would be. Vendors have capitalized on the fact that large quantities of memory are available at relatively inexpensive rates. The previous section offered the user the procedure for upgrading the amount of memory available to the user. RAM disks are one of the reasons the user should consider maxing out the system RAM. Software was written to allocate a portion of the total memory available, up to 640K, to emulate a hard disk, hence the term RAM disk. Once memory is allocated for the disk emulator, a drive ID is assigned to the emulated disk. Files from a floppy disk may then be copied to the emulated disk for high-speed access. This copy routine may be part of the AUTOEXEC.bat file, which contains commands to be processed upon system reset or startup. Because all UNIX systems discussed in this text include hard disk systems, RAM disks are not used.

## PC 6300 CLOCK

The PC 6300—regardless of configuration, either dual floppy or hard disk version— has a built-in clock. The user may need to set the clock initially when the computer is unboxed. However, thereafter, when the computer is in use, the battery is recharging so that when "Power off" occurs, the time and date are maintained. MS-DOS has access to the clock at any time, as do all application programs running on the system.

To change or set the date of the clock, simply key in the command DATE and hit Return. The computer will display the current date with a prompt for a new date in the following manner.

```
Current date is MON 9-03-1984
Enter new date:
```

Simply key in the new date and press Return.

To change the time, the user follows the same sequence as the DATE command. Type TIME and press Enter. The current time and a prompt for the new time will be displayed as follows:

```
Current time is 15:34:13.20
Enter new time:
```

Merely enter the correct time according to the current time format and press Enter. The clock/calendar is now set.

## PRINTERS

To produce a written record of your results or programs, you must have a printer. The two most common types of printers are dot matrix and daisy wheel.

*Dot matrix printers* form characters by making patterns of dots in a rectangular grid. For example, the AT&T 473 and 475 Matrix Printers use a nine-dot-by-nine-dot grid. Figure 4-5 shows how these printers construct the letters T and H.

Dot matrix printers are generally fast and inexpensive. The 47X Matrix Printers produce 120 characters per second. This is about 1500 words per minute, 10 to 15 times the speed of the fastest typists.

Because of the gaps between the dots, the output of dot matrix printers is not as clear and readable as the output of a typewriter. Of course, the more dots in the printer's grid, the better its output looks, since the gaps are smaller. Dot matrix

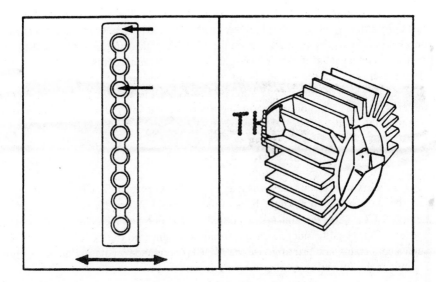

**Figure 4-5** Dot-matrix printing technique

printers also have the advantage that they can produce plots and pictures, since they can create any pattern of dots (say, for example, a rectangle) as opposed to being limited to printed characters.

By contrast, a *daisy wheel printer* works like a typewriter. That is, it actually imprints entire characters on the paper. Daisy wheel printers cannot draw pictures, but a user can obtain different typefaces and character sets (e.g., Greek letters or mathematical symbols) by changing character wheels. In general, daisy wheel printers are more expensive than dot matrix printers and are much slower. AT&T offers multiple letter-quality printers including the 455 printer, capable of printing at 55 characters per second. They also offer slightly slower printers for environments with lighter use. The 457 and 458 printers output data at 45 cps, differing only in the port used for local connection.

Which type of printer should you buy? If you do not need letter-quality output, a dot matrix printer is the best choice because of its higher speed. But if you need typewriter-quality print for business letters or documents, you should invest in a daisy wheel printer.

These printers are connected to the PC 6300 through one of two types of interfaces, serial or parallel. The serial interface used on the PC 6300 conforms to the Electronics Industries Association RS-232-C standard. It may be used to connect printers and other peripherals. However, the default port for connection of a hardcopy device is the parallel port. This port is a standard feature on the AT&T PC 6300. This feature does not require the addition of a special board to the computer, freeing up another slot in the computer system. This port is compatible with the IBM PC/XT parallel port and supports the same set of peripherals.

## PRINTING WITH THE PC 6300

For our purposes, assume that the user of the PC 6300 has a printer attached via a parallel interface. The parallel port on the PC 6300 is the same shape as the RS-232 port except that it is of the female gender. The default address of the printer is 'LPT1:'. Insure that the printer is powered on, is on-line, and has paper in it. To print the contents of the PC 6300 screen, merely hold down the shift key along with the PrtSc key. This action will cause the information displayed on the monitor to be output to the printer. Should hardcopy of all activity be desired, hold down the Ctrl key along with the PrtSc key. Everything that appears on screen hereafter will also be printed on the printer. To negate this and turn the printing off, merely repeat the action of holding down both keys.

Printers with serial interfaces may be used with MS-DOS. These printers plug into the male RS-232 port on the back of the PC 6300. To use this port instead of the default 'LPT1:', the user must first set up the serial port and then reassign the output address. COM1 is the address of the serial port built into the PC 6300. To enable such a connection and printing, use the MODE command by entering the following, excluding the quotation marks.

```
"MODE COM1:96,N,8,1 Return'   :sets up the port
```

```
"MODE LPT1:COM1   Return'        :redirects output to the
                                  serial port
```

This assumes 9600 bits per seconds, no parity, 8 bits, and 1 stop bit. If your printer requires different options, please enter them using the same MODE command sequences.

MS-DOS offers a command, PRINT, to print the contents of a file on the printer. This command offers the ability to print a text by merely issuing the following command sequences:

```
                PRINT filename
```

This is a nice feature, as it does not tie up the computer (see the section on spooling in Chapter 3).

### PC 6300 Spooling

The command that allows the PC 6300 to print using a spool function is PRINT. Discussed before, this command can dump the contents of a text file onto a printer. There are four options with command as follows:

```
'PRINT filename /T Return'   TERMINATE stops the printing
                             and removes all jobs from the
                             queue that have not been
                             printed.

'PRINT filename /C Return'   CANCEL suspends the printing
                             of the filename in the
                             command sequence and all
                             subsequent files until the /P
                             option is entered.

'PRINT filename /  Return'   PRINT begins the printing
                             operation. The preceding
                             file and all subsequent ones
                             are added to the queue.

'PRINT Return'               PRINT with no options
                             displays the contents of the
                             print queue on the screen of
                             the PC 6300.
```

## COMMUNICATIONS MANAGER

Refer to Chapter 3 for specifics on communication environments for the PC 6300. AT&T offers a combination communication software and board-level modem package known as the Communications Manager. This is a half-size card containing a

212A-compatible modem. This modem incorporates not only data communication functionality, but also support for simultaneous and voice communication. This board-level modem is plugged into any of the slots on the motherboard in the PC 6300. Follow the same procedures for removing the system unit cover as found in the memory section of this chapter. Once removed, the user merely plugs in the modem to acquire full- or half-duplex asynchronous communications. The interfaces for connections are modular jacks for a voice line, data line, and telephone set. Standard analog telephone sets are supported with this package. Key sets, of the 1A key type, are supported with the appropriate adapters to give them modular connections. This modem's features shine when used in conjunction with the communication software included with the product. This feature is discussed later in this chapter.

### Stand-Alone Modems

AT&T offers a number of stand-alone modems loaded with intelligence. Both the models 2212C and 4000 series modems will work with the PC 6300. All that is required is a serial port. Because the computer is equipped with an RS-232 serial port, the modems can be connected directly to the system unit. The user should note that the serial port on the computer is addressed as COM1, when setting up the appropriate communication software.

### Communication Software

If the user is not familiar with communication software, he/she is advised to review Chapter 3 prior to the next section discussing AT&T's Communications Manager.

### AT&T'S Communications Manager

Included with this offering, in addition to the 212-compatible modem discussed earlier, is voice and data communication software. This software offers many of the standard comm-software capabilities, as well as terminal emulation of a DEC VT100 terminal emulation. Some of the features include a call timer function, uploading and downloading of files, as well as many keyboard features. Also, both Touchtone and rotary pulse dialing are supported in addition to auto answer.

XON/XOFF flow control is included for communication with other systems that support this. The software offers the ability to monitor incoming data and append characters to the end of each line of text when received from a remote system.

Context-sensitive help is a very nice feature of the communication software. This is the ability to request help for any portion of the software when questions arise. As a user is using the Communications Manager, on-line help may be requested at any point during a session. This frees the operator from having to keep up with books of documentation.

Because the system supports both voice and data call activities, the directory capability is significant. The user has the ability to add, change, or delete entries into the directory, with a maximum capacity of 200 entries. Directory searches are possible with the inclusion of a find function. The directory may also be printed on an attached printer. These directory entries can be expanded to include all relevant information about a call destination. The user merely selects an entry to place either a voice or data call.

If a hard disk is available, the procedures are included for copying the system to that drive. This procedure is menu-driven, offering the user many options. The Communications Manager install routine allows the program to be placed in any subdirectory within the system. All loading is done automatically based on the selections the user makes during the install procedures.

## CONTEXT SWITCH

Because of the rapid growth in the number of personal computers requiring communication capabilities in addition to all other application support, a means of allowing both these operations had to be devised. The MS-DOS user is used to dealing with data files when working with a single application program. Because of the nature of DOS, only a single operation can occur at a time. However, this may not be acceptable as the user becomes more proficient and demanding with his/her system.

The best way to demonstrate this is by example. A word processing user may discover the need to access information stored on a different system while in the middle of document preparation. In most environments, the DOS user must exit the word processing program, load a communication program, connect with a remote system, retrieve the file, reload the word processing program, load the original document, and then merge the newly retrieved information. As you can tell, this is a laborious process for the simple requirement of adding a piece of text not currently resident on the PC's disk.

AT&T's Context Switch offers a means of overcoming this time-consuming process. As the name implies, this software package allows switching back and forth between two contexts or processes. Context Switch is a piece of software that resides in some obscure location in the PC's RAM and allows the user to bounce between two applications with ease by freezing one and enabling the other.

Using our previous example of the word processing environment, Context Switch could be used in conjunction with the word processing package and a terminal emulation package, such as the Communications Manager or EM4410. The user would load all three software packages: Context Switch, terminal emulation package, and the word processing software. The user would proceed through the word processing package software in the normal fashion. When the requirement of a foreign text file arises, the user would access the terminal emulation package through a function key supported by Context Switch. CS would then freeze the word processing program and enable the terminal emulation software. The user, not exiting any software, would access the remote system and perform the download operation of the file to the PC's disk system. Once completed, the terminal emulation program would be suspended while the user bounced back to the word processing program. Now the user could merge the newly retrieved text into the existing document through the standard word processing routines. This is accomplished without having to exit any programs, but merely by switching between the two applications, word processing package and terminal emulation.

The connection to the other computer is not limited to dial-up environments. It could be a permanent connection, enabling instant access to the computer with the PC acting as a terminal. When the remote computer is acting as a file server in addition to a host, this feature is of even greater value. Refer to Chapter 8 for environments where this would be appropriate.

# 5

## the AT&T UNIX PC

**Figure 5-1** AT&T Unix PC Model 7300 (Courtesy of AT&T Information Systems, Inc.)

## PRODUCT DESCRIPTION

The UNIX PC is a desk-top UNIX System V-based computer that can support up to three users. The UNIX PC incorporates telephone functionality into its basic system design. In addition, the UNIX PC includes the ability to have twelve active windows in a multitasking environment and a user-friendly front end to allow the naive user to operate the computer with minimum start-up training.

The following table summarizes the basic components of the UNIX PC:

| | |
|---|---|
| Processor | MC 68010 |
| Clock speed | 10 MHZ |
| Virtual memory | 4 MB |
| Internal memory | 0.5 to 2 MB |
| Address/data bus | 32/16 |
| Floppy disk | 320KB (IBM PC/AT compatible) |
| Hard disk | 10 or 20 MB Integral |
| Display bit mapped | 720 × 348 monochrome |
| Keyboard | 103 key detachable |
| Mouse | 3 button (keyboard attached) |
| Clock/calendar | Included on system board |
| RS232 port | 1 standard |
| Parallel port | 1 standard |
| Modem | 300/1200 included |
| Graphics | Standard |
| Windowing | Standard (12 windows max) |
| Telephone lines | 2 lines can be connected and a standard telephone |
| Expansion slots | 3 |
| Operating system | UNIX System V |

## SYSTEM ARCHITECTURE

The UNIX PC is based on the Motorola 68010 microprocessor running at 10 MHZ. In addition to standard UNIX System V features, the UNIX PC includes such features as demand paging, high-resolution bit-mapped graphics, and integrated telephone management.

**Modem**—The system board includes a modem-on-a-chip. This modem is a 212A-compatible 300/1200 bps intelligent modem that can be used to connect to other computers and time-sharing services.

**Floppy disk**—The 5 ¼-inch 320 KB floppy is compatible with IBM PC/AT floppy disks and can read an IBM-formatted data disk.

**Hard disk**—The UNIX PC can support a single 10MB or 20MB drive integral to the system unit. UNIX occupies 2.5 to 5 MB of space on the hard disk, depending upon the utilities loaded.

**Display**—The display is rigidly mounted to the system and cannot be detached. The standard display is a 12-inch monochrome green phosphor bit mapped unit featuring 720-by-348 resolution.

## WINDOWS

The UNIX PC can support 12 multiple active windows in a true multitasking environment. The user interface is Macintosh-like and makes heavy use of icons and context-sensitive help to aid the user. In addition, screen-labeled keys aid the user within the office manager function as well as application programs such as dbase III and Multiplan which have been written to take advantage of the windows on the UNIX PC.

Windows can be moved or resized by using the mouse in conjunction with icons that border individual windows. In fact, the UNIX operating system itself can be brought up in a window if so desired.

The standard funtions included with the UNIX PC include the windows, the Office Manager and the Telephone Manager, along with a core set of UNIX utilities.

The Office Manager window provides access to the all-administration-type functions as well as the office file cabinet and wastebasket.

The Telephone Manager includes the ability to place and receive voice calls, data calls, and electronic mail. It provides the ability to support either one or two telephone lines and a standard telephone that all plug into the back of the PC using standard telephone jacks.

## I/O PORTS

The RS232 port can support speeds up to 9600 bps and can be used to connect to a terminal, printer modem, or another computer. The Centronics parallel port provides a 36-pin interface to connect to a parallel printer such as the AT&T 470 and Epson FX/MX series printers.

## EXPANSION

Three slots are included on the rear for expansion. The memory expansion board plugs into one of these slots as well as the STARLAN local area network access unit.

## MULTI-USER

You can connect up to two users to the UNIX PC by using the RS232 interface and the on-board modem for access to install log-ins and passwords for these additional users.

## UNIX

The core UNIX system includes all the commands most users would ever use in addition to the window software and help files. The UNIX utilities include commands that are geared toward the experienced UNIX system user and software developer. This set includes nroff, vi, edit and bfs, for example. The Development Set includes ISAM, Sort/Merge, as well as the C compiler sccs utility and 68010 Assembler.

Because of the size of the UNIX operating system (2.5 to 5 MB), it may not be desirable to load all the utilities on an end-user system.

## THE AT&T UNIX PC 7300

One of the newest additions to the AT&T computer product line is this UNIX-based desk-top computer. The 7300 has some unique features that are not available in the current work-station marketplace. For example, included in the purchase price you get a machine with a minimum of 512K, a high-resolution monitor with a resolution of 720 by 348, an integrated 300/1200 bps modem, an RS232 port, a Centronics parallel port, a 10 MB hard disk, an IBM-compatible floppy disk drive, a keyboard equipped with a mouse, and a very sophisticated version of the UNIX operating system. In addition to all that, the system comes equipped with integrated telephone management features. You can plug your telephone into the system and use the computer to manage your calls. The Telephone Manager allows you to keep notes on each call, keep a history of all calls made, manage a telephone directory, place calls on hold, time the length of a call, and call another computer—all with software supplied with the standard system.

### Flavors of UNIX

The PC 7300 runs a version of the UNIX SYSTEM that is totally System V-compatible, conforming to the standards as set forth in AT&T's System V Interface Definition Document. This version of the UNIX system does provide some very interesting features beyond those included in the System V Interface Definition, such as demand paging, which greatly enhances system performance; graphics support for the bit-mapped display; support for the mouse; and windows. The system can communicate with other UNIX machines and exchange files and mail.

### Human Interface

Best of all, the system is simple to operate. The philosophy behind the design is that the user need not have any understanding of UNIX commands to operate the system. In keeping with that philosophy, AT&T has included such things as icons, pop-up windows, screen-labeled function keys, and context-sensitive help, all to aid the user. You will see throughout our discussion of the 7300 that it is an extremely user-friendly computer.

### Special Features

The PC 7300 comes equipped with some features not found in any other desktop UNIX-based system. The most predominant feature is of course the window interface that shields UNIX from the naive user. Beyond the windows, the most impressive feature is the integrated Telephone Manager, which will certainly appeal to all of us who rely on the phone for our business. The integrated modem and standard I/O ports add to the overall slick design of the product. This product is truly designed for the office, and I think you'll agree that even though it may not meet all your wildest expectations, you will want one on your desk.

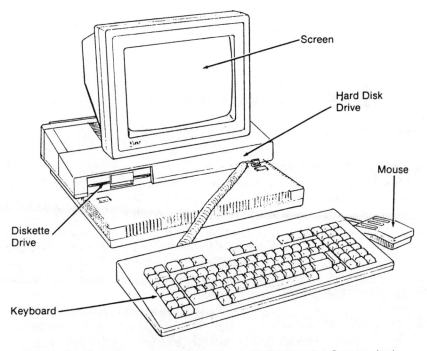

**Figure 5-2** Unix PC components (Courtesy of AT&T Information Systems, Inc.)

## HOW TO INITIALIZE YOUR AT&T UNIX PC MODEL 7300

The first step is to locate the installation guide. This book describes the unpacking process and identifies all the components. After unpacking the system you should assemble the mouse by installing the tracking ball in the underside of the mouse. Complete the installation by plugging the mouse into the right side of the keyboard, then drape the cable through the guides. Now plug the keyboard cable into the left side of the keyboard and the other end into the receptacle on the right side of the system housing.

### INSTALLING THE OPTIONAL MEMORY

If you have purchased any additional memory, you should verify that the power is off and remove the screws holding the cover of the first expansion slot. The expansion slots are located on the rear of the machine. Now plug in the memory card taking care not to touch the edge connector. Make sure that the card is fully seated in the slot. That's it.

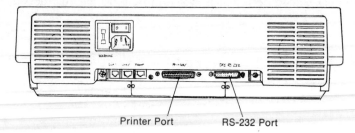

Printer Port                RS-232 Port

**Figure 5-3** Rear Unix PC (Courtesy of AT&T Information Systems, Inc.)

### APPLYING POWER TO YOUR PC 7300

Plug the power cord into the plug on the back of the computer and the other end into an 110V outlet. Reach behind the system and operate the power switch to the one position. The system will present a message and begin searching the hard disk. Eventually you will receive a message that tells you that you must set the date and clock. After pressing the enter key a window will pop up and present you with a form to fill in. To use the form, move the highlighted area to date by using the arrow keys or by pointing with the mouse. Press the (cmd) key to display all possible entries. Choose an item from this menu by depressing the <next> key until the month desired is highlighted, then press the <enter> key. The month will then be inserted into the form. Proceed to select and item and press the <cmd> key to se-lect the appropriate item. When the form is completely filled in you can press the <enter> key or point to the [OK] icon at the bottom of the window. The system will then display a window similar to the following:

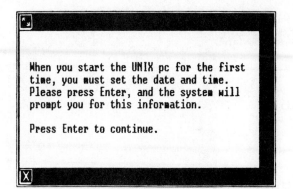

**Figure 5-4** Start-up Procedure

Ignore the message to shut down the system. We'll do this later. Ignore the message concerning the telephone setup by pressing the <enter> key. The following will be displayed:

```
VOICE 1: ACTIVE      Tue, F 8:49am

Welcome to the AT&T PC7300
Please login: tutor
```

Type in **tutor** in response to the log-in prompt and press <return>. The system will then display the office window.

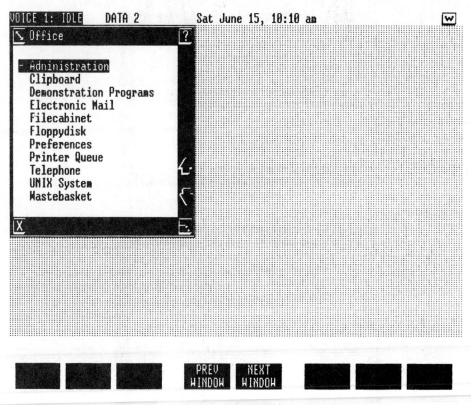

Figure 5-5 Office window

## HOW TO USE THE MOUSE

The mouse has three buttons that correspond to three keys on the keyboard.

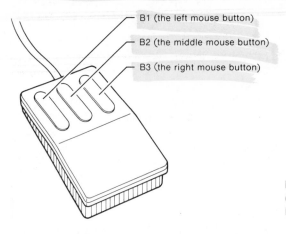

Figure 5-6 Unix PC Mouse
(Courtesy of AT&T
Information Systems, Inc.)

<B1>—This button corresponds to the <enter> key. It is used to select objects. You can alternate between the <enter> key and <B1> as you wish, since they perform the same function.

<B2>—This button corresponds to the <cmd> key on the keyboard. It is used to display the commands available with a given menu selection. You can alternate between the <cmd> key and <B2> since they perform the same function.

<B3>—This button corresponds to the <mark> key on the keyboard and is used to select multiple objects for action such as deleting several files in one step. You can alternate between the <mark> key and <B3>, as they perform the same function.

## WINDOWS

What's a window? A window is an area of the screen that looks physically like a window in a house. The casing or border surrounds the window and serves to separate a particular window from other windows. Windows are used to operate on different tasks either all at the same time or separately. For example, you could have a window performing a spreadsheet recalculation, another window sending mail to another system, and more windows performing other functions. This ability to have more than one task running at a given time is called *multi-tasking,* a built-in feature of the UNIX operating system.

## ICONS

An *icon* is a symbol that represents a familiar object. For example the ? icon is used to access the help facility. All you need to do is point to the icon with the mouse and press <B1> or the Enter key. Instantly you have help, which also labels the keys F1 through F8. Another icon is the exit window icon X. By pointing to the X and pressing <B1> or pressing the Enter key, you can exit an active window, which will cause it to be erased from the screen. Note that you cannot exit from the office window. The figure below will summarize the icons used in the PC 7300.

The **active** window is the window that is highlighted. You must make a window active in order to use its icons. To do this, move the mouse, point into the window, and press <B1>. This window now becomes the active window. You could also use the <next> <previous> keys to perform the same function.

To **move** a window, point to the icon and press and hold down the mouse button <B1>. Then "drag" the window outline slowly to the desired location. Once at the correct location, release <B1> and the window will be instantly moved.

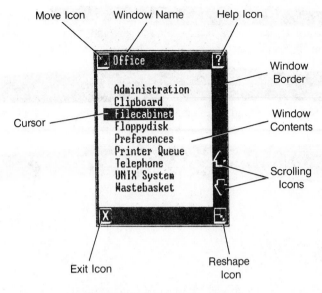

**Figure 5-7** Office windows icons

To **shrink** or **expand** a window, point to the resize icon and press and hold the mouse button <B1>. Then "push" the window outline up to the left to shrink it, or "pull" the outline down to the right to expand it. Once in place, release <B1> and the window will size to fit the outline.

## THE PC 7300 SCREEN

The PC 7300 screen provides four separate areas to display. First, the top line contains the status of the two telephone lines on the left, the date and time in the center, and a special icon W that is used to access the window manager, a special utility used to control multiple windows. The second area is the largest portion of the screen; it is the area where all windows will be displayed, such as the office window. The third area, known as the status area, is where the PC 7300 will tell you what commands it is executing. It is also where the working symbol will be displayed to indicate that the system is busy performing a task. The fourth and last area is the area at the very bottom of the screen that is used to label functions for the keys just below these boxes on the keyboard. These keys are numbered F1 through F8 and can be relabeled by the application as it so desires.

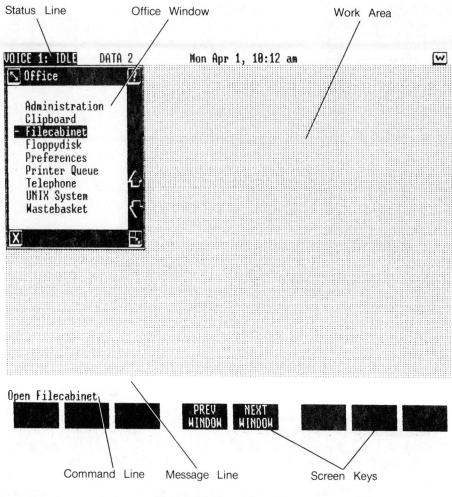

Status Line          Office Window                          Work Area

**Figure 5-8** Screen layout

## HOW TO SELECT ITEMS FROM THE OFFICE WINDOW

To select an item from any window, you must first highlight the item by using the mouse to move up or down the selections, using the keyboard ROLL UP and ROLL DOWN keys, typing the first letter or letters of the desired selection, and then pressing the Enter key or mouse button <B1>. A second window will appear and become the active window (highlighted). Notice the **prev window** and **next window** screen-labeled keys. You can use these keys to move back and forth between these windows. Remember, the active window is the highlighted window.

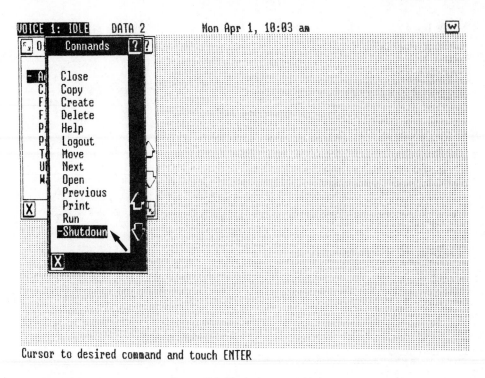

Cursor to desired command and touch ENTER

**Figure 5-9** Displaying commands

In addition to being able to open and close windows, you can display all the optional commands in a window by pressing mouse button <B2> or the <cmd> key on the right side of the keyboard. This will display the command menu. To select an item, just point and press <B1> or <enter>. The following screen display represents the following actions: Open the administration window and press the cmd key.

You should practice using the mouse, windows, icons, and help before continuing with the initialization process.

## INITIALIZING YOUR AT&T PC 7300

The process of initializing the PC 7300 includes the following steps:

1. Setting the system clock.
2. Setting up user log-ins/passwords.
3. Configuring the line printer.
4. Setting up the Preferences files.
5. Setting up the Telephone Manager.

6. Installing application software.

7. Backing up your system.

We will discuss how to perform these steps in detail and provide some tips on successful initialization techniques.

## SPECIAL LOGINS

The PC 7300 comes with two log-ins already installed. The first is **tutor,** which is provided for users to get acquainted with the system. The second is the log-in you should be using to initialize your system. This log-in is called **install,** and will allow you privileges that tutor does not provide. Now if you are logged in as tutor, you should exit any open windows and return to the office window. Highlight administration and then press the <cmd> key on the keyboard. This will bring up the list of commands; highlight **Logout** and press the <enter> key or <B1>. After a short time the system will present you with another log-in message and the windows will have disappeared. Type in **install** in response to the log-in message; eventually you will be back into the office window. Notice this time that the UNIX system appears as a selection in the office window. In addition, the administration window will provide many more functions than you had when you were logged in as tutor.

## EXPERT STATUS

The reason for expert status is that install, unlike tutor, has a log-in created with expert status set to yes. You, as the administrator, can control who has expert status and who does not when creating log-ins for other users.

## SETTING THE SYSTEM CLOCK

If you have not already done so or if you made a mistake on the initial power-up prompt, you should select administration from the office window and then highlight the second entry **Date and Time** and press <enter> or <B1>. The system will then present a form for you to fill in or change.

## HOW TO FILL IN A FORM

If you wish to change the month, highlight the month if it is not already highlighted and press <B2> or the <cmd> key; a list of months will appear. Highlight the month and press <B1> or <enter>. You will be back to the date and time window, and you can perform the same function for each field in the form. Once the form is complete, press <B1> or <enter> or optionally you can point to the {OK} at the bottom of the window and press <B1>.

This is standard procedure for filling in any form that is presented by the system. The mouse button <B1> or <cmd> key provides you access to all the possible admissible choices, and all you need do is highlight the entry and press <B1> or <enter>.

## HOW TO INSTALL USER LOG-INS AND PASSWORDS

We'll start at the office window and select administration just as we did when we set the date and time. The administration window appears and we'll select the very last item, User Log-ins; the following window appears:

After a few moments you will see the User form:

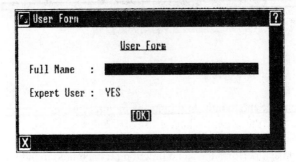

**Figure 5-10** Creating log-ins

The entry **show** is highlighted and the log-in by default is **install,** the current log-in. To add a log-in called **bill,** make sure that **show** is highlighted and press <B2> or <cmd> select **add** from the commands menu and press <B1> or <enter>. When you return to the user's window, the field **Log-in name :** will be highlighted. Since install already exists, we can begin to type in our new log-in **id bill.** Notice that as we begin to type, the field clears, and we can continue typing. Use the backspace key to correct any errors or the clear line key to start the line over.

Once form is filled in we can make the change by pressing <B1> or <enter>. At this point we will get another form to fill in, asking for the user's full name. Fill in this field with the user's name (makes sense!). In keeping with our example, type in **William Jones** and press <return>. The next field we are asked to either change or accept is **Expert User.** The default is yes, which will allow the user to have access to the UNIX operating system and the expanded administration functions. Consider the implications here; when in doubt, change the yes to **no** by listing the commands (you know how, <B2> or <cmd>) and highlighting **NO.** When you return to the user form, make the change by pressing <B1>, <enter> or pointing to the [OK], and pressing <B1>.

The system then will ask you to confirm the information you just entered. To cancel, press the **Cancl** key. We can continue entering log-ins in the same manner. When done, exit the user window by pointint to the X and pressing the <B1> or

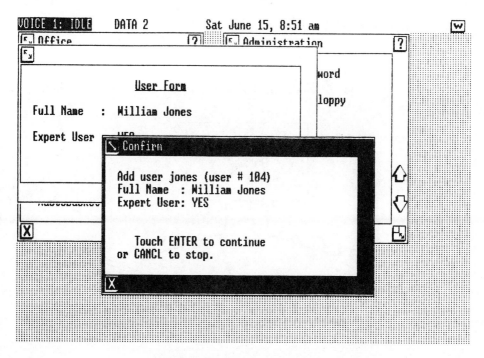

**Figure 5-11** Log-in administration

<enter> key, or optionally press the <exit> key on the keyboard. With the PC 7300 there are many ways to accomplish the same task.

Each user, expert status or not, has the ability to change or remove his/her own password. The default is no password. If you would like to add a password, you will have to log-in under the user's id and change password from the administration window.

For advanced UNIX users: If you want to make changes directly to the password file, you should log in as root and edit the /etc/passwd file.

## PREFERENCES

The UNIX PC allows you the ability to change the way files and menus will appear, what your editor of choice is, and the shell you will use. If all this sounds confusing to you, then you will be able to operate just fine without making any changes here. If you would like to make changes, highlight Preferences on the office window fill-in or change the entries as desired. If your editor of choice is the screen editor **vi,** make sure it is installed (Editing Utilities Package) and enter /bin/vi as the default editor. Do not make any changes to the default shell unless you know what you are doing.

## CONFIGURING THE PRINTER ON YOUR PC 7300

The UNIX PC comes equipped with both a serial RS 232 port and a Centronics parallel port. You have the option of either interface for your printer. The major difference from an installation point of view will be the cabling used to connect the

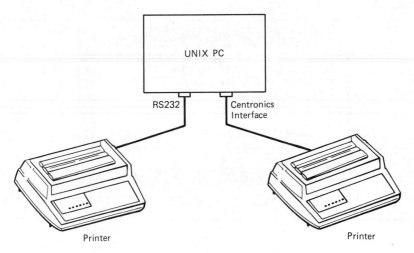

**Figure 5-12** Printer connection

printer to the system. Thus, the first step is to connect the printer to the selected port.

## CABLES

If you have purchased an AT&T printer such as the Model 475, the proper cabling should be provided. If you are installing your own non-AT&T printer, you should consider the cable very carefully. The parallel port on the PC 7300 presents a female (receptacle) type connector that conforms to Centronics standard 36-pin interface. Do not confuse this with the parallel port on the IBM PC or compatibles. The interface on these machines is Centronics compatible but uses a different connector DB25, which, believe it or not, is a 25-pin interface. Thus, the cable from an IBM PC or compatible will not work on the AT&T UNIX PC's parallel interface. What cable should you buy? A 36-pin Centronics male-to-male connector of the desired length to connect to your printer.

The RS232 port on the AT&T UNIX PC is also a female connector (receptacle) that uses a DB25 connector. This interface is configured for DTE, data terminal equipment, meaning that your printer should emulate a DCE (data communication equipment) device. If not, a special cable known as a null-modem cable may be required. For more information on connecting devices to RS232 interfaces, see Martin D. Seyer's book *RS232 Made Easy*.

## SETTING UP YOUR PARALLEL PRINTER

Make sure you are logged in as **install** and the printer is cabled to the system. Insure that the printer has a fresh supply of paper installed and the power is turned on. Next open the administration window from the office window and from there select Hardware Setup. Your screen should look like this:

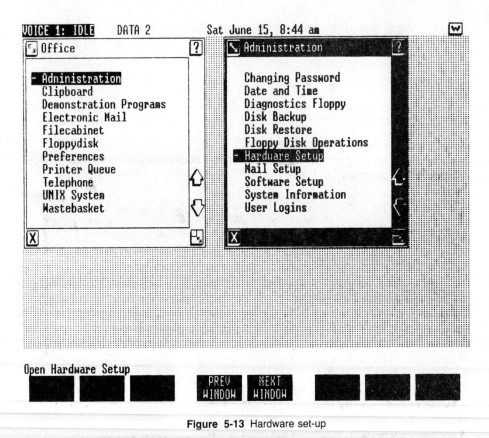

Figure 5-13 Hardware set-up

From the hardware window open Printer Setup and select the first entry, **Parallel Setup.** The next window displays the following:

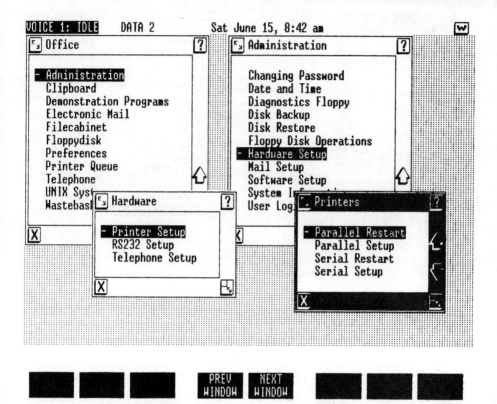

**Figure 5-14** Installing a printer on the UNIX PC

Press the <cmd> key for possible choices and you will see the following:

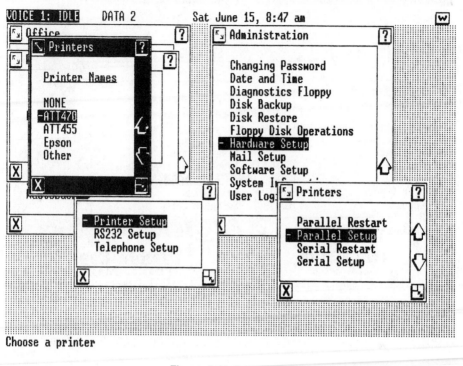

Choose a printer

**Figure 5-15** Printer selection

These printers are the ones currently supported by the UNIX PC. The entry NONE means that no printer is installed. The entry OTHER is used as a generic printer definition and can be used for most printers. The entries ATT470 and ATT455 are for AT&T's draft-quality and letter-quality printers, respectively.

## HOW TO INSTALL AN EPSON PARALLEL PRINTER

Because Epson is the predominant printer in the micro industry, we will indicate the steps to set up the Epson MX/FX series parallel printers. If you are using the AT&T printers, you should make the selection for those printer names in place of Epson.

With the parallel printers window displayed, press the <cmd> key and highlight Epson, then press <B1> or <enter>. This will return you to the parallel printers window; press <B1> or <enter> and the change is made. Touch <enter> when you get the warning message.

Make sure that the cables are seated and either locked in place or screwed in.

## TESTING THE PRINTER

To test the printer, you can press and hold the <shift> key while simultaneously pressing the <print> key. This will dump the contents of the screen to the printer. Be patient, as this can take up to 20 seconds before the printing begins. Of course if your printer does not support Epson-compatible graphics, the printout will not match the screen contents. You can use this procedure to print and screen currently displayed.

We experienced no problems disconnecting an Epson MX-80 from an IBM PC and setting it up on the UNIX PC. The windows were easy to use and the printer worked the first time without modification. However, if you have followed the steps and your printer is not working, check the printer options, especially flow control. If there is an option for flow control it should be set to XON/XOFF. In addition, check the printer queue via the office window to see if there are any requests queued for the printer. If there are requests in queue and the printer is not printing, you may have to perform a parallel restart. Do this by choosing administration from the office window. From administration take Hardware Setup and then Printer Setup from the hardware window. You will now be in the printers window and you can highlight Parallel Restart and press the <enter> key.

Now that the printer is installed and working, let's proceed with the next step and set up the Telephone Manager.

## SETTING UP THE TELEPHONE MANAGER

The UNIX PC can work with either one or two telephone lines and a standard telephone. First unplug the cord from the back of your telephone (the one that connects to the wall jack) and plug it into the UNIX PC line 1 jack. Next, if you have another

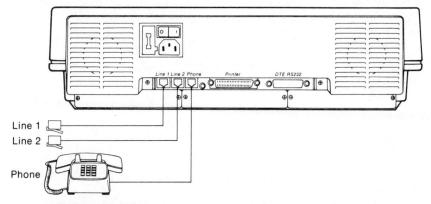

**Figure 5-16** Telephone jacks on rear of UNIX PC (Courtesy of AT&T Information Systems, Inc.)

line, plug that cord into the line 2 jack on the PC 7300. For the final connection, plug your telephone into the UNIX PC phone jack, using one of the two cords included with your system.

**What to do if you do not have the right connection**   Many of the "older" non-miniplug-type jacks still exist in some areaas. In order to use this type of line with the PC 7300 you'll have to convert the small block on the wall to the new miniplug-type jack. You can purchase the necessary hardware to do this at most department stores that carry telephones. This process is quite simple and requires no prior experience with telephone installation.

**What phones will work?**   The UNIX PC will work properly with any standard telephone, either rotary (dial) or Touchtone (pushbutton). Most telephones that will work in the home will work with the UNIX PC.

**What phones will not work?**   Some business telephone systems have multiline telephones with integrated electronics that provide the ability to have many lines on a telephone with 4–8 lead-type jack. The technology used here requires that the telephone transmit control information to a master unit or circuit pack. The master unit or circuit pack then returns dial tone for the proper line. This category of telephone is known as an **electronic telephone;** it will not work with the UNIX PC.

### Configuring the Software

Make sure you are logged in as **install.** If you are not, highlight administration and press the <cmd> key, highlight and select **Logout.** You can then log back in as install.

Open the administration window from the office and then open Hardware Setup. For the hardware window, select and open **Telephone Setup.** Your screen should look like:

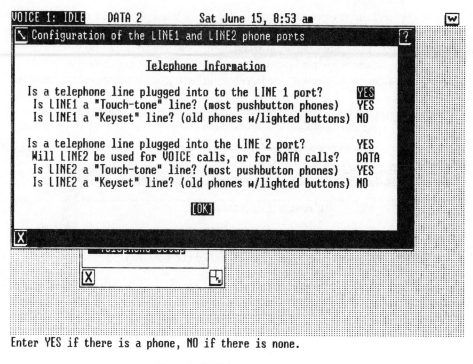

**VOICE 1: IDLE    DATA 2        Sat June 15, 8:53 am**                        [w]

**⬙ Configuration of the LINE1 and LINE2 phone ports**                         [?]

### Telephone Information

Is a telephone line plugged into to the LINE 1 port?      **YES**
Is LINE1 a "Touch-tone" line? (most pushbutton phones)    YES
Is LINE1 a "Keyset" line? (old phones w/lighted buttons)  NO

Is a telephone line plugged into the LINE 2 port?         YES
Will LINE2 be used for VOICE calls, or for DATA calls?    DATA
Is LINE2 a "Touch-tone" line? (most pushbutton phones)    YES
Is LINE2 a "Keyset" line? (old phones w/lighted buttons)  NO

                          [OK]

[X]

Enter YES if there is a phone, NO if there is none.

**Figure 5-17** Telephone setup

This screen allows you to define whether you have one or two lines, pushbutton or rotary dial, key telephone, and whether line 2 will be used for data or voice. The choices are made in the same manner we have used to fill in forms— using the <cmd> and <enter> keys.

**What if I have only one line?**   Fill in the information for line 1 and answer NO to the question "**Is a telephone line plugged into the line 2 port?**" You will still be able to use the UNIX PC to send both voice and data. If you need to change later to a two-line configuration, this can be done via the same process.

**Why does the system ask VOICE or DATA for line 2?**   The modem included with the PC 7300 can be switched between either line 1 or line 2. However, if you want your machine to be able to answer an incoming data call automatically, the modem should be on line 2 at all times. By choosing DATA for line 2 you are accomplishing just that. Any incoming calls on line 2 will be answered by the internal modem. If you have a two-line system, this will allow you to make a voice call on line 1 and receive mail from another system on line 2.

**What is a keyset?**  A keyset is a type of telephone found mostly in businesses. This type of telephone is an old-style set that has five buttons for lines and a hold button. The buttons light up when a line is activated or put on hold. The PC 7300 can connect to these type systems; when it places the call or puts a call on hold, the lights on the rest of the keysets will light up, letting the others know the line is busy.

The following screen represents a single-line configuration with Touchtone capability (pushbutton phone).

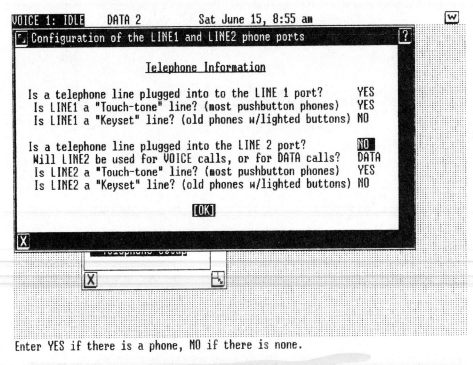

Enter YES if there is a phone, NO if there is none.

**Figure 5-18** Telephone setup, single-line connected

Once you have entered the form, the top line of the screen will indicate the status of the line and the mode. For example, **Voice 1: Idle** indicates that you have a single line, the line is idle, and it is in voice mode. We will see that this line will change as we use the Telephone Manager to initiate calls.

### Setting Up the Phone Manager Preferences

From the office window, select and open the item **Preferences.** Then select and open the item **Phone Manager.** Your screen should look like this:

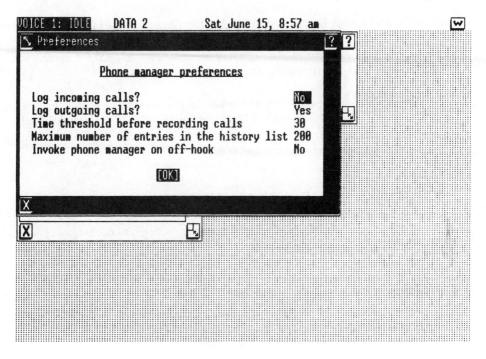

**Figure 5-19** Telephone preferences

**Log incoming calls?**   You have the option of answering yes or no. If you answer yes, you will be prompted for the name and telephone number of the calling party for each and every call. This information will be put into the call history file. Recommendation: Unless you have a specific need, answer no to this question.

**Log outgoing calls?**   Same yes or no option. However, on outgoing calls you don't have to do anything—the system does it all. It knows the name and number it dialed from the directory entry and will create the history entry with no intervention. The exception is if you use the keyboard dial feature, whereby the system will prompt you for the name. Recommendation: Leave set to yes.

**Time threshold before recording calls?**   This entry is the number of seconds that will transpire before a call entry is created in the history file. It is set at 30 seconds as a default, but can be adjusted from 1 second up to 999 seconds (16.65 minutes). Recommendation—leave it set to 30 seconds unless you have a specific need.

**Maximum number of entries in the history list?**   This entry determines the number of call records that can be created in the history file. Once the list is full you will be prompted to save the file, and the recording process starts over. You can have up to 999 entries in the history file. Your business or personal needs should dictate the size of the list. If you want to keep a month's calls at a time and save them in files labeled by the month, then take an educated guess and the number of calls you expect to receive during this period.

   **Invoke phone manager on off-hook?**   If you answer yes to this question every time you pick up the receiver of the phone connected to your system, the call screen will be displayed. This feature seems to be more of an annoyance than a benefit. Recommendation—leave it set to no.

## HOW TO USE THE TELEPHONE MANAGER

You can access the Telephone Manager by either selecting and opening telephone from the office window or by pressing <shift>-<F2> at any time. The call screen will look like:

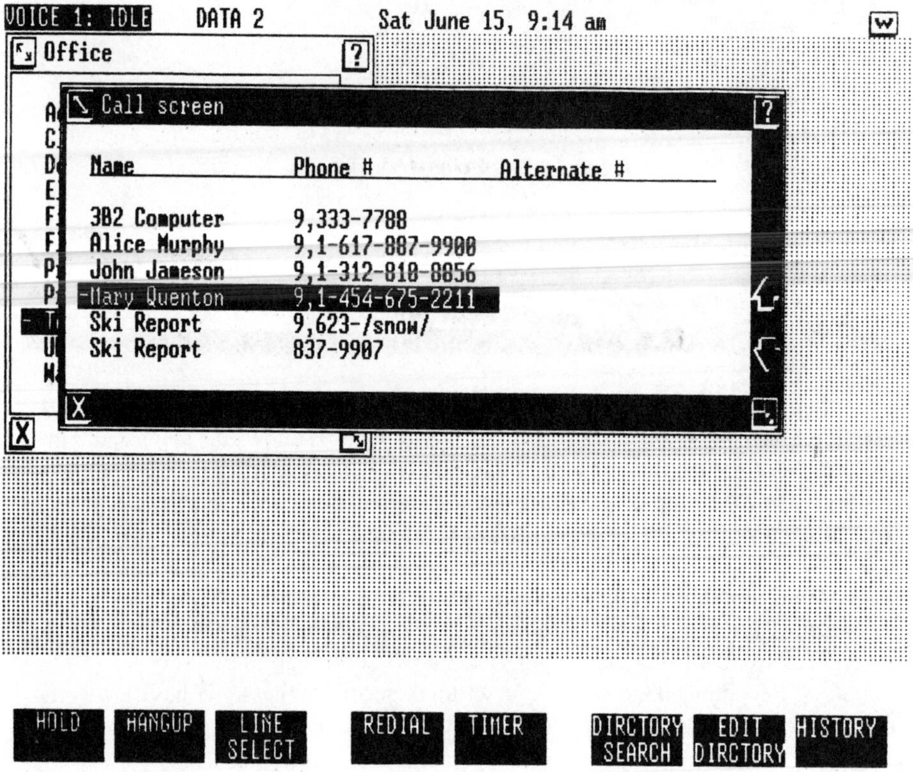

**Figure 5-20** Call screen

Notice that the screen has relabeled the function keys F1 through F8. These keys can be used to access all the major functions of the Telephone Manager. These keys perform the following functions:

HOLD—By pressing this key you can place a call on hold and return to it later. When activated, an asterisk will appear under the word HOLD. In addition, the line status will change from ACTIVE to <HOLD. You can return to your call by pressing the hold button.

HANGUP—This button allows you to hang up any call.

LINE SELECT—If you have two lines connected, you can use this button to alternate between line 1 and line 2. If you have a single line connected, this button will allow you to switch from voice to data.

REDIAL—Will redial the last number dialed.

TIMER—Press once and begin a stopwatch timer that appears in the upper right-hand corner of the screen. Press a second time to stop and a third time to clear. This timer can be used to time the length of an expensive call or a call to your mother-in-law, for example.

DIRECTORY SEARCH—Allows access to another window to search the directory upon any field you so desire. You can also dial from the directory.

EDIT DIRECTORY—Brings up another window from which you can enter new entries, modify existing entries, modify field labels, and so on.

HISTORY—Displays the history file and enables you to print the list or display any notes for calls in the file.

## How to Make a Voice Call

Use the EDIT DIRECTORY function key to access the edit window. Select **Create Voice Entry** and fill in the form:

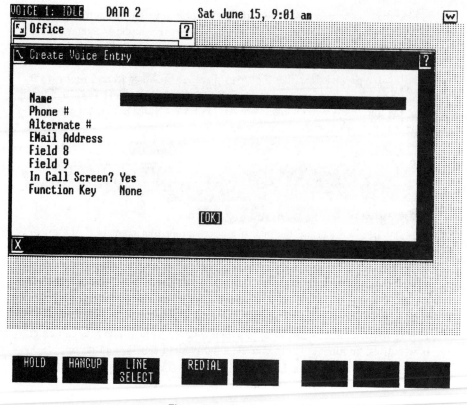

**Figure 5-21** Create voice entries

NAME—up to 50 characters of your choice

PHONE #—up to 50 characters; it can include special dial features for PBX (private branch exchange) systems.

Alternate #—up to 50 characters. This could be an alternate office telephone number, home number, or secretary telephone number.

EMAIL ADDRESS—up to six-character name for the computer at the distant end. Allows you to send "pink slips" to a remote PC 7300.

FIELD 8 and FIELD 9—These two 50-character fields can be customized by you. For example, you may want to include a customer identification code, organization number, Social Security number, employee id, and so on.

IN CALL SCREEN—The CALL screen can hold 15 numbers for display. Once the screen is full you will have to place your entries in the directory file. If you answer yes to this question, the entry will appear in the screen. If you answer no, the entry will appear in the directory. Recommendation—answer yes for the most commonly used numbers; answer no for infrequently used numbers.

FUNCTION KEY—By pressing the <cmd> key when this entry is high-lighted you can assign a telephone number to one of the function keys F1 and F3 through F8. By pressing <shift> Fx you can dial the number immediately. You might want to put the number of your secretary, home, or an emergency number on one of these keys.

Fill in the form with the information you desire and press the <enter> key. To dial the entry simply point to the entry; once it's highlighted press <B1> or <enter> and you will hear the system begin to dial the number. There is a slide switch on the lower right side of the keyboard to adjust the volume of the internal one-way speaker.

Practice creating and modifying voice entries to become familiar with the features of the Telephone Manager.

## COMMUNICATING WITH OTHER COMPUTERS

The PC 7300 can communicate with other systems using its internal modem. These systems can be other UNIX systems; however, any system that supports ASCII asynchronous communications should work fine.

The steps necessary to connect to another system seem somewhat convoluted after having set up voice entries. To begin the process, you must first create a **Modem Profile** in the filecabinet, then create a data entry in the Telephone Manager.

What do you need to know about the other system?

Name—the name you want to call the system. Note if you want to use the EMAIL ADDRESS to send pink slips this name must be six characters or less.

Telephone number—number of the system.

Speed—300 bps or 1200 bps (bits per second).

Parity—no, even, or odd parity and whether parity will be checked by your PC 7300 upon reception.

### Steps to Create a Data Entry

1. Log in as install.
2. Highlight and open filecabinet in the office window.
3. Press the <creat> key located on the left side of the keyboard.
4. Highlight and open Modem Profile.
5. Type in a name for your system. Write this name down on a piece of paper; you'll need it in step 13.

6. Press <enter>.

7. Highlight and open Terminal Setup.

8. Fill in the form using the <cmd> key to choose from the available entries. Press the <enter> key when the form is completed.

9. Exit all the open windows and return to the office window.

10. Highlight and open Telephone.

11. Press the Edit Directory key (F7) and open **Create Data Entry**.

12. Fill in the name and phone number, pressing <return> after each field.

13. For the field data profile name, type in the name from step 5 and press <return>. Note: Earlier, the system called this name a terminal profile name.

14. Press the <enter> key.

This process is complicated by the fact that the terminology is confusing. The name of the profile is called by different terms. In step 5 the name is called a terminal profile name and in step 13 it's called a data profile name. Consistency will avoid the confusion caused by this situation.

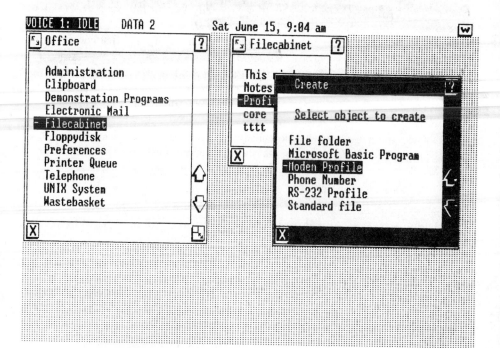

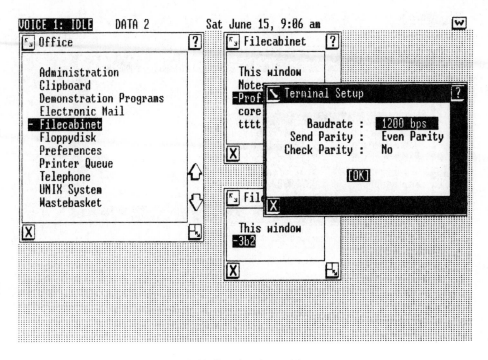

**Figure 5-22** Creating data entries

## How to Make a Data Call

Bring up the call screen by either pressing <shift>-<F2> or selecting Telephone from the office window. Next, highlight the entry for the computer you wish to dial and press <enter> or <B1>. Shortly you will hear the dialing take place and a short beep. The internal modem and the modem at the distant computer will complete an exchange of signals; finally the screen will clear and the line status will indicate DATA. If you do not see a log-in from the other computer, press the <return> key two or three times. When you get the log-in message you can begin your session.

## How to Exit a Data Call

When you've completed your session you can exit by pressing <shift>-<exit> to disconnect the line.

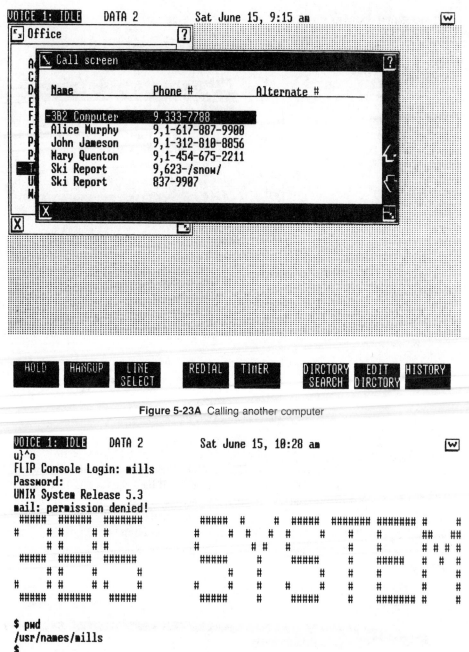

**Figure 5-23A** Calling another computer

```
VOICE 1: IDLE    DATA 2        Sat June 15, 10:28 am              W
u}^o
FLIP Console Login: mills
Password:
UNIX System Release 5.3
mail: permission denied!
#####  ######  #######        #####  #     #  #####  ####### ####### #     #
#     # #     # #              #      #     # # #        #       #     # ##   ##
     # #       # #            #        #    # # #        #       #     # # # # #
 #####  ######  ######        #####    #    #   #####    #    ##### #  #   #
      # #     # #                   #  #    # #       #  #       #     #     #
 #     # #     # #     #            #  #    # # #     #  #       #     #     #
  #####  ######  #####             #####    #   #####    #    ####### #      #

$ pwd
/usr/names/mills
$
$
```

**Figure 5-23B** Sample terminal session

# HOW TO BACK UP YOUR PC 7300

The PC 7300 allows you the option of backing up the complete system, backing up only those files that were modified since the last backup, or backing up a single user's files. The backup medium is the 5¼-inch floppy disk drive. It takes approximately 25 floppy disks to back up a full 10 MB hard disk. You must first format enough disks to back up the system. This is important as it will be difficult to abort the backup process once intitiated. Recommendation: Format enough disks for a full hard disk (25 floppy disks). You can always use spare formatted disks. To format a floppy, choose Administration from the office window and open Floppy Disk Operations from that window. Next, highlight and open Floppy Disk Format. You will be prompted to insert the disk, and the disk formatting will take place. Perform this process for all the disks that will be used for backup. See Fig. 5-24 for formatting steps.

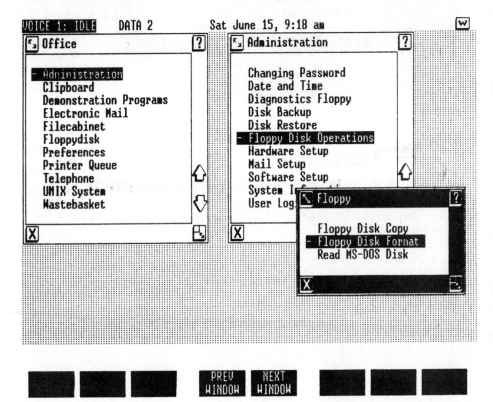

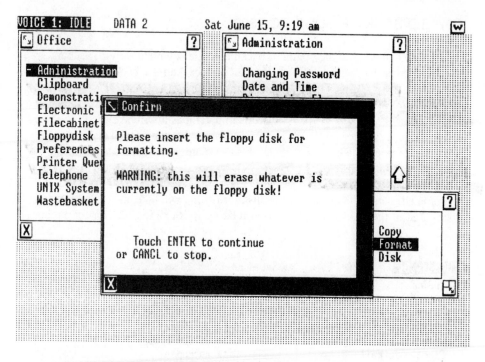

**Figure 5-24** Formatting floppy disks

Now that all your disks are formatted, you can select Disk Backup from the administration window and select and open Disk Backup. From the disk backup window, highlight and open Complete Backup and follow the instructions. You should be prepared to set aside enough time to perform this process, as it can be quite time-consuming. Figure 5-25 illustrates the backup options available.

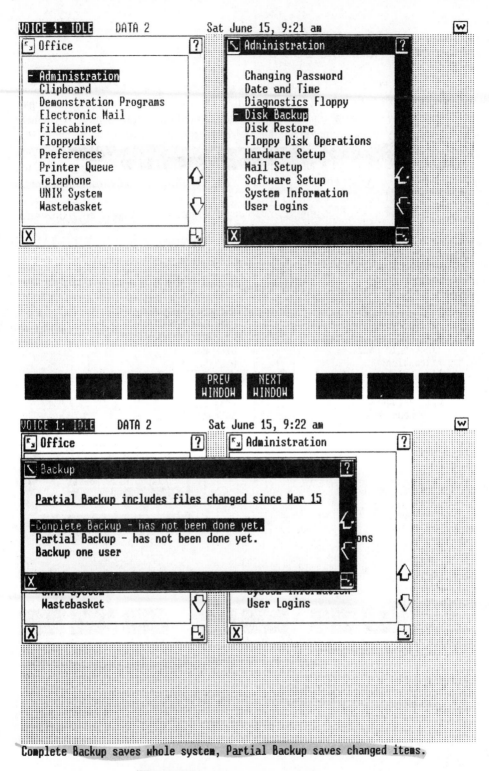

Figure 5-25 Backing up the UNIX PC

## HOW TO READ MS-DOS DATA DISKETTES

The UNIX PC can read in data from an IBM-formatted diskette and place the data into the system filecabinet for use by other programs in the system. For example, you may want to read in a text file and use the mail program to send it to a remote system, or you may want to read in a multiplan spreadsheet for use in the UNIX PC.

You have the capability of reading the directory on the MS-DOS disk and opening the file(s) you want to import into the UNIX PC. By selecting a file, the system will copy the contents into the UNIX PC's filecabinet and from there can be manipulated just like any other file.

The process of reading MS-DOS disks is straightforward; Fig. 5-26 illustrates the steps necessary to use this utility.

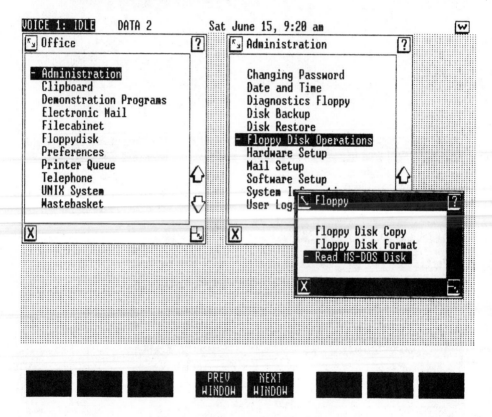

**Figure 5-26** Reading MS-DOS disk

## SHUTTING DOWN THE UNIX PC

Unlike most MS-DOS PCs, UNIX-based computers are rarely shut down to the point of removing power. These machines are intended to be left on and shut down only to perform maintenance or for shipment of the system to a different location. The UNIX PC fits into this latter category.

What does shutdown do? The process of shutting down the system insures the integrity of all open files and performs any outstanding disk writes by flushing the system buffers. The process is known as a "graceful" shutdown and is the preferred means of removing power to the system.

To shut down the system, from the office window highlight administration and press the <cmd> key. Select shutdown from the commands menu and press <enter>. The system will take a few minutes to present a message indicating that it is safe to remove the power. Remove power by setting the on/off switch to off. Figure 5-27 indicates the steps necessary to shut down the system.

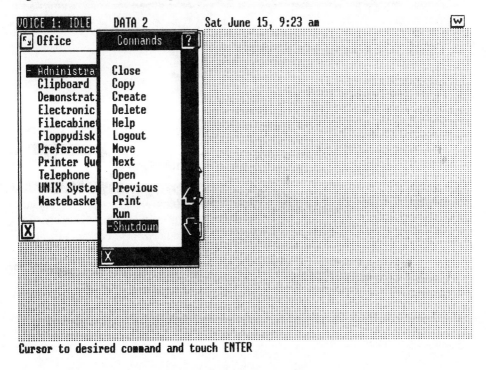

Figure 5-27 Shutting down the UNIX PC

# 6

# the AT&T
# 3B2 super micro

## PRODUCT OVERVIEW

The AT&T 3B2 computer is a 32-bit desk-top multi-user UNIX-based computer. The 3B2 is typically configured as a four-to-ten-user system; it supports applications written for UNIX System V. Some of the applications written for the 3B2 include INFORMIX, Multiplan, dBase II, and INGRES. AT&T has actively pursued software vendors to port their packages to the 3B2; the results of this effort are starting to pay off in the increased number of vertical and horizont al packages available for the 3B line.

At the low end, the 3B2 is priced below $10,000, but a more typical system is in the range of $16,000. This price does not include terminals for end users nor application software. The system includes four feature card slots for expansion and the connection of an add-on expansion module.

## CONFIGURATION

The following configurations represent the minimum, typical, and maximum arrangements for the 3B2:

|                    | Minimum | Standard | Maximum |
|--------------------|---------|----------|---------|
| Internal memory    | 512K    | 1MB      | 2MB     |
| Hard disk          | 10MB    | 32MB     | 104MB * |
| RS232 ports        | 2       | 6        | 18 (14) * |
| Parallel ports     | 0       | 1        | 4 (3) * |
| Floppy disk drives | 1       | 1        | 2 *     |
| Tape backup        | 23MB *  | 23MB *   | 23MB *  |

*Note that the XM (expansion module) is required to achieve this feature. The XM requires a slot in the 3B2 for connection of the cartridge tape controller. By adding the XM, this effectively reduces the maximum number of RS232 ports to 14 (3 slots × 4 ports each + the 2 system ports).

## EXPANSION MODULE (XM)

The XM can be added to the 3B2 computer; it provides the ability to connect one each of the following devices: floppy disk, hard disk, (either 32MB or 72MB drive), 23 MB streaming-tape drive. Maximum capacity is achieved by adding an XM with a 72MB hard disk, streaming tape drive and an additional floppy disk.

The XM is required for all configurations that desire tape backup. The tape unit provides a much faster medium for backup of hard disk data than the floppy disk alternative.

## SYSTEM ARCHITECTURE

The 3B2 is based on the WE32000 microprocessor and includes memory management firmware to enhance performance. The WE32000 microprocessor is a full 32-bit processor that was designed to run UNIX. It is part of a family of microprocessors that appear in other 3B products. The WE32000 can handle data in full 32-bit words, half words, or bytes. The following diagram depicts the overall bus structure of the 3B2.

**Memory management unit**—The MMU provides translation from a virtual address to a physical address used by the system.

**Memory**—Main memory is not plugged into the system board, but rather is contained on plug-in memory boards that plug into the system board.

**Memory boards**—These are available in two configurations, 256K and 1 MB boards. These boards plug into the two available memory slots located on the main

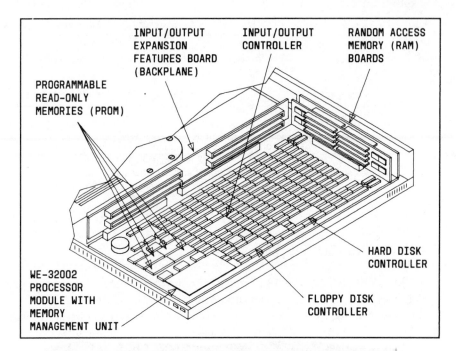

INPUT/OUTPUT
EXPANSION
FEATURES BOARD
(BACKPLANE)

INPUT/OUTPUT
CONTROLLER

RANDOM ACCESS
MEMORY (RAM)
BOARDS

PROGRAMMABLE
READ-ONLY
MEMORIES (PROM)

HARD DISK
CONTROLLER

WE-32002
PROCESSOR
MODULE WITH
MEMORY
MANAGEMENT UNIT

FLOPPY DISK
CONTROLLER

**Figure 6-1** 3B2 inside view (Courtesy of AT&T Information Systems, Inc.)

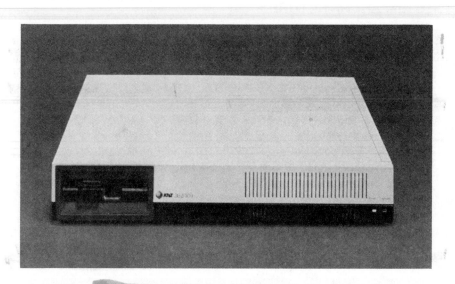

**Figure 6-2** 3B2 Computer (Courtesy of AT&T Information Systems, Inc.)

system board. The memory on the 3B2 is dual ported, meaning that there are actually two channels to access main memory. One channel is used by the main cpu and the other by DMA (direct memory access) devices such as intelligent I/O controllers.

**Hard disk**—The 3B2 has a single integrated hard disk that can be either 10 MB or 32 MB configuration.

**Floppy disk**—The 3B2 includes an integral 720KB 5.25 in floppy disk drive. The drive uses 96 TPI double-density, double-sided diskettes. All software for the 3B2 is supplied on floppy disk. In addition, floppy diskettes can be used to back up the system if so desired.

**I/O controllers**—The 3B2 uses intelligent I/O controller cards to provide connections to terminal, printers, and modems. Each I/O card has four RS232 ports and a parallel port and contains an on-board Intel 80186 to assist in I/O processing. The RS232 ports use a eight-pin (phone-type) jack to connect to RS232 devices. Cables and eight-pin-to-RS232 connectors are also provided to connect the RS232 interface.

**Ethernet/3Bnet card**—This card supports the lower levels of the Ethernet protocol and allows the 3B2 to connect to an Ethernet-type network running at 10 MB per second. In addition, this card also supports 3B Net, a high-speed 10 MB area network compatible with Ethernet at the lower levels. 3B Net can be used to interconnect 3B2s and 3B5 computers in a tightly coupled arrangement.

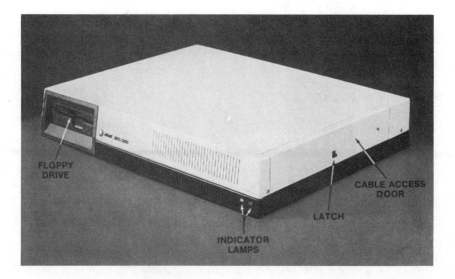

**Figure 6-3** Side view 3B2 (Courtesy of AT&T Information Systems, Inc.)

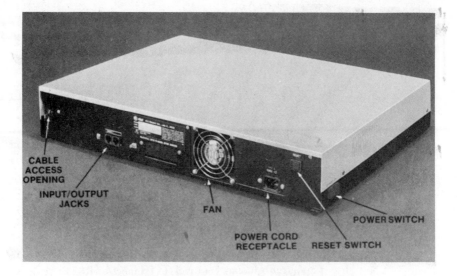

CABLE
ACCESS
OPENING

INPUT/OUTPUT
JACKS

FAN

POWER CORD
RECEPTACLE

RESET SWITCH

POWER SWITCH

**Figure 6-4** Rear view 3B2 (Courtesy of AT&T Information Systems, Inc.)

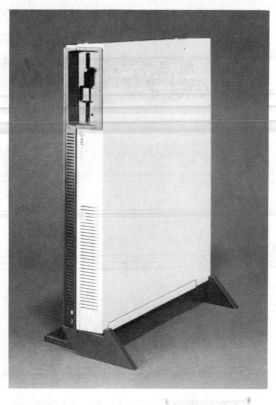

**Figure 6-5** 3B2 computer vertical mount (Courtesy of AT&T Information
Systems, Inc.)

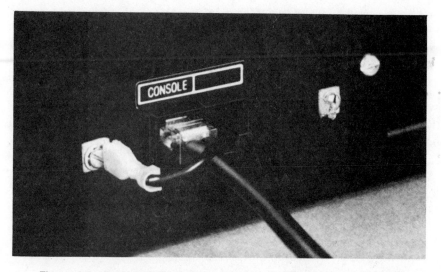

**Figure 6-6** 3B2 Console/Contty ports (Courtesy of AT&T Information Systems, Inc.)

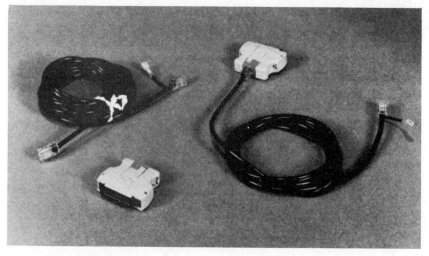

**Figure 6-7** 3B2 Cables and connectors (Courtesy of AT&T Information Systems, Inc.)

## SYSTEM INITIALIZATION

The process of initializing (bringing up) your system can be quite simple, as in the case of the PC 6300 and the AT&T UNIX PC 7300, or moderately complex, as in the case of the 3B2 Model 300 computer. The process involved is similar, but the method of execution is very different.

The PC 6300 is a clone of the IBM PC/XT; the initializing process is almost identical, using MS-DOS commands to perform functions. The AT&T UNIX PC, on the other hand, provides a windowing environment similar to the Apple Macintosh that allows the user to use pop up windows, icons, help, and forms to simplify the process. The 3B2 does not provide this windowing capability but does use menus to aid the user in performing many functions.

The process of installing memory, clock/calender, terminals, printers, modems, and add-on application packages is known as *system initialization*. For the PC 6300 and the UNIX PC Model 7300, the person performing this function may be the only user of the system, while the person performing this function on a 3B2 may be acting as an administrator for a system that supports multiple users.

**What documents are available?**    All 3B2 computers include the following documents:

*3B2 Owners/Operators Manual*

*UNIX System V User Guide*

*UNIX System V Release 2.0 Reference Manual*

*3B2 Computer Utilities Guide*

In addition, there are individual documents for each of the optional utilities, such as programming languages. If you have ordered the software, the documentation will be included.

Use the *3B2 Owners/Operators Manual* in conjunction with the steps recommended in this chapter. Read and note any documents describing **updates,** as these documents usually indicate known bugs and fixes.

This chapter is not meant in any way to replace the documentation you have received with your system. Rather, it is intended to complement the information within these volumes.

**What do I need to know before I start?**    It is certainly helpful if you have read the 3B2 *Owner's Operators Manual* for an overview of the major components, cables, and adaptors. The only tool required for assembly is a standard screwdriver for use in removing the cover.

You may think that a UNIX System is a UNIX System. Well, that's almost true. Each version of the UNIX system includes features not found in prior versions. The most current version is UNIX System V Release 2 Version 1. All references in this section refer to this version of the UNIX system on the 3B2 Model 300 Computer.

## INSTALLING MEMORY

The 3B2 can utilize two types of memory cards: 512K memory cards or 1 MB memory cards. Both of these cards are the same physical size but cannot be mixed in the same system. To install the memory boards, first remove the cover by removing the four screws located at the corners of the computer. See Fig. 6-1 for view of internal components. Make sure the power is off. Locate the two connectors marked M0 and M1, respectively. These slots are located behind the system board toward the back of the computer. Refer to Fig. 6-1 for exact location. Plug the memory board(s) into these slots and look in place with the retaining clip provided. Place the cover back on the computer and reinstall the four screws.

## CONNECTING THE SYSTEM CONSOLE

The 3B2 computer arrives with two connectors that resemble telephone jacks on the back of the main system unit. These eight-pin connectors are used in conjunction with special cables and RS232 adapters to connect to terminals, printers, and modems. First locate the port marked "console." This is the port (jack) on the left as viewed from the back of the computer. Plug one of the cables supplied with the system into this jack and plug the other end into an eight-pin-to-RS232 adapter marked terminal/printer. Plug the RS232 adapter into the terminal you intend to use as the console. This terminal could be a PC running a terminal emulator. In that case, the RS232 adapter would plug into the RS232 port on the PC. Once the console terminal is connected you must option the terminal for 9600 bps, full duplex, 8-bit ASCII, and no parity. You should refer to the information supplied with your terminal for the correct option settings, as they differ for each device. If you are using the AT&T 5420 terminal, set the parity to space parity for the terminal to function properly.

The port next to the console port can be used to connect to another terminal but is typically used for the modem connection. This port is known as the *contty port*. If you intend to to use a modem in the future, leave this port available, as it will make the installation process much easier.

## APPLYING POWER TO YOUR 3B2

Now that the system console is connected and optioned properly, you can switch the power on by operating the power switch on the left rear side of the computer. The system will then go through its "boot up" diagnostics. This process will test memory, the processor, hard disk, and floppy disk. If any errors are found, an error message will be displayed. Once everything tests properly, the system will display the "Console login :" message. UNIX provides a special log-in called setup that has special privileges. This is the log-in used to perform initial system functions. Type in the word setup (all small letters) in response to the Console log in: prompt. The system will respond with some text and will prompt you for some user information relative to log-ins and passwords. Establish log-ins and passwords for each user on the system. When you are entering passwords they do not display on the terminal as security precaution.

SELF-CHECK

DIAGNOSTICS PASSED

UNIX System V Release 2.0 3B2 Version 1
unix
Copyright (©) 1984 AT&T Technologies, Inc.
All Rights Reserved
                    Time of Day Clock needs Restoring:
                    Change using "sysadm datetime" utility
The system is coming up.  Please wait.
This machine has not been used as a customer machine yet.  The messages that
follow are from checking the built-in file systems for damage that might have
occurred during shipment.  As long as you do not see either of the messages
                            BOOT UNIX
or                     FILE SYSTEM WAS MODIFIED
all is well. If either message does come out, call your service representative.
However, the machine is still usable unless I tell you otherwise.
I will now start checking file systems.

  /dey/dsk/c1d0s2
  File System: usr Volume: 1.1

  ** Phase 1 - Check Block and Sizes
  ** Phase 2 - Check Pathnames
  ** Phase 3 - Check Connectivity
  ** Phase 4 - Check Reference Count
  ** Phase 5 - Check Free List
  xxx files xxxx blocks xxxxx free

The machine appears to be usable.


          Welcome!
This machine has to be set by you. When you see the "login' message type
                        setup
followed by the RETURN key. This will start a procedure that leads you through
those things that should be done the "first time' the machine is used.

The system is ready.

Console Login:


# SETTING THE BACKSPACE KEY

The UNIX system uses the sharp character # as the default erase character. You can
set this to the backspace key on your terminal by typing:

```
$ stty echoe erase "^h" <cr>
```

Note: The <cr> indicates carriage return and will be used throughout this book to indicate function performed by depressing the return key on the keyboard. The ^h stands for control-h, which is the backspace key on most terminals. If this is not true on your terminal, substitute the control sequence for backspace using the circumflex character ^ to represent the control character.

After issuing this command the backspace key will work properly until you log off the system. You can place this command in a special file called **.profile** so it will be executed every time you log in. See the section on profiles later in this chapter for more information.

## HELP FUNCTION

With UNIX System V Release 2 you get a great utility called help. Want to learn how to use some common UNIX commands? Need to know what **white space** is? What is a directory? Help to the rescue! All you need to do is execute the help utility. Help is a menu-driven program that allows new users to learn how to use some of the most commonly used commands by providing descriptions, examples, and a list of options for 42 UNIX commands. In addition, help also provides a glossary function that allows users to look up over 100 terms used in UNIX systems and computers in general. For example, if you did not know what the term **argument** meant you could look it up in the on-line glossary.

The help utility can also be modified or added to by the system administrator. Commands are provided as well as recommendations for customization of the help screens.

### Before Using Help

Because help is a screen-oriented program, you must let the program know what type terminal you are using. To accomplish this, the UNIX system provides a terminal database called *termcap* that has over 200 terminal characteristics already defined. The termcap file is quite large; if you were to list it to your terminal it would go flying by, making it impossible to read. You can, however, freeze the screen and then restart the listing. The sequence ctrl-s (press and hold down the control key while simultaneously depressing the s key) will freeze the listing and ctrl-q (press and hold down the control while simultaneously depressing the q key) will restart the listing from the point where it left off.

The command to list a file is called **cat,** short for concatenate, and your termcap file is located at the location /etc/termcap (more on this later). To list the file we would type:

```
$ cat /etc/termcap

d0|vt100| vt100-am|vt100| tnis one:\
        :rf=/usr/lib/tabset/vt100:ku=\EOA:kd=\ EOB:kr=\EOC:kl; oe\EOD:kb=^H:\
d1|vt100| vt100-nam|vt100 w/no am:\
        :am@:xn@:tc=vt100-am:
        :al=99\E[L:dl=99\E[M:ip=7:dc=7\E;P:ei =\E[41:im=\E[4h:xn:dN#30:tc=vt100:
di|vt100-23| vt100 for use with vt100sys:\
        :li#23:is=\E[1;23r\E[23;1H:tc=vt100-am:
ds|vt100-s| dec vt100 132 cols 14 lines (w/o advanced video option):\
        :li#14:tc=vt100-w:
dt|vt100-w| dec vt100 132 cols (w/advanced video):\
        :co#132:li#24:rs=\E>\E/[?3h\E/[?41\E[?51\ E[?8h:tc;o evt100-am:
dt|vt100-w-nam| dec vt100 132 cols (w/advanced video):\
        :co#132:li#24:rs=\E>\E[?3h\E[?41\E[?51\ E[?8h:vt@:tc=vt100-nam:
vt100am:tc=vt100-am:
vt100nam:tc=vt100-nam:
vt100s:tc=vt100-s:
vt100w:tc=vt100-w:
```

Then find the abbreviation that fits your terminal type—for example, vt100 for a DEC VT 100 terminal or 5420 for an AT&T 5420 terminal. If you are using a PC to access the system, most terminal emulators provide VT100 emulation. Once you find the correct terminal type you should type in the following commands, substituting your terminal type where noted:

```
$ TERM=your_terminal_type
$ export TERM
```

Watch the case. The word TERM is in capital letters. After executing these commands the help program will know what type terminal you are using. It's too bad that help didn't help you set your terminal type, as this task can be confusing for first-time users who need the help utility.

## A Help Scenario

```
$ help:
help: UNIX System On-Line help
        choices                   description

           s                      starter: general information
           l                      locate: find a command with keywords
           u                      usage: information about commands
           g                      glossary: definitions of terms
           q                      Quit

Enter choice > s
```

```
starter: General UNIX System User Information
```

starter provides general information for system users. Enter
one of the choices below to proceed.

| choices | description |
|---|---|
| c | Commands and terms to learn first |
| d | Documents for system users |
| e | Education centers for UNIX System training |
| l | Local UNIX System information |
| t | Teaching aids available on-line |
| q | Quit |
| h | Restart help |

Enter choice > c

Commands & Terms to Learn First

The most basic UNIX system commands and terms are listed here. New system users should master these commands and understand the meaning of
these technical terms before going on to anything else.

```
        Commands                |        Technical Terms
                                 |
 cat    ed     mv                | command      password
 cd     grep   pwd               | directory    pathname
 chmod  ls     rm                | file         program
 cp     mail   who               | file system  shell
 date   mkdir                    | login        UNIX system
                                 |
 for command information:        | for definitions:
 1. enter:  q   to quit          | 1. enter:  q   to quit
 2. type: usage cmd_name,        | 2. type: glossary tech_term
where cmd_name = a command name  |    where tech_term = a term
                                 |    from the list
------------------------------------------------------------------------
Choices:    s (restart starter), h (restart help), q (quit)
------------------------------------------------------------------------
```

# SIMPLE ADMINISTRATION

Most UNIX systems require a dedicated person to oversee the day-to-day administrative tasks such as backing up the system, creating log-ins, and so on. This individual, known as the system administrator, typically has to know quite a lot about

UNIX COMMANDS to perform these tasks. In some instances system administrators have been known to resort to wizardry to accomplish certain goals. Most of us are not in this category and thus would have a difficult time filling the administrator's role. Nor would a small (3–18 user) system warrant hiring a full-time UNIX System guru. Fortunately, this is not a problem. Simple administration consists of a set of interactive commands presented in menu format that allow the normal user the ability to act as an administrator. It is supplied as part of your 3B2 system.

## Menus

The menu system provided with simplified administration is a series of submenus and commands accessed from either the main menu or used explicitly in command strings. A view of the menu structure is on the next page.

To access simplified administration, you would type sysadm at the system prompt $ or #. The # is the standard system prompt, but can be changed to your own prompt easily. The # indicates the root or **superuser** prompt. You will receive this prompt if you log in as root. The root log-in is a special log-in that can override any file permission and perform tasks no other log-in can perform. From the **sysadm** menu you would choose items from the menus to perform functions such as formatting floppy disks, installing and removing software, creating and modifying log-ins passwords, backing up the system, changing the system date and time, and so on. To exit submenus you can type **q** or press the (break) key on your terminal. It's a good idea to practice using the menus and submenus to understand how they work and what commands are available.

Soon you will become familiar with the menu structure and you will be able to access the command explicitly by typing **sysadm function** where function represents one of the subcommands. For example, to install additional software packages you would type:

```
$ sysadm installpkg
```

This would run the **installpkg** command under the Software Management menu.

## Installing Log-ins

To add additional users you would type:

```
$ sysadm adduser
```

This would execute the command **adduser** under the User Management menu. Consider the following scenario for adding a user log-in:

```
$ sysadm
```

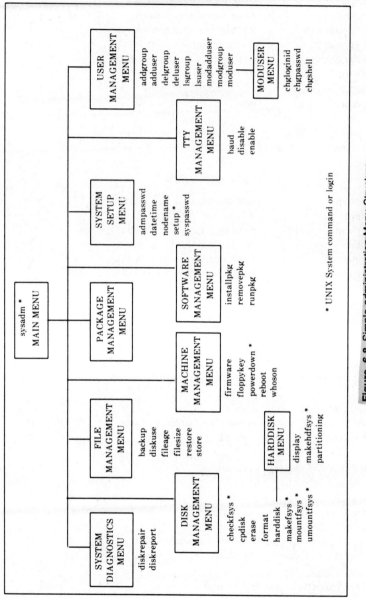

**Figure 6-8** Simple administration Menu Structure

119

SYSTEM ADMINISTRATION

| | | |
|---|---|---|
| 1 | diagnostics | system diagnostics menu |
| 2 | diskmgmt | disk management menu |
| 3 | filemgmt | file management menu |
| 4 | machinemgmt | machine management menu |
| 5 | packagemgmt | package management |
| 6 | softwaremgmt | software management menu |
| 7 | syssetup | system setup menu |
| 8 | ttymgmt | tty management menu |
| 9 | usermgmt | user management menu |

Enter a number, a name, the initial part of a name, or
? or <number>? for HELP, q to QUIT: 9

USER MANAGEMENT

| | | |
|---|---|---|
| 1 | addgroup | add a group to the system |
| 2 | adduser | add a user to the system |
| 3 | delgroup | delete a group from the system |
| 4 | deluser | delete a user from the system |
| 5 | lsgroup | list groups in the system |
| 6 | lsuer | list users in the system |
| 7 | modadduser | modify defaults used by adduser |
| 8 | modgroup | make changes to a group on the system <not available> |
| 9 | moduser | menu of commands to modify a user's login |

Enter a number, a name, the initial part of a name, or ?
or <number>? for HELP, ˆ to GO BACK, q to QUIT: 2

Anytime you want to quit, type ''q''.
If you are not sure how to answer any prompt, type "?" for help,
or see the Owner/Operator Manual.

Enter user's full name:   john doe
Enter user's login ID:    doe
Enter user ID number. (If you don't, I'll pick one):
Enter group ID number or group name.
(If you don't, I'll pick one):
Enter user's login (home) directory name.
(If you don't I'll use ' /usr/doe'):

This is the information for the new login:
            User's name:   john doe
            login ID:      doe
            user ID:       102
            group ID:      1          (other)

```
       home directory: /usr/doe
Do you want to install, edit, or skip this entry [i, e, s, q]? i
Login installed.
Do you want to give the user a password? [y, n] y
New password: 'xRe-enter new password: S|Do you want to add another login?
[y, n,
       Type  y  for yes, n  for no.   q  to quit.
Do you want to add another login? [y, n, q] n

Press the RETURN key to see the usermgmt menu [?, ^, q]:
```

Of course, you could always proceed through the menus to perform the same function. First select the User Management menu, then the adduser function from that
menu. The *Owners/Operators Manual* for the 3B2 describes simplified administration in detail. If you have ever worked on a UNIX system that does not have this
feature you will learn to depend on its presence. If this is your first UNIX system,
enjoy! Life has been made simple for you.

     Most functions can be performed by using the simplified administration fea-
ture. However, some functions may require knowledge beyond this level. In this
chapter we will indicate sections for advanced users and systems administrators
where prior UNIX command knowledge is required to accomplish customization of
some tasks.

## CLOCK/CALENDAR

The time-of-day timer maintains a time-of-day clock which provides tenths of seconds, seconds, tens of seconds, minutes, tens of minutes, day of week, day, tens of
days, months, and tens of months. The system clock is maintained by a battery located on the system board. There are two ways to set the system clock. When you
first power up the system and log in as **setup,** you are prompted for time, day of
month, and so on. You also could type **sysadm datetime** from the system prompt **$**
or superuser prompt **#** to enter the same data.

```
$ sysadm datetime

Current time and timezone is: 14:30 CDT
Change the time zone? [y, n, q, ?] y<CR>
       Available time zones are...
       1.  Greenwich  (GMT)
       2.  Atlantic   (AST & ADT)
       3.  Eastern    (EST & EDT)
       4.  Central    (CST & CDT)
       5.  Mountain   (MST & MDT)
       6.  Pacific    (PST & PDT)
       7.  Yukon      (YST & YDT)
```

```
   8.  Alaska      (AST & ADT)
   9.  Bering      (BST & BDT)
  10.  Hawaii      (HST & HDT)
Enter zone number:  4<CR>

Does your timezone use Daylight Savings Time during the year? [y, n, q, ?]
y<CR>
Time zone now changed. Next time you turn on the machine
ALL times will be reported in the new time zone. Most will be right
next time you log in.
Current date and time: Fri. 06/22/84 14:30
Change the date and time? [y, n, q, ?] y<CR>
Month   default 06      (1-12):  7<CR>
Day     default 22      (1-31):  2<CR>
Year    default 84      (70-99): <CR>
Hour    default 14      (0-23):  12<CR>
Minute default 30       (0-59):  27<CR>
Date and time will be set to:   07/02/84 12:27.   OK? [y, n, q, ?] y<CR>
Mon Jul  2 12:27:01 CDT 1984
The date and time are now changed.
```

## ADDING MORE PORTS

The 3B2 model 300 system has two RS232 ports on the system unit and four slots to hold feature cards. These feature cards could be networking interface such as 3B net or I/O expansion cards. The I/O expansion card supplies four RS232 ports and one Centronics parallel port. The total system capacity is four of these cards, providing a total of 18 RS232 ports (four on each expansion card and two on the system unit) and four Centronics Parallel ports (one on each I/O expansion card).

To add more ports, shut the system down by issuing the **powerdown** command and allowing the system to perform a graceful shutdown and remove power to the system. Simply plug in the I/O cards and switch the power switch to on. The system will recognize the card on boot up. You then would install the port specifics, such as speed, using the TTY Management menu under simplified administration.

## HOW TO INSTALL PRINTERS ON THE 3B2

The 3B2 computer can support both RS232 serial printers as well as Centronics parallel printers. These two major types cover the majority of printers available today. Typically, draft-quality printers are of the Centronics parallel type, while most letter-quality printers are of the RS232 type. Either type can be supported simultaneously and interchangeably on the 3B2.

### Which Type Is Best—RS232 or Parallel?

There are many answers to this question, causing much debate in the printer industry. However, in light of the 3B2 and its porrt configuration, with each I/O card having a parallel port included, the preference would be to use this port to connect to a parallel printer. In addition, though RS232 is considered a standard, the industry will only guarantee that two compatible RS232 devices will not smoke when plugged together, therefore making the cabling of these devices a nightmare. On the other hand, the Centronics parallel interface is more of a standard, and the cabling of these types of printers is usually not a problem. If you are planning to use a parallel printer that is currently connected to an IBM PC or compatible, you should be aware that you will have to purchase a new cable in order to connect to the 3B2's interface. The reason for this is that IBM did not follow the standard 36-pin plug on the PC, IBM chose to use a 25-pin DB25-type connector. The interface on the 3B2 uses a 36-pin connector, rendering the IBM PC parallel cable incompatible.

## LINE PRINTER SPOOLING UTILITY PACKAGE

This is an optional utility available from AT&T that is required for support of a printer on the 3B2 computer. Spooling is a technique that is borrowed from the mainframe environment; it is used to allow multiple print requests to be queued for output on an attached printer. The files in the queue are serviced on the first-in, first-out basis, however, this can be modified through the use of administrative commands supplied with the package.

With the LP spooling utility installed you do not have to wait for the printer to print your file. Once the request is issued your terminal is free to continue with other activity.

Because of its mainframe orientation, the terminology used within LP spooling utility (sometimes referred to as lp spooler) can be ambiguous. The following summarizes some of these terms and their meaning:

device—This is the physical port on the 3B2 called ttyxx. See Table 6-A for a list of these port names.

printer name—This is the name you have chosen for the printer-for example, lpl or prl. This "logical" name can be up to 14 characters long.

class—Printers can be grouped into classes of printers—for example, deptA or letter-quality versus draft-quality.

default—Print requests can be directed to certain printers or be printed on the system default printer. The default printer can be assigned and use LP administration commands.

model—The 3B2 comes equipped with certain printer driver programs supplied. These programs are located in a "model" directory. When installing the package, you must choose from this list of supported printers.

scheduler—This is a process that, when running, will allow print requests to print on the printer(s). This process is started automatically by the system when the package is installed.

printer driver—A shell program that determines how the output will look for a particular printer. There is a shell program for each model printer supported.

enable—Allows a printer to print requests that are in the queue.

disable—Prevents a printer from printing requests that are in the queue. This can be used to take a printer out of service to change paper or for maintenance. Requests will continue to queue for the printer, and when the printer is "enabled" the requests will start to print.

accept—Allows requests to be queued for a printer. This command is used to tell the system that a "new" printer exists.

reject—Prevents requests from being queued for a printer. This is the opposite of *accept*.

lpstat—This command displays the status of the printer(s) and the requests that are in queue.

lpadmin—Used to install and modify printers.

lpsched—Starts the scheduler if it is not already running.

lpshut—Stops the scheduler if it is running.

cancel—Used to cancel an outstanding print request.

lpmove—Used to move requests from printer A to printer B.

**I/O Port Names**

| Port # | Card #1 | Card #2 | Card #3 | Card #4 |
|--------|---------|---------|---------|---------|
| RS232 #1 | /dev/tty11 | /dev/tty21 | /dev/tty31 | /dev/tty41 |
| RS232 #2 | /dev/tty12 | /dev/tty22 | /dev/tty32 | /dev/tty42 |
| RS232 #3 | /dev/tty13 | /dev/tty23 | /dev/tty33 | /dev/tty43 |
| RS232 #4 | /dev/tty14 | /dev/tty24 | /dev/tty34 | /dev/tty44 |
| Parallel | /dev/tty15 | /dev/tty25 | /dev/tty35 | /dev/tty45 |

## BEFORE INSTALLING THE LP SOFTWARE

Make sure the user environment utility is installed in the system. This utility is included with the system and should be installed before using the LP spooler commands.

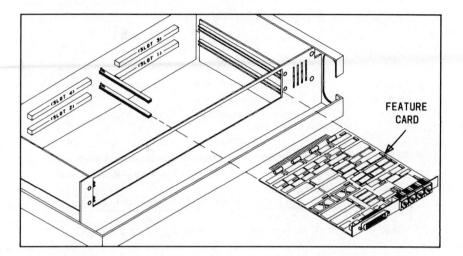

**Figure 6-9** I/O card installed in 3B2 (Courtesy of AT&T Information Systems, Inc.)

Connect the printer to the system. Refer to Fig. 6-9 for the location of the ports on the I/O ports card. Note the "name" of the port. Refer to Table 6-A for the names of the ports. Make sure you have an adequate supply of paper installed in the printer and that it is on-line and ready.

## INSTALLING THE LINE PRINTER SPOOLING UTILITY SOFTWARE

The LP spooler software is installed using the simplified administration commands available through the sysadm menu system. The command used would be **sysadm installpkg.**

In addition, the LP spooler utility includes a program that will prompt you for information concerning the printer you are installing. This program is run automatically at installation time and is not available once the installation is complete. However, you can still make changes and additions without the aid of this program.

The next section covers both these situations, first using the LP spooler installation aid program, then using UNIX commands to perform the same functions.

### Steps to Install LP Spooler:

1. sysadm installpkg—Once the sysadm installing command is executed, the system will display a list of directories it is installing on the system. You can ignore this listing.

The system will display the following:

```
Available printers are:

"lqp40"        for LQP-40 Letter Quality Printer,
"dqp10"        for DQP-10 Matrix Printer,
"hp"           for Hewlett Packard 2631A line printer
               at 2400 baud,
"prx"          for Printronix P300 at 4800 baud using
               XON/XOFF protocol on a serial interface,
"1640"         for Diablo 1640 at 1200 baud using XON/XOFF
               protocol,
"dumb"         for a line printer with no special functions
               or protocol,
"done"         if no more printers are to be configured.
```

Enter type of printer to be added to the LP system:

You then must choose a printer type from this list. If you do not have a printer on this list, choose "dumb" or "dqp10" and we will show you how to customize interfaces to fit most printers.

The dqp10 interface supports a CITOH 8510 printer. This printer is OEM from CITOH and is called the AT&T 470 printer. The lqp40 interface supports the QUME Sprint 55 Plus printer; under AT&T's label it is called the Model 455 printer.

For this example we will respond with **"dqp10"**.

2. Enter type of printer to be added to lp system:

```
dqp10
```

The system will respond with:

```
The printer name is dqp10__1
```

If you would prefer another name enter name:

```
To accept the default name dqp10__1 press <return>.
```

For our example we will call our printer "lp1".

3. Enter printer name:

```
lp1
```

The system responds with:

```
The choices for device names are:

/dev/tty11    /dev/tty12    /dev/tty13 /dev/tty14
/dev/contty

Enter the device name:
```

The devices listed will be adjusted to reflect the number of I/O ports cards installed in your system. Refer to Table 6-A for port (device) names. You should be aware that any parallel ports—tty15,tty25, tty35, tty45—are not listed. This is a glitch in the installation procedure supplied with the system. You can still respond with a parallel port device even though it is not listed. Consider that we wish to have our printer called "lp1" and with a type of dqp10 installed on the first parallel port device /dev/tty15.

   4. Enter the device name:

```
/dev/tty15
```

The system will start the print scheduler and will display:

```
destination "lp1" now accepting requests
printer "lp1" now enabled.
```

The system will then ask if you have any other printers to be installed; if not, type **done**.

   5. If no more printers are to be installed type done to exit. If other printers are being installed repeat steps 1-4.

   To check the status of the printer spooling package, type **lpstat -t.** The following will be displayed.

```
$ lpstat -t
scheduler is running
system default destination: dqp10_1
device for dqp10_: /dev/tty15
dqp10_1 accepting requests since Mar 13 09:32
printer dqp10_1 disabled since Mar 13 10:53 -
```

You are done installing the package and can begin to use the printer.

# HOW TO USE THE LINE PRINTER SPOOLER

## Creating Test File with ed

If you are not familiar with UNIX editors or permission requirements, skip to the section, "Using an Existing File."

Create a sample file called testfile using a UNIX editor such as ed. This can be done by the following steps:

```
$ ed testfile
? testfile
a
this is a test file that will print on the line printer
.
w
56
q
$
```

## Using an Existing File

If you have created a file using the ed editor, skip this section. Learning to use the editor at this point may not be prudent, so as an alternative you could print the password file. This file already exists in the system at the location /etc/passwd. You can use this file to test the printer by first copying the file into a new file called testfile.

```
# cp /etc/passwd testfile a
```

This will copy the contents of the password file into testfile. We should now have some text in testfile to print on the printer. To verify this, list the file on the screen by typing:

```
$ cat testfile
root: 5a12eYJpd7uDQ: 0: 1: 0000-Admin(0000) : /:
daemon: NONE: 1: 1: 0000-Admin(0000) : /:
bin: NONE: 2: 2: 0000-Admin(0000) : /bin:
sys: NONE: 3: 3: 0000-Admin(0000) : /usr/src:
adm: NONE: 4: 4: 0000-Admin(0000) : /usr/adm:
uucp: NONE: 5: 5: 0000-uucp(0000) : /usr/lib/uucp:
```

If all these steps are performed properly, you then can direct output to the printer. To print a file on a UNIX system you would type:

```
$ lp testfile
request id is pr1-123 (1 file)
$
```

You would receive a request id number and your request would be queued for printing. If the print queue were empty, the printer would begin printing your file. If the print queue were not empty, the request would wait its turn in the queue before printing.

Another way to print a file is to **pipe** the output of the **cat** command to the input of the lp command, as in:

```
# cat testfile | lp
$
$ cat testfile:lp
request id is pr1-124 (standard input)
$
```

## LP SPOOLER FOR ADVANCED USERS
## AND ADMINISTRATORS

This section assumes some familiarity with basic UNIX commands such as **cd,ed,cat,rm,** and **cp.** If you are not familiar with these commands, read Chapter 7 and practice these commands before proceeding.

What do you do if your printer is not included on the list? What if you want to add or change a printer after the initial installation? What if you made a mistake when you first installed the printer (not very difficult to do)?

The solution is to dig in and understand the commands and directories that are manipulated under the menus. One of the most confusing areas of the UNIX system is the relationship of the files within some of the utility software. Once you understand the commands and file relationships, although they appear rather cryptic at first, you will be able to make modifications to these files with ease.

Situation: We need to install an Epson FX 80 printer on the first parallel port of I/O card # 1. Log in to the system as **root** and type in the following command:

```
/usr/lib/lpadmin   -pptrname   -dptrname  -v/dev/portname
-mmodelname
```

Where ptrname is the name you choose to call your printer and modelname is a model in the directory /usr/spool/lp/model .

First we'll choose a name for our printer. We'll call the printer **lp1.** Next we must choose a **printer driver script** from the **/usr/spool/lp/model** directory. The model we'll use is called dqp10. This script is supplied for the AT&T 470 draft-

quality printer, but we can customize it to work with our Epson printer. The lp1
printer will also be the default printer, meaning that if a destination is not supplied,
the request will print out on this printer.

```
# /usr/lib/lpadmin -plp1 -dlp1 -v/dev/tty15 -mdqp10
```

This command installs the printer with a logical name lp1 and relates it to the physical device /dev/tty15; it will use the dqp10 printer driver script to produce output on
the printer.

The next step is to change "ownership" of the devices that the LP spooler is
using to print requests. You can perform this by typing:

```
# chown lp /dev/ttyxx      (where xx is the actual device used)
# chmod 600 /dev/ttyxx          "     "
```

The output of these two commands will be the UNIX super-user prompt # if completed successfully. You can verify the results by:

```
# cd /dev

# ls -1 tty*

crw-rw-rw-   1 root      sys      20,  0 Jul 15 11:35 tty
crw--w--w-   1 craig     appeng    1,  0 Jul 15 14:08 tty11
crw--w--w-   1 root      appeng    1,  1 Jul  5 09:01 tty12
crw--w--w-   1 bittmann  other     1,  2 Jul 15 12:55 tty13
crw--w--w-   1 root      10        1,  3 Jul  3 15:28 tty14
crw-rw-rw-   1 lp        root      1,  4 Jul  3 10:53 tty15
crw--w--w-   1 lp        root      2,  0 Jul 15 13:35 tty21
crw-r--r--   1 root      root      2,  1 Jul  3 15:15 tty22
crw-r--r--   1 root      root      2,  2 Jul  3 15:15 tty23
crw-r--r--   1 root      root      2,  3 Jul  3 15:15 tty24
crw-r--r--   1 root      root      2,  4 Jul  3 15:15 tty25
```

Next you must turn off the "getty" process for the device (port) the printer is connected to.

The place the getty exists is in the /etc/inittab file. You can cat this file to see if '
there is a getty active on the port. To remove the getty, use the sysadm tty management menu and select disable to turn off the tty line.

The next step is to remove a lock on the scheduler.

```
# rm -f /usr/spool/lp/SCHEDLOCK
```

Now start the scheduler.

```
                              # /usr/lib/lpsched
```

Tell the system that the printer is ready to accept requests.

```
                              # enable lp1
                              # /usr/lib/accept lp1
```

Now check the status of the scheduler and printer(s).

```
                 # lpstat -t
                 scheduler is running
                 system default destination: pr1
                 device for pr1: /dev/lp1
                 pr1 accepting requests since Apr 2 11:27
```

## Customizing Printer Driver Scripts

This is the last step in the process. A printer driver script is a shell program that controls the way files are printed on printers attached to the system. The following is a listing of the dqp10 printer driver script.

```
# cat/usr/spool/lp/model/dqp 10
# lp interface for DQP-10 Matrix Printer
#
#
```

```
1XXXXXXXXXXXXXXXXXXXXXXXXXXXXXXXXXXXXXXXXXXXXXXXXXXXXXXXXXX
2 stty -parenb -parodd 9600 cs8 cread clocal ixon 0<&1
3 stty -ignbrk -brkint -ignpar -parmrk -inpck -istrip 0<&1
4 stty -inlcr -igncr -iuclc -ixany 0<&1
5 styy opost -ocrnl onlcr -onlret tab3 0<&1
6 echo ''\033N''                    escape sequence to reset AT&T 470 Printer
7 echo ''\033]''
8 id=$1
9 name=$2
10title=$3
11copies=$4
12shift; shift; shift; shift; shift
13files=''$*''
14echo "\014\c"                     form feed
15echo ''\n\n\n\n\n\n\n\n\n\n''
16echo ''$x\n$x\n$x\n$x\n\n\n\n\n\n''
17banner ''$name''
18echo ''\n''
19echo ''Request id: $id''
20date
```

```
21echo ''\n''
22if [ -n ''$title'' ]
23then
24          banner $title
25fi
26echo ''\n\n\n\n\n''
27echo ''$x\n$x\n$x\n$x\n\n\n\n\n\n''          new line
28echo ''\014\c''          form feed
29i=1
30while [ $i -le $copies ]
31do
32          for file in $files
33          do
34                    case $file
35                    in
36                              *.g/*.n/*.mm)
37                              stty -opost 0<&1
38                              ;;
39                    esac
40                    cat ''$file'' 2>&1
41                    stty opost -ocrnl onlcr -onlret tab3 0<&1
42                    echo ''\033N''
43                    echo ''\033]''  escape sequence to reset AT&T 470 Printer
44                    echo ''\014\c''          form feed
45          done
46          i='expr $i + 1'
47done
48echo ''\n\n\n\n\n\n\n\n\n\n''
49echo ''$x\n$x\n$x\n$x\n\n\n\n\n\n''
50banner ''END''
51echo ''$x\n$x\n$x\n$x\n\n\n\n\n\n''
52echo ''\014\c''
53exit 0
```

This shell program is fairly easy to decipher. Use the UNIX System V Release 2 Version 1 programmers reference manual as an aid. Lines 2–5 set printer options with the stty command such as speed, line ending sequence, parity, and so on. Lines 14–28 print the header at the beginning of each print request. Lines 29–46 do the actual printing of the file sent via the LP command. Finally, lines 47–53 print a trailer message.

There is no magic here. With a little bit of investigation we can modify the script to work with most any printer. Before we begin to make changes to the file, let's make a copy.

```
# cd /usr/spool/lp/model
# cp dqp10 epson
```

Now we can use an editor such as ed or vi to make the necessary changes. Below is the modified script that will work with an Epson FX 80 printer.

Steps to modify dqp10 interface for an Epson printer:

1. Delete lines 6,7 and 42,43.
2. Change the onlcr in line 5 to read -onlcr.

```
1       # lp interface for EPSON FX80 Matrix Printer
2       #
3       #
4
5       xxxxxxxxxxxxxxxxxxxxxxxxxxxxxxxxxxxxxxxxxxxxxxxxxxxxxxxxxxxxxx
6       stty -parenb -parodd 9600 cs8 cread clocal ixon 0<&1
7       stty -ignbrk -brkint -ignpar -parmrk -inpck -istrip 0<&1
8       stty -inlcr -igncr -iuclc -ixany 0<&1
9       stty opost -ocrnl  -onlcr  -onlret tab3 0<&1
10      id=$1
11      name=$2
12      title=$3               does not sent carriage return on line feed
13      copies=$4
14      shift; shift; shift; shift; shift
15      files=''$*''
16      echo ''\014\c''
17      ''\n\n\n\n\n\n\n\n\n\n''\
18      echo ''$x\n$x\n$x\n$x\n\n\n\n\n\n\n''
19      banner ''$name''
20      echo ''\n''
21      echo ''Request id: $id''
22      date
23      echo ''\n''
24      if [ -n ''$title'' ]
25      then
26              banner $title
27      fi
28      echo ''\n\n\n\n\n''
29      echo ''$x\n$x\n$x\n$x\n\n\n\n\n\n\n''
30      echo ''\014\c''
31      i=1
32      while [ $i -le $copies ]
33      do
34              for file in $files
35              do
36                      case $file
37                      in
38                              *.g/*.n/*.mm)
```

```
39                                    stty -opost 0<&1
40                                       ;;
41                              esac
42                              cat ''$file'' 2>&1
43                              stty opost -ocrnl -onlcr -onlret tab3 0<&1
44                              echo ''\014\c''
45                    done
46                    i='expr $i + 1'
47          done
48          echo ''\n\n\n\n\n\n\n\n\n\n''
49          echo ""$x\n$x\n$x\n$x\n\n\n\n\n''
50          banner ''END''
51          echo ""$x\n$x\n$x\n$x\n\n\n\n\n''
52          echo ''\014\c''
53          exit 0
```

Now that we have a modified script, we must put it into the correct location. The model directory contains all the scripts, but these scripts are not really the one(s) executed. This sounds confusing, but remember the command we issued earlier:

```
# /usr/lib/lpadmin -plp1 -dlp1 -v/dev/tty15 -mdqp10
```

The section of this command line -mdqp10 actually copies the dqp10 printer driver script into the **/usr/spool/lp/interface** directory and gives it a file name that is the same as the logical printer name. In our example we chose lp1 as a logical name for our printer. Therefore, we should have a file called lp1 in the interface directory. We can check this by:

```
# cd /usr/spool/lp/interface
#
#
#pwd
/usr/spool/lp/interface
# ls -1
total 2
-rwxr-xr-x    1 root      other        1007 Apr  1 21:08 lp1
#
```

The file lp1 is a duplicate of the dqp10m file in the model directory. Now that we have our printer driver script in a file called Epson, the last step is to copy it into the interface directory.

```
# cp /usr/spool/model/epson/usr/spool/lp/interface/lp1
```

Because we have added our new printer driver to the model directory we can use -mepson to install any additional Epson (or Epson-compatible) printers.

This completes the process of installing our printer. Refer to the section on how to use the LP spooler to test the printer.

## What to Do if the Printer Is Double-spacing

If your printer is double-spacing when it shouldn't, you can either change the options in your printer or modify the printer driver stty commands to not add carriage return after line feed.

Note: We could also have used the printer driver called dumb and modified it to perform the same function. The dumb printer driver is a generic driver and, with minor modification, can be used to support most printers.

## What to Do if the Printer Is Not Working at All

Execute the lpstat -t command. Make sure the scheduler is running and the printer has been enabled. If the scheduler is not running, start it by typing:

```
# /usr/lib/lpsched
```

If the printer is disabled, type:

```
#
# enable lp1
printer "lp1" now enabled
#
```

Check the cabling and make sure the printer is optioned properly. Especially check the speed setting.

The print spooling program will disable the printer if there is a paper jam, the power is turned off to the printer, or the printer is not cabled correctly. A good tool with which to diagnose a problem on an RS232 port is a break-out box. With a break-out box you can isolate the leads and verify that data can be sent out the port. If your printer is connected to the parallel port, check the Centronics cable, as it has a tendency to come unseated very easily and can cause "interesting" problems.

Another potential problem is "ownership" of some of the devices that the LP spooler is using to print requests. You can verify this by typing:

```
# chown lp /dev/ttyxx        (where xx is the actual device used)
# chmod 600 /dev/ttyxx         "      "
```

A final suggestion is to verify that the device is turned off in the /etc/inittab file. To do this, use the sysadm tty management menu and select disable to turn off the tty line.

## WHY INSTALL A MODEM ON YOUR 3B2 COMPUTER?

The UNIX operating system includes many built-in communication features such as electronic mail, networking, and UNIX-to-UNIX file transfer capability. With these features it is very easy to mail an entire program to a user on another machine or send memos, meeting notices, or customer files to users on other computers, local or remote. In conjunction with the ability to schedule this transfer to happen immediately or at some later hour, day of the week, or day of the month, communications proves itself to be one of the highlights of UNIX and the 3B2 computer.

## ALL ABOUT THE MODEM

The modem that AT&T offers for the 3B2 is an intelligent modem manufactured by Penril corporation. It is a dual modem capable of communicating at 300 bps and 1200 bps. Do computers still communicate at 300 bps? AT&T calls this modem the AT&T 3B2 Computer Auto Dial Modem, and it is the recommended modem for use on the 3B2. The modem works in conjunction with communication software called the Basic Networking Utilities package. This package is an optional utility and must be purchased if you wish to have your computer originate calls. If all you want to do is call your computer from another computer or terminal to perform the functions of a locally connected terminal, then you do not need to install this utility.

**Figure 6-10** AT&T Auto Dial Modem (Courtesy of AT&T Information Systems, Inc.)

## INSTALLING THE AT&T 3B2 COMPUTER AUTO DIAL MODEM

The modem comes supplied with all the necessary hardware to complete the installation. In addition, it is factory optioned to work with the 3B2. We can leave the manual for future review at this point. To connect the modem to the computer, first make sure all the push-button switches on the front of the modem are out (that means in their nonoperated mode). The back of the modem has two switches: echo and HS (high speed).

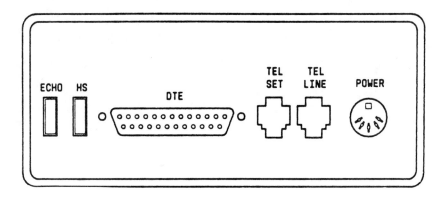

**Figure 6-11** Rear AT&T Auto Dial Modem (Courtesy of AT&T Information Systems, Inc.)

If you plan to communicate at 1200 bps, push the HS switch into its operated position. Now connect the power transformer to an AC outlet. Because of the size of the transformer, you may need to purchase an AC outlet strip that will plug into the wall outlet. Now that we have power to the modem we can connect the cable from the modem to the port on the 3B2. The recommended port on the 3B2 is the contty port. This is the port adjacent to the console port. If this port is already used you can use any spare RS232 port. Plug one end (the end without the tail) into the eight-pin-to-RS232 adapter provided with your modem. This is important. It should be marked ACU/MODEM connector. Do not use a TERMINAL/PRINTER connector. Plug the other end of the cable (the one with the ground tail) into the port on the 3B2. Finally, connect the telephone line to the jack marked Tel Line on the back of the modem.

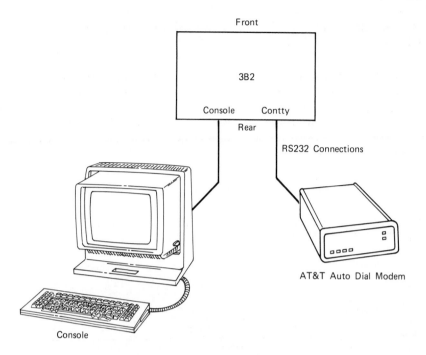

**Figure 6-12** Connecting modem to 3B2

If all you want to do is call your computer from another terminal or your PC from home, you are done. You will be able to call the computer and act as a terminal with full function, just as if you were locally connected.

However, if you want your computer to be able to send and receive mail, files, and programs, then the computer must be able to carry on these sessions. This will require the Basic Networking Utility Package.

## INSTALLING THE BASIC NETWORKING UTILITY PACKAGE

The following scenario depicts the steps necessary to install the AT&T Auto Dial Modem (Penril) on the contty port of the 3B2 computer.

1. sysadm installpkg <cr>

```
        The machine is currently ""denver''
        Do you want to change it? [y,n,q,] n <cr>
```

As part of the initial installation of the Basic Networking Utility Package, you should select the following items from within uucpmgmt:

devicemgmt: To provide Basic Networking Utility Package with information about devices it can use for outgoing traffic.

portmgmt: To permit incoming calls on the I/O port(s) or set it/them up for outgoing bidirectional traffic.

systemgmt: To provide Basic Networking Utility Package with the names of the systems you wish to contact.

pollmgmt: To initiate the polling of other systems by this system "denver".

2. Choose packagemgmt from the sysadm main menu and then select uucpmgmt by choosing item 1 from this submenu.

The system displays:

```
Basic Networking Utilities Management

1. devicemgmt  manages devices (list,add,delete)
2. pollmgmt    manages poll entries (list,add,delete)
3. portmgmt    manages I/O ports (list,modify)
4. systemmgmt  manages remote sys entries (list,add,
               delete, call)
```

3. Choose item 1 devicemgmt by typing 1 <cr>

Then choose add from the submenu. The system will then display:
Enter device name:
4. Respond by typing the device name from Table 6-A. For our example we will respond with contty.
Enter device name:

```
                    contty <cr>
```

The system then displays:
Enter device type to call on.
Select one from the list:

1. 801

2. direct

3. develcon

4. hayes

5. micom

6. penril

7. rixon

8. ventel

5. Choose an item from the list. If you using the AT&T Auto Dial Modem, you can accept the default (penril) by pressing <cr>.

The system responds with:

This is the device entry generated for device "contty":

```
CALLER TYPE:    ACU
PORT NAME   :   contty
SPEED       :   1200
DEVICE TYPE:    penril

CALLER TYPE:    ACU
PORT NAME   :   contty
SPEED       :   300
DEVICE TYPE:    penril

Do you want to add this entry to the devices file ?
[y, n, q, ]
```

6. Type y to add the entry to the system tables.

The system will confirm the installation by displaying:

```
****   Device "contty" has been added to the
/usr/lib/uucp/Devices file.
Add another entry to the Devices file? [y, n, q, ]
```

7. Type q to quit.

8. Choose **portmgmt** from the Basic Networking Utilities Management menu by selecting item 3 and pressing <cr>.

9. Next select **modify** from the submenu.

The system will display:

```
            enter port name you want to modify [q]
```

10. Type contty <cr>

The system will respond with:

```
Found the following entry in "/etc/inittab"
PORT contty
SPEED contty
DIRECTION incoming
Do you want port "contty" to be for incoming, outgoing, or
bidirectional traffic?
```

1. incoming

2. outgoing

3. bidirectional

11. Choose item 3, bidirectional, by typing: 3 <cr>
The system responds with:

```
The current speed is contty.
If you want to change the speed enter speed
300, 1200, 1800, 2400, 4800, 9600, 19200
```

12. Leave it set to contty by typing <cr>.
The system responds:

```
**** The entry for "contty" is now:
PORT contty
SPEED contty
DIRECTION bidirectional
```

13. Exit the menus and sysadm by typing q <cr>.

# BASIC NETWORKING SOFTWARE

The Basic Networking software includes numerous commands and options. In addition, there are many directory locations and administrative commands that can overwhelm the uninitiated. The good news is that if you are installing a "standard" modem that is in the list of supported devices, you may not need to understand all the intimate details of Basic Networking. For this situation the next section describes how to use the most common Basic Net commands.

However, if you need to make any modifications or are using a modem that is not in the supported devices list, you will need to understand Basic Networking at a much more detailed level. For this situation there is a section that provides details on the directory structure and file relationships as well as description of some important administrative directories.

**User Commands**

| Command | Description |
| --- | --- |
| ct | Used to call a remote terminal from the 3B2. |
| cu | Used to call a remote computer from the 3B2. There are many subcommands under cu that allow the user to perform file transfer and data capture. Note that cu does not provide error-checking protocol. |
| uucp | Used to perform UNIX-to-UNIX file transfers. This command allows the sender to receive confirmation of the sent material and options to notify the recipient via electronic mail, just to name a few capabilities. uucp does provide error checking on in-and-out data transfers. |
| uux | Allows a command script to be executed on a remote UNIX computer. |
| uuname | Provides the names of computers you are allowed to call. These systems are defined by the administrator and can be added or changed as desired. |
| uulog | Displays a list of status messages for a specific computer. |

## HOW TO USE BASIC NETWORKING

Basic Networking provides two major commands and numerous subcommands. The two most commonly used commands are **cu** (call UNIX) and **uucp** (UNIX-to-UNIX copy program).

The cu command is used to call another computer system, mainframe, another 3B2, or any computer supporting plain vanilla ASCII async communications (most computers). For example, if a user on the 3B2 needs call Dow Jones to retrieve stock quotes, the cu command will perform this function nicely.

The **uucp** command is used to perform file transfer and mail to other UNIX machines. Unlike cu, which can be used to call non-UNIX computers, uucp depends upon a protocol for file transfer currently only supported by other nonUNIX-based computers. Once a uucp command is issued to send files to another system, the user is free to go about other tasks. The uucp program will take care of the file transfer and will notify you upon completion if you so desire. Requests for transfer are queued in a manner similar to the line printer spooler, with requests being handled in a FIFO manner (first in, first out).

### How to Use cu

We would like to call a time-sharing system that is at the home office. The following command can be issued from any terminal on the 3B2:

```
$ cu -s1200 1,312-555-1212
```

After the modems at each computer complete their handshake, you will be connected on-line to the computer.

The -s1200 identifies the speed we wish to transmit to the other computer. Once we are ready to disconnect from the remote system, we issued the disconnect command (tilde period). The line will disconnect and return you to the local system. The following table summarizes the most commonly used cu subcommands.

**User Commands**

| Command | Description |
| --- | --- |
| ~. | Used to end communications and return to the local 3B2. |
| ~ ! | Allows the user to escape to the shell on the local 3B2 to execute some commands without disconnecting the on-line communication. To return to the on-line communication, type ‹ctrl›-D. |
| ~$ | Used to issue a command on the local 3B2 and send the output to the remote system. |
| ~%take | Used to extract files from the remote system and store them on the local 3B2. |
| ~%put | Used to transfer files from the local 3B2 for storage on the remote system. |
| ~%break | Send a break character to the remote computer. |

### How to Use uucp

The uucp command is used to transfer files or programs to remote UNIX systems. Once a uucp command is issued, the user is free to continue with other activity. The actual transmission may not take place for some time and is managed by the uucp program. There are commands associated with uucp that will provide that status of the transmission.

In order to use uucp you must know the:

name of the remote computer

telephone number

recipient's log-in id

The remote system needs to have the same information about your computer if you intend to be able to originate and receive transmission from either end.

To find out the name of your computer, type:

```
$ uname -n
denver
```

To find out what systems your computer can send to, type:

```
$ uuname -a
bostn
nyc
chic
```

Assuming that all the definitions are in place, we can send small files using the mail command. Let's send a file called sales to a user named john on a machine with the name chic. We would type:

```
$ mail chic!john < sales
```

The ! character separates the machine name from the user id of the recipient on that machine. That's all there is to it.

To send large files, we can use the uucp command. In this scenario we have a payroll database that has 10,000 entries called pay.dbf, and we intend to send it to a machine called nyc to a user on that machine called alice. We want to place the file in alice's log-in directory which is /usr/alice. Consider the command line

```
$ uucp pay.dbf nyc!/usr/alice/pay.dbf
```

The uucp command then would queue this request for transmission to the nyc machine. There are other commands included with uucp to check the status of the file once this command is issued. The system administrator also has control over the queue and outstanding requests.

**Word of caution:** Because uucp is such a powerful utility, its complexity can be overwhelming. It is no trivial task to set up and administer uucp properly. It's very easy to get into trouble and find yourself in a perplexed state. For this reason the following approach is recommended:

1. Install the modem, making sure you can call the system and log in. This will at least prove that the cabling, modem, and port are working properly.

2. Install the Basic Networking Utility software—test the outgoing capability with the cu command. We know now that the modem and computer can initiate calls.

3. Administer uucp and set up machine definitions.

4. Test uucp using the uucp command and sysadm call function.

## BASIC NETWORKING FOR ADVANCED USERS AND SYSTEM ADMINISTRATORS

This section assumes some basic knowledge of UNIX commands and auto dial modems. If you are using a modem that is supported by the Basic Networking Utility, you may not need to read this section. However, if you need to understand directory relationships and customization techniques, this section is for you.

This section includes a description of how to add nonsupported modems to the 3B2 and make them work. In addition, there is a description of how to hard-wire the 3B2 computer to another computer and transfer files. Finally, there is an overview of the important files and directories that make up the Basic Networking Utility package.

### Nonsupported Modems

When the Basic Networking package is installed, a list of supported modems is displayed. If your modem is not in that list you still may be able to make it work. The Basic Networking software uses files that contain information specific to the actual device used. For example, the actual dial commands that the modem expects to see are imbedded in the /usr/lib/uucp/Dialers file. In addition, there are dependent entries in the /usr/lib/uucp/Devices and /usr/lib/uucp/Systems files.

Most intelligent modems expect input from a terminal device—your keyboard. Since the actual dialing sequence will be sent from the 3B2 we need to detail the specific sequence on paper before proceeding. To gather this information, arm yourself with the manual supplied with your modem and connect a terminal to the modem. Next, write down every step necessary to cause your modem to dial a remote system. Consider the following example using a Hayes Smartmodem 1200:

1. Type AT <cr>                     (wake up)
2. The modem responds with: OK <cr>         (all set to dial)
3. Type ATDT12125551212 <cr>        (wake up and dial)
4. The modem responds with : CONNECT

You should also note the pause character used by the modem to wait for second dial tone supplied by most PBX systems. The Hayes, for example, uses the comma (,) for a two-second pause.

### Devices File

The /usr/lib/uucp/Devices file contains information relative to the modem and actual devices being used for communication. The format of the devices entries is:

```
Type Line Class Dialer
```

Type—This can be DIRECT for systems that are hard-wired together without a modem, or
ACU for systems that will use an intelligent auto dial modem.
Line—This is the actual device name that the modem will be connected to. Refer to Table 6-A for device names—for example, contty for a modem connected to the contty port.
Class—This field indicates the speed at which the modem is to transmit. For example, -1200 indicates that the modem initiates transmission at 1200 bps. For dual- or triple-speed modems, you should create an entry for each speed.
Dialer—This is an entry with the same name as your modem. For example, "penril" for the penril modem or "hayes" for the Hayes modem. This entry must be the same name that appears as the first entry in the dialers file for the specific modem. If you were hard-wiring two computers together, this entry would be DIRECT.

Example

The following entry in the /usr/lib/uucp/Devices file is for a Hayes Smartmodem communicating at both 300 and 1200 bps and using an entry in the dialers file called hayes.
The modem is connected to the contty port of the 3B2 computer

```
ACU contty -1200 hayes
ACU contty -300 hayes
```

## Dialers

The /usr/lib/uucp/Dialers file contains the actual dialing sequences your modem must use to communicate with another system. Now that you have your list of actual keyboard entries, we can begin to build the entry.

The dialers file uses a pseudo language to create entries in the file. The commands under this pseudo language can be used to perform dialing sequences. The following list summarizes these commands:

\p pause approx 0.25 to 0.50 of a second before continuing

\d delay approximately two seconds before continuing

\D insert telephone number without translation

\T insert telephone number with translation

\K insert a break character

\E enable echo checking

\r carriage return

\c no new line

\n add a new line

\nnn send octal code nnn

The construction of the dialers entries is in a "wait for" "then send" sequence. For example, the following entry will wait for nothing, as indicated by "" then send Dial9 to the modem.

```
modem name "" Dial9\r
```

Another example might be to wait for nothing "" then delay two seconds, wait for OK, then send ATDT.

```
modem name "" \d OK ATDT\r
```

All entries are separated by spaces in the "wait for " "then send" sequence.

**Putting it all together:** The following is a complete entry for a Hayes Smartmodem 1200:

```
hayes =,-,  "" \dAT\r\c OK\r \EATDT\D\r\c CONNECT
```

The first field—hayes—is a pointer to the device entry dialers field. The second field—=,-,—tells the system to translate = and - in a telephone number string to the Hayes pause character comma. The rest of the entry is translated as:

```
expect nothing ""
```

then send a two-second delay followed by AT, which is the Hayes wake-up command, followed by a carriage return without a new line.

Except OK from the modem, then turn on echo checking followed by ATDT, which is the Hayes dialing sequence followed by the actual telephone number, nontranslated, followed by a carriage return without a new line.

Expect CONNECT from the modem. This is the indication that the Hayes modem has made a connection with a modem at the distant end and is ready to transmit and receive data.

## Systems File

The /usr/lib/uucp/Systems file contains an entry for each computer you intend to send or receive using Basic Networking. Just like the dialers file, the systems file has its own syntax. In addition, fields in the system entry are related to fields in the devices and dialers files.

Each entry in the systems file has the following format:

```
System-Name Time type class phone# log-in
```

System-Name—The name of the remote system, for example, boston.

Time—The time permissible to contact the remote system.
    This can be
                Su Mo Tu We Th Fr Sa
    for the days of the week, or

```
WK for any weekday
```

Any—indicates any day is permissible.

type—This is the type that is included in the devices

entry—for example, ACU.

class—Indicates the speed for transmission. Again, this is an entry that uses a field in the devices file for lookup. The system will search for an available device at the requested speed, then use the dialers entry for that device to perform the actual dialing.

phone#—This is the actual phone number of the remote system. The = and - can be used to include a pause in the dialing sequence.

log-in—This is the actual log-in message that the remote system will send. Here again, the "expect" "send" sequence is used. For example, expect the word "login" and then send "dallas," then expect "password", then send "texas."

Consider the following entry for a system called Boston using any ACU-type device at a speed of 1200 bps. The remote system will send the word "login:" and the login we will send is "nuucp." The remote system will send the word "password:" and password we will send is "beans."

```
Boston Any ACU 1200 9,16175551212 login: nuucp password: beans
```

When creating entries in the systems file, take care to include all the actual characters in the "expect" "send" sequence. For example, if the remote system sends the word "login" followed by a colon and a space, you must include this in your entry. If not, the system will never see the "expect" sequence and hence will never log in to the remote system.


## HARD-WIRED COMPUTER-TO-COMPUTER CONNECTIONS

The uucp command can be used to communicate to a system that is hard-wired to the local system. The first step in connecting the 3B2 to another computer is to build or purchase a special cable called a *null modem cable*. This cable configures the data leads in a manner that is compatible for both systems.


### Building the Null Modem Cable

Make the following modifications to the cable. Connect:

pin 1 to pin 1
pin 2 to pin 3
pin 3 to pin 2
strap pin 4 to pin 5 in the same plug
pin 6 to pin 20
pin 7 to pin 7
pin 8 to pin 20
pin 20 to pin 6
pin 20 to pin 8


### Device and Systems Entries

Make sure the device type is direct and the desired speed is included, for example, 9600 bps.

## IMPORTANT FILES FOR BASIC NETWORKING

| | |
|---|---|
| /usr/lib/uucp/Devices | device definitions |
| /usr/lib/uucp/Dialers | modem dialer entries |
| /usr/lib/uucp/Systems | remote system definitions |
| /usr/lib/uucp/Permissions | read write security |
| /usr/lib/uucp/locks | lock files |
| /usr/lib/uucp/uucppublic | public area |
| /usr/lib/uucp/Dialcodes | dialing abbreviations |
| /usr/lib/uucp/Poll | polling table |
| /etc/inittab | device specifics |

## CREATING USER PROFILES

Each user on the 3B2 has a file called .profile (dot profile) in his/her home directory. This file is executed each time the user logs in to the computer. This file is where you should put commands such as setting the backspace key, defining your TERM variable, checking your mail, or any other function you would like to have automatically executed each time you log in. The DOS analogy would be the autoexec.bat files that are executed when the system is booted.

Profiles are usually customized by the user to provide features that suit the individual. Consider the sample .profile:

```
HOME=/usr/bill
PATH=: $HOME/bin: /bin: /usr/bin:
PS1="HI BILL > "
stty -tabs echoe erase "^h"
TERM=vt100
export HOME PATH TERM
date
```

HOME is the user's home (log-in) directory
PATH is where the system will search for commands
stty sets the backspace key
TERM sets our terminal type
export makes these variables known to other programs
date will print the system date and time upon log-in.

## Formatting Floppy Disks on the 3B2

The process of formatting floppy disks "prepares" the disk to accept data. This process defines the actual layout of sectors and also creates the necessary headers required by the system read/write routines.

To format a floppy disk, use the sysadm command and choose the diskmgmt submenu. When the submenu is presented, choose format (item 4) and follow the instructions.

The process of formatting floppy disks takes approximately 3.5 minutes per floppy disk. Following the recommendations in the *System Administration Guide* to format a full box of ten floppy disks would take approximately 35 minutes.

An alternate way to format floppy disks is to log in as root, insert a blank disk in the disk drive, and issue the following command:

```
# fmtflop -v /dev/rdiskette<cr>
```

Remove the floppy disk when the light on the drive is off.

## How to Back Up the 3B2 Hard Disk

The 3B2 provides the capability to back up the complete disk, called a volume backup; or back up only those files that have been modified since the last backup, called incremental backup; or files of your choice, called selected backup.

To back up any file system (/ /usr), you must begin with enough formatted floppy disks to perform the back up procedure.

**How to determine how many floppy disks to format.** Issue the following command after logging in as root:

```
# du -s filesystem              (eg / or /usr)
```

The system will respond with the number of blocks (512-byte) the file system occupies. Consider the following:

```
# du -s /usr
12484 /usr
```

Now divide the number of blocks by 1300 (approximate capacity of a floppy disk) and round to a whole number. For example:

```
12484 ÷ 1300 = 9.6031 round up =10 diskettes
```

Perform this procedure for each file system, typically the root /file system and the user /usr file system. Add the number of floppy disks arrived at for both systems and format this number of diskettes.

## Procedure to Perform Complete Volume Backup

1. Format the required number of floppy disks.
2. Log in as root.
3. Type init 1 to put the system in single-user mode.
4. Type fsck followed by the file system(s) to be backed up.
5. Mount the /usr file system by typing:

> # mount /dev/dsk/c1d0s2 /usr<cr>

6. Type sysadm backup and follow the instructions.
7. When finished, dismount the /usr file system by typing

> # umount /dev/dsk/c1d0s2<cr>

8. Return the system to multi-user state by typing:

> # init 2<cr>

## CREATING DATA DISKS ON THE 3B2

The 3B2 provides utilities for backing up the total hard disk, file systems as well as individual files. These utilities are accessed via the *sysadm* menu system. The underlying assumption is that the backup will be performed by the "system administrator." In most small system configurations there may be no one assigned to this role and therefore the concern for file integrity can be comprised. The best solution is to use the cartridge tape on the optional XM (expansion module) for backup. This requires a minimal amount of effort and can be a scheduled function that in some cases requires no human intervention.

In addition to these utilities the users can also create their own diskettes to store and retrieve files. These "data disks" can become a safety net for a missed backup. In addition, coming from a PC background you may feel insecure without a physical copy of just your files in your hands. Another reason for creating data disks might be to move files to another 3B2 that may not have the cartridge tape mechanism.

## WHAT YOU NEED BEFORE YOU START

You will need at least one blank 5.25 in double-sided, double-density floppy diskette. These disks should be certified at 96 tpi (tracks per inch). You should either own all or have write permission for the files you wish to backup. Of course if you are logged in as superuser then you will by default have write permission for all files.

The process of creating a data disk is done in four steps: formatting the disk, making a file system on the disk, copying files to the disk, and unmounting the file system.


# STEPS TO CREATE A 3B2 DATA DISKETTE

### Format the Disk

Just as in DOS you must prepare the disk to receive data. To format the disk type in *sysadm* and choose item #2 *diskmgmt* from the main system administration menu. This will display the diskmgmt sub menu. Choose item #4 *format* from this menu and follow the instructions. If the system reports any disk errors try another disk.


### Making a File System on the Diskette

The Unix operating system understands file systems as collections of files that are "mountable." The term mountable is a carryover from the days of magnetic tape when a computer operator would physically mount the tape to be read by the system. The thing to remember here is that before a file system can be accessed it must be mounted and before you can store files on a blank formatted floppy you must first make a file system on the diskette.

To do this choose #6 *makefsys* from the diskmgmt submenu. The process will indicate when to insert the disk and then will prompt you for some information necessary to initialize the disk. The first piece of information that you must provide is a label. The label must be less than 6 characters. For example, we could use the initials jmg. The next prompt will ask for the name of the file system. You should enter a name that makes sense to you, for example your first name, the word bkup for backup, and so forth. For our example we will call the file system jim. The next prompt will ask for the maximum number of files and directories that will be on the disk. The default 200 will be sufficient for most situations but I choose to answer with 710, the maximum allowable files and directories. This process reserves enough space in the inode table for files and directories.

At this point the system will initialize the diskette to the parameters that you have chosen. The final prompt will ask if you would like to leave the file system mounted and since we will be copying files to the disk we should answer yes. If you have already answered no and exited the sysadm menu you can still mount the file system by choosing item #7 *mountfsys* from the diskmgmt submenu.

## Copying Files to the Diskette

Now that we have a diskette that has been formatted, contains a file system, and is mounted we can proceed to copy files to the diskette.

Because UNIX treats all file systems in a similar manner the diskette once mounted can be treated just as any other "normal" Unix directory. If you remember our example we called our file system jim. So to see what is contained on the floppy disk we can cd to /jim and then list the files on the disk. We can also copy files to the diskette by using the /jim directory as the target directory.

## Copying Selective Files

To copy the file called sales.results from the current directory you would type:

```
$ cp sales.results /jim
```

To copy all files that begin with north you would type:

```
$ cp north* /jim
```

The * and ? metacharacters operate the same here as they do with any UNIX directory.

This is fine for copying files selectively to the disk but what if you wanted to copy all files in all directories under your login directory? Well you could cd to each directory and the cp * to /jim but that can be quite tedious. A better solution is the following command line issued from your login directory:

```
$ find . -depth -print ¦ cpio -pdl /jim
```

This will descend the tree and copy all files and directories recursively from your login directory down. To verify that the copy took place correctly:

```
$ cd /jim
$ ls -l
```

This will list all files on the disk and one system file called lost+found. To copy files from the floppy diskette to the hard disk we would reverse the process and copy from /jim to the target directory.

For example, to copy new.results from the floppy disk to the /usr/gill/sales directory we would type:

```
$ cp /jim/new.results /usr/gill/sales
```

## Unmounting the File System

This step is absolutely necessary. The files must be closed and the system device status tables updated. How do you know if the floppy disk is mounted? As long as the device is still mounted the light on the floppy drive will be on and will stay on until unmounted. To unmount the device choose item #8 *unmount* from the sysadm diskmgmt submenu and follow the instructions. Do not remove the disk until the light is off.

Once a disk has been prepared using the steps discussed above you can use the diskette by first performing a mount and lastly performing a unmount.

# 7

# DOS/UNIX
## command comparison

The authors of this text have experience with both operating systems. Having both grown up in a DOS world, the transition proved to be more difficult than originally anticipated. (For example, UNIX commands are generally expressed in lowercase, while the MS-DOS world will accept either. For our purposes we will denote DOS sequences in uppercase). However, once the transition was made, the UNIX power was unleashed. When a user logs into a UNIX system, the commands will prove to be similar in functionality yet different in actual command entry. Once understood, the user has the ability to operate in both environments with great success. In this chapter the user will be provided a command comparison between available MS-DOS versus UNIX commands. This will aid an experienced DOS user to accomplish the same desired functions under UNIX system, as well as allowing a UNIX user to understand command syntax within an MS-DOS environment.

Certain commands under DOS are used more frequently than others. The intent is to cover the most frequently used commands common to both environments. Movement within and between directories, display functions, system functions, and file commands will be covered. The following commands will be covered: CHDIR, DIR, MKDIR, RMDIR, TREE, MORE, DATE, PROMPT, TIME, VER, PRINT, TYPE, DISKCOMP, PATH, COMP, COPY, DEL, FIND, REN, SORT, DATE, TIME, and CHKDSK. UNIX treats every action as if it were working with a file. Because of this, prior to actually discussing each of these commands, the user should understand the basics of a file sytem. If the reader is familiar with file systems, he/she is encouraged to proceed to the section dealing with the movement within directories.

## INTRODUCTION: WHAT IS A FILE?

A file can best be viewed as a collection of data organized in some logical order. A good example is the file cabinet that exists in abundance in most offices. In the process of organizing your files in the file cabinet, you would place things in folders that make some logical sense: all files for Company XYZ, for example, or all monthly reports. It is also possible to have folders within folders. You might have an insurance file folder and within that folder have additional folders for auto, life, and medical insurance, each containing information specific to its respective area.

This analogy carries over to the electronic filing of data. A file is a collection of bytes of data, with a byte being analogous to a character. A file system is nothing more than a collection of files. The file system structure is normally integrated into the operating system; therefore, the operating system controls the way we must deal with files. Most operating systems allow us to view our files on a single level. The UNIX operating system was one of the first to pioneer a file system that allowed the user to view files on multiple levels. This multiple-level concept is known as a *hierarchical file system*. Data is organized in a multilevel format similar to an inverted tree. MS-DOS and PC-DOS since version 2.0 have also incorporated this scheme.

In this chapter we will explore the similarities and differences of both implementations. We will learn the benefits and uses of this powerful structure. This chapter also provides an overview of the most common commands used to create and manipulate files. It is intended as an overview and does not provide the level of detail some readers may desire.

All efforts have been made to include the latest features of both UNIX Systems V Release 2 and PC-DOS/MS-DOS 2.XX.

## THE HIERARCHICAL FILE SYSTEM (TREE STRUCTURES)

The hierarchical file system allows files to be categorized on multiple levels, allowing the user to view them in a more organized and logical way. Figure 7-1 represents our insurance file organized into a hierarchy.

Each major grouping is known as a directory. The directories in Fig. 7-1 are insurance, auto, life, and medical. Insurance in turn contains the subdirectories auto, life, and medical. The auto directory contains the files Mercedes and Porsche, while the life directory contains the files self and Alice, and the medical directory contains files John, Mary, and Dave. To access the file Mercedes we must first reference the directory insurance, then the directory auto, then the file Mercedes. Our path then is vertical down the tree to the target file. Once at the appropriate level, in

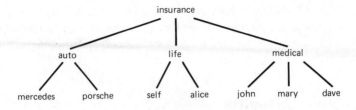

**Figure 7-1** Hierarchical structure

this case Mercedes, we must travel up the tree and then down to access the file self in the directory life. This is similar in concept to climbing up and down the branches of a tree, hence the name "tree structure." This is done by using the branches as they are connected. Understanding of this concept allows users to move very effectively within both DOS and UNIX environments.

Both UNIX and DOS (MS/PC DOS 2.0 and later) systems support this type of file system. Initially this structure may not appear to be a benefit. It is not until you have created many files that you can appreciate the logical format. Figure 7-2 is another example of how you might use this file structure to gain better categorization of your files.

Thus the games directory in Fig. 7-2 would allow games to be categorized by type. Some other examples would be: a directory of word processing packages, a directory of terminal communication software, a directory of spreadsheets, and so on.

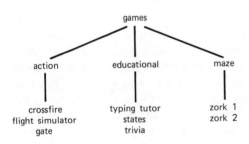

**Figure 7-2** Subdirectory hierarchy

## THE UNIX FILE SYSTEM

Why is the UNIX file system important to DOS users? UNIX features became the driving force for Microsoft to include such things as installable device drivers, redirection of I/O, piping, and the hierarchical file system—all features found in UNIX systems! It is clear since the introduction of DOS 2.0 that Microsoft's strategy will be to include more UNIX-like features in further releases of DOS.

The DOS user, therefore, can learn quite a lot about how to maximize the use of current DOS by exploring some examples included in this section. In addition to the inevitable convergence of both systems, the current DOS user can get a head start on the features and utilities that are sure to appear in future releases of DOS. Also, users of both UNIX and DOS operating systems will find the summary of commands extremely useful.


## DIRECTORY COMMANDS

Prior to actually focusing on all the commands available to super users, certain operator particulars must be covered. These relate to keyboard operation.

KILL A LINE: Under DOS, the user is used to killing a line by hitting the ESC key. Under UNIX systems the @ key accomplishes the same result. Both of these allow the user to start over with a command sequence.

INTERRUPT: Once the command sequence is successfully entered and executing, the user may need to stop the process. Under DOS, a Control C or a Control Break sequence will accomplish this. UNIX operators hit the Delete key on their terminal/PC to kill a command.

BACKSPACE: Backspace on the PC is a key on the top of the computer. The left arrow on the UNIX terminal is generally set up as the backspace. A command, stty erase ctrl H, may be entered to set this up.

METACHARACTERS: These characters, *, ?, are the same under both operating systems.

PIPES and REDIRECTION: Piping and redirection function the same way under both operating systems. Examples will be given later in this chapter.

COMMANDS: MS-DOS offers two type of commands, internal and external. Internal commands are those that are always resident in main memory. Examples of these include DIR, COPY, and TYPE. External commands are those that are included with the operating system, yet are stored on disk rather than in main memory. Examples of external commands include SORT, EDLIN, and CHKDSK. ALL UNIX commands are external due to the large nature of the core operating system.

CASE: UNIX uses lowercase for command sequences, whereas DOS does not care. Because of this, DOS commands will be capitalized in the text for distinction from their UNIX equivalents.

### Root Directory Command Comparison

| DOS | UNIX |
|:---:|:---:|
| \ | / |

The UNIX file system structure begins at the / (slash) directory, which is known as the root. Within DOS, it is also the root directory, but a backslash is used instead of a slash. Consult the next chapter for a means of modifying the DOS delimiter, (\), to be equivalent to the UNIX (/). It is the source from which all other directories originate.

## Directory Command Comparison

| DOS | UNIX |
|-----|------|
| DIR | ls -l |

The command used within DOS to yield a listing of all the files within a given directory is the DIR command. DIR without any options displays all entries on the default drive. If a particular drive is desired, DIR d: should be used, with d being the desired drive. There are many different options available for this command. The command to list files on a UNIX system is ls. Each command in a UNIX environment has numerous options designated with the -n parameter. To list files once at the root directory, we would issue the ls -l command for listing files with the long format.

| DOS | UNIX | Action |
|-----|------|--------|
| DIR | ls -l | Lists directory entries |
| DIR k* | ls -l k* | Lists directory entries beginning with the letter *k* |
| DIR/W | see Chapter 8 | Lists entries in a wide fashion across the screen |

The results would look like those in Fig. 7-3.

For dir output, the first two columns are the filename plus the optional extension. The third column yields a count of the bytes contained in the file. The last two columns indicate the date and time of the last update of the file. In the case of a new file, this indicates the date and time the file was created.

For the UNIX directory listing, the first line indicates the number of blocks (1024 bytes) that the listed files use. The next line can be deciphered by breaking it into sections.

1. Type and access permission: drwxrwxrwx
2. Links: 2
3. Owner: root
4. Group: sys
5. Number of characters in file: 32768 (32 × 1024)

DOS
C)dir

```
Volume in drive C has no label
Directory of  C:/

COMMAND   COM     15957    11-10-83    12:03p
SORT              429      3-27-85     5:13p
CHKDSK    COM     6468     10-19-83    7:51p
COMP      COM     2713     6-05-84     2:03a
DISKCOMP  COM     2758     5-30-84     1:54a
DISKCOPY  COM     3276     5-31-84     6:14p
FORMAT    COM     6636     5-31-84     6:52p
SYS       COM     2498     5-30-84     1:48a
MODE      COM     5308     6-07-84     3:50p
PRINT     COM     3808     2-23-84     11:25a
GRAPHICS  COM     656      6-08-84     10:48a
FIND      EXE     6331     10-19-83    7:51p
MORE      COM     4364     10-19-83    7:51p
SORT      EXE     1632     10-10-84    12:44a
ANSI      SYS     2504     6-11-84     1:05p
ASSIGN    EXE     15872    6-11-84     6:13p
```

UNIX

```
$ ls -l
total 416
drwxrwxr-x   2 root    sys        32 Mar 16 17:55 bck
drwxrwxr-x   2 bin     bin      1408 Mar 16 17:55 bin
drwxrwxr-x   2 root    sys       320 Jun 18 12:57 boot
drwxrwxr-x   7 root    sys      3280 May 31 15:12 dev
-r-xr-xr-x   1 bin     bin     19108 Mar 16 17:55 dgmon
drwxrwxr-x   2 root    root      112 Mar 16 17:55 dgn
drwxrwxr-x  10 root    sys      1648 Jun 27 10:43 etc
-r-xr-xr-x   1 bin     bin     13636 Mar 16 17:55 filledt
d---------   2 root    root       32 May  3 07:14 instal
drwx------   2 root    sys        32 Mar 16 17:55 install
drwxrwxr-x   4 bin     bin       304 Mar  4 10:20 lib
drwxrwxr-x   2 root    root     3104 May  8 02:03 lost+found
drwxrwxr-x   2 root    sys        32 Mar 16 17:55 mnt
drwxrwxr-x   2 root    other      32 Jan 31 16:38 root
drwxrwxr-x   2 root    sys        32 Mar 16 17:55 save
drwxrwxrwx   2 sys     sys       176 Jun 27 22:05 tmp
-rwxr--r--   1 root    root   159916 Jun 18 12:59 unix
drwxrwxr-x  24 root    root      400 Jun 24 20:01 usr
```

**Figure 7-3** Directory listings for DOS and UNIX

6. Date/time (the file was last modified feb 25 1:01)

7. Name of file, and so on.

**Permission Bits**—The first character, if a d, tells UNIX this file is a direct-ory. If it is, then it is an ordinary file; if it is b,c, or p, then the UNIX operating system understands this to be a special file used to perform I/O operations. The next group of characters, rwx, indicates the owner's ability to read, write, or execute files within that directory. The next three characters indicate the group permission to read, write, or execute files. The last three characters pertain to any other user on the system. The same read, write, and execute permission scheme pertains to this section as well. The following syntax is used in the listings. The -rwx,rwx,rwx permission bits relate to owner, group, and other, respectively.

**Links**—The number in this field indicates the number of files this file relates to. These files are aliases (duplicates with possible different names) that refer to the same physical file.

**Owner**—This field identifies the owner of the file or directory. This is the log-in name of the owner (creator).

**Group**—This field identifies the group the owner belongs to. This entry relates to the group permission bits. If you were a member of this group, your permission would be determined by the group's permission status.

**Characters in the File**—This is the total number of characters in the file.

**Date/Time Last Modified**—This the actual date and time the file was last changed. Time is indicated in military time. 1:00 P.M. would be indicated as 13:00.

**Filename**—This is the filename that was used at the time of creation.

## Moving Between Directories: Change Directory Command Comparison

| DOS | UNIX |
|------|------|
| CD or CHDIR | cd |

The command used to move from one directory to another is called cd (change directory). These commands are very similar between MS-DOS and UNIX Systems. Within MS-DOS, either CD or CHDIR is allowed to change between directories. However, UNIX environments only support cd, not chdir. In order to change from the root directory to a subdirectory called etc, we would issue the following command.

| DOS | UNIX | Action |
|------|------|--------|
| cd etc | cd etc | changes current directory to etc |

We would then be located at that directory level. We are now located at the etc directory, which is a subdirectory of root as shown in Fig. 7-4. The hierarchy from root to etc is known as the path to that directory. We learned earlier that the backslash and slash are used as delimiters in the directory hierarchies. So the path to the etc directory under DOS is \etc, or /etc under UNIX systems.

DOS

C)cd etc

C)dir

```
Volume in drive C has no label
Directory of  C:/etc

.               <DIR>      5-24-85   3:26p
..              <DIR>      5-24-85   3:26p
        2 File(s)    3297280 bytes free
```

UNIX

```
$ cd etc
$ ls -l
total 3706
-rw-rw-r--  1 root    other      1845 May  8 22:41 OLDgettydefs
-r--r--r--  1 root    sys          66 Apr  1 22:03 TIMEZONE
-rwxr--r--  1 root    sys         386 Sep 14  1984 bcheckrc
-rwxr--r--  1 root    sys          70 Sep 14  1984 brc
-rwxr--r--  1 root    sys         344 Sep 14  1984 bzapunix
-r-xr--r--  1 root    bin       23636 Dec 17  1983 cgetty
-rw-------  1 root    other       293 Oct  8  1984 checkall
-rw-rw-r--  1 root    sys           0 Sep 14  1984 checklist
-r-xr-xr-x  1 bin     bin       11660 Sep 20  1984 chroot
-r-xr-xr-x  1 root    root      10168 Sep 14  1984 ckauto
-r-xr-xr-x  1 bin     bin       11240 Sep 14  1984 clri
-rwxr-xr-x  1 root    sys         800 Oct  6  1984 coredirs
-r-xr-xr-x  1 bin     bin       75752 Sep 20  1984 crash
-r-xr--r--  1 bin     bin       36444 Sep 14  1984 cron
-r-xr-xr-x  1 bin     bin       24588 Oct  5  1984 dcopy
-r-xr-xr-x  1 bin     bin       12304 Sep 14  1984 devnm
-r-xr-xr-x  1 bin     bin       16784 Sep 20  1984 dfsck
-r--r--r--  1 root    sys         570 Sep 14  1984 disketteparm
-rwxr-xr-x  1 bin     bin       25720 Sep 14  1984 drvinstall
-rwxr-xr-x  1 bin     bin       23640 Sep 14  1984 edittbl
```

**Figure 7-4** Changing directories

## Current Directory Command Comparison

| DOS | UNIX |
| --- | --- |
| CD | pwd |

Because you are only one level into the hierarchy and have just completed changing directories, you know exactly where you are. However, after continued use and bouncing around both DOS and UNIX file systems the user may lose track of which directory he/she is actually in. Both operating systems provide commands to display the path to the current directory.

To find out where we are in a DOS or UNIX directory, we would enter the following command sequence.

| DOS | UNIX | Action |
| --- | --- | --- |
| CD | pwd | displays current directory |

## Returning to Root Directory Command Comparison

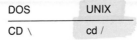

| DOS | UNIX |
|-----|------|
| CD \ | cd / |

To return to the root directory, we would issue the cd command and reference the root directory. This can be done in MS-DOS by issuing the command sequence CD \, and in UNIX with cd /. See Fig. 7-5 for a sample session. Note the difference between the slashes used. Refer to Chapter 8 for assistance in solving this discrepancy.

| DOS | UNIX | ACTION |
|-----|------|--------|
| C>cd etc | $ cd /etc | move to etc directory |
| C>CD | $ pwd | displays current directory |
| C:\ETC | /etc | current directory |
| C>CD \ | $ cd / | move to root directory |
| C>CD | $ pwd | displays current directory |
| C:\ | / | current directory |
| C> | $ | system prompt |

**Figure 7-5** Displaying correct directory

Within both systems there is a means of moving up one level within the directory hierarchy. The .. refers to a special directory known as the *parent directory*. That is the directory one level up from the present directory in the hierarchy. Thus, root is exactly one level up from etc in our example. To move back one level from the etc directory, issue the following commands:

| DOS | UNIX | Action |
|-----|------|--------|
| CD .. | cd .. | moves up one level in the hierarchy |

With a path of \etc or /etc, depending on the operating system, the user will be at the root directory upon issuance of this command.

Users begin to rely heavily on their ability to move around a file system with the change directory sequences. However, it is sometimes awkward to have to know where a user is in the hierarchy. Rather than display the current directory with a CD or pwd command, both MS-DOS and UNIX provide the capability to move directly to a directory. This is accomplished by giving a path to the directory relative to the root.

To move down the tree, you can refer to the full path name separated by the \

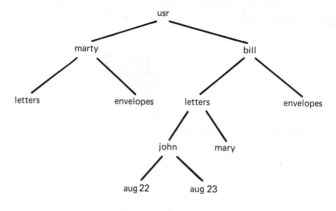

**Figure 7-6** Tree structure

or / character, for DOS or UNIX, respectively. Consider the following example using the tree structure in Fig. 7-6.

In order to access the letter aug22 in the john directory you would issue the following:

| DOS | UNIX | Action |
|---|---|---|
| C> CD \usr\bill\letters \john | $ cd /usr/bill/letters/john | moves to john directory |
| C> CD | $ pwd | prints current directory |
| C> DIR AUG22 | $ ls -l aug22 | display entry |

These sequences will place you in the directory containing the directory john which contains the file aug22. The final command merely lists the directory entry for confirmation that the user is truly at the proper location.

This type of reference is known as *full path name* in UNIX jargon. Once at the correct directory, the next step would be to list the contents of the file. Refer to the section appearing later in this chapter for how to list the contents of a file.

## Making Directories Command Comparison

| DOS | UNIX |
|---|---|
| MD or MKDIR | mkdir |

We generally don't appreciate why more than one directory is needed on a system until we use the additional ones, then their merits are overwhelming. The DIR and ls commands were used to get a listing of all the files on a disk or directory. If many files are present, they quickly scroll off the screen upon command issuance. This may prove to be unacceptable. Enter one of the reasons for subdirectories. A directory may be created to hide files that are not relevant to the current user's activities. For example, if a user were developing word processing text files for later editing, a special directory could be set up. All text files could then be stored in the word processing directory. Unless the user specifically wanted to view the text filenames, they would not appear in a directory listing. Only those files that were stored in the current or working directory would be displayed. This is a rather simple reason to build subdirectories, but will suffice in our explanation of how to create subdirectories.

To create a new directory, the mkdir command is issued in both DOS and UNIX with a valid filename. To create a new directoy called "proposal" to add to the existing structure of Figs. 7-6, you would perform the following steps:

| DOS | UNIX | Action |
|---|---|---|
| C> CD \USR\BILL | $ cd /usr/bill | move to proper place |
| C> MKDIR PROPOSAL | $ mkdir proposal | build the directory |
| C> DIR | $ 1s -1 | insure that it is there |

The results of issuing the mkdir command created our new directory "proposal" under the existing /usr/bill directory. Figure 7-7 illustrates this change. It is really not necessary to move to the directory that you want to be the parent of your subdirectory. The user merely issues the mkdir command followed by a full pathname, including the name of the new directory, mkdir /usr/bill/proposals. The same command using the backslashes would be issed in the DOS world.

Now that the proposals directory exists, we can begin to create and place files into that directory. The steps that we would perform to create files would be to first

```
DOS
C>cd \usr\bill

C>mkdir proposal

C>dir

    Volume in drive C has no label
    Directory of  C:\usr\bill

.               <DIR>      4-03-84    3:10p
..              <DIR>      4-03-84    3:10p
PROPOSAL        <DIR>      5-24-85    3:56p
        3 File(s)     4083712 bytes free
UNIX
$ cd usr/bill
$ mkdir proposal
$ 1s -al
total 3
drwxr-xr-x   3 var      spl         48 Jun 27 22:16 .
drwxr-xr-x   3 var      spl         48 Jun 27 22:13 ..
drwxr-xr-x   2 var      spl         32 Jun 27 22:16 proposal
$
```

**Figure 7-7** Making directories

cd to the proposals directory and then use the editor to create our file(s). The full path name to our new directory is /usr/bill/proposals.

### Removing Directories Command Comparison

| DOS | UNIX |
|---|---|
| RD or RMDIR | rmdir |

Our example has been modified to show the existence of two new files; xyz_inc and kiwi_inc. These two new files have been placed in the recently created proposal directory. Note that the underscore character _ has been used where a space may appear more appropriate. The reason for this is that UNIX filenames by convention do not contain spaces. Figure 7-8 illustrates the current condition of our directory structure.

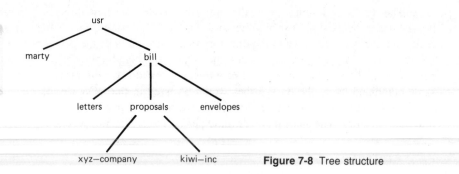

**Figure 7-8** Tree structure

If we were to change directories to the proposal directory and then display the directory we would see that the files xwz_company and kiwi_inc are in fact there. Use the DIR or 1s commands as in the following:

| DOS | UNIX | Action |
|---|---|---|
| C> CD \usr\bill\proposal | $ cd /usr/bill/proposal | change directory |
| C> CD | $ pwd | current directory |
| C> DIR | $ ls -l | lists files |

Now that we have created a directory and placed files into it, how do we remove a directory? The rmdir command used in both systems has a built-in safeguard. It will not allow you to remove a directory that contains existing files—a nice feature once you consider that it is real easy to remove multiple files with a single typo. To remove our proposal directory, we would use the rmdir command. The rmdir command will fail if we still have files in the proposals directory. The files and directory will not be modifed as result of a failure. The correct procedure is first to remove any existing files and then to remove the directory. Our next step would be to remove the files. In order to do this, we must understand the DOS ERASE and the UNIX remove files command rm. These commands, like so many other commands, need only the filename or names separated by spaces in order to remove a file or files. The rm command will be discussed further in this chapter. However, for our purposes, please accept that the command does indeed work and do the following.

| DOS | UNIX | Action |
|-----|------|--------|
| C> CD \usr\bill\proposals | $ cd /usr/bill/proposals | Moves to directory |
| C> ERASE *.* | $ rm * | Deletes all files |
| C> DIR | $ 1s -1 | Checks directory |
| C> CD .. | $ cd .. | Move to parent directory |
| C> CD | $ pwd | Proper directory?? |
| C> RMDIR proposal | $ rmdir proposal | Removes directory |

It is possible to combine more than one command on a single line. The UNIX command separator is the semicolon ;. UNIX systems execute commands in the order that they appear. For example, we could type the following and obtain the same results as the previous example:

```
$ cd /usr/bill/proposal ;pwd ;1s -1
$ rm *.* ;1s -1 ; rmdir /usr/bill/proposal
```

The use of multiple commands on a single line can greatly reduce the number of steps necessary to perform a function. However, a single mistake in typing could cause the total line to have to be reentered or, a worse disaster, removing forever some very important files. The beginning UNIX user should be very comfortable with the results of combined commands before attempting to make use of this feature.

## FILE MANIPULATION

MS-DOS and UNIX operating systems provide a comprehensive set of commands to manipulate files. These include the capability to list, copy, remove, sort, and compare files. All of these features are provided in the operating systems and can be combined to provide some extremely powerful tools.

Files are created using one of the standard DOS or UNIX editors such as edlin, ed, ex, vi, or sed. Edlin is included with the basic MS-DOS operating system, while some or all of the other editors may be included in your release of UNIX. Some, such as vi, are considered enhancements to UNIX and may be considered optional. You can be sure that the original editor, ed, will be included with the core system. Use of the editors is covered later in this chapter. Consider for the following discussion that the file kiwi_inc has already been created using one of these editors.

## File Listing Command Comparison

| DOS | UNIX |
| --- | --- |
| TYPE | cat |

Both operating systems provide the user the capability to display the contents of a file. Under DOS, the command TYPE is used, followed by a filename. As before, the user may issue this command from any directory by giving the appropriate path as a filename after the TYPE command.

The UNIX command cat is used to list the contents of a file. Unlike the ls command, which lists the names of files and directories, the cat command lists the contents of a file.

Therefore, to list the contents of our kiwi_inc file, we would type:

| DOS | UNIX | Action |
| --- | --- | --- |
| C> CD \USR\BILL\PROPOSAL | $ cd /usr/bill/proposal | Move to directory |
| C> DIR K* | $ ls -l k* | Lists files |
| C> TYPE KIWI_INC | $ cat kiwi_inc | Lists file |

We would not actually have to move to the proposal directory to list the file kiwi_inc. From the root directory, or anywhere else, we would issue the commands as shown in Fig. 7-9.

```
DOS
C> cd
C:\

C> type \usr\bill\proposal\kiwi_inc
This is the contents of the kiwi_inc file.

C>
```

```
UNIX
$ pwd
/
$ cat /usr/bill/proposal/kiwi_inc
this is the contents of the kiwi_inc file.
$
```

**Figure 7-9** Listing file contents

## Scroll Control Command Comparison

| DOS | UNIX | Action |
|-----|------|--------|
| Control Num Lock | Control s | To hold/stop |
| any key | Control q | To continue |

Both the TYPE and cat commands correctly list the contents of the file. It can be quite annoying to list a very long file and see it disappear from the screen. Both DOS and UNIX systems provide ways to deal with this problem. By typing ctrl-s under UNIX, the screen can be stopped until a restart character ctrl-q is typed. MS-DOS uses Control s or a Control Num Lock to accomplish the same scroll control. Typing any key will resume scrolling. This is a typical way to read very long files and should work on most systems. Later we will review other UNIX utilities such as pr and pg in addition to the DOS MORE command, which will allow you to view or print your data a screen at a time.

## Copy/Move Command Comparison

| DOS | UNIX |
|-----|------|
| COPY | cp |

When the user desires to copy a file from one directory to another or one file system to another, the copy facilities of the operating systems are invoked. Under DOS, the ability to copy a file from one disk to another or one directory to another is provided by issuing a COPY command followed by a source and destination file or drive. The cp command is used to copy the contents of one file to another under UNIX. The syntax is COPY/cp source_file target_file. The target file need not exist. It is created automatically if it does not already exist. If the target file already exists, then its contents are overwritten by the results of the cp command. An example is in order.

If we decided we would like a copy of our kiwi_inc file to be duplicated and placed in our letters directory, the copy commands should be used. We will call our new file kiwi.bk. To perform this function we would type:

| DOS | UNIX | Action |
|-----|------|--------|
| C> CD \usr\bill\proposal | $ cd /usr/bill/proposal | Go to parent directory |
| C> COPY kiwi_inc \usr \bill\letters\kiwi.bk | | Performs copy function |
| | $ cp kiwi_inc /usr/bill/letters/kiwi.bk | |
| C> CD \usr\bill\letters | $ cd /usr/bill/letters | Move to destination directory |
| C> DIR k* | $ ls -l k* | Insure sucessful copy |

We now have an exact copy of our kiwi_inc in the letters directory with the name kiwi.bk. It should be noted that if kiwi.bk already existed in the target directory, its contents would have been overwritten. Neither DOS nor UNIX systems provides any check for this situation; thus, the responsibility is left to the user.

## Rename Files Command Comparison

| DOS | UNIX |
|-----|------|
| REN | mv |

There are many situations where it is necessary to rename a file. The UNIX move command provides this function along with a dual capability to move files from one directory to another. DOS provides a mnemonic command, REN, to rename a file. REN simply replaces the directory entry with the new name. The UNIX command is called mv. The syntax is mv source target. Unlike cp, which copied the source file into the target file, leaving the source unaltered, mv "removes" the source file as it executes. Consider the following, where we desire to rename a file within the proposal directory.

| DOS | UNIX | Action |
|-----|------|--------|
| C> CD<br>   \USR\BILL\PROPOSAL | $ cd /usr/bill/proposal | Move to proposal directory |
| C> DIR K* | $ ls -l k* | List directory entry |
| C> REN kiwi_inc aussie | $ mv kiwi_inc aussie | Renames filename |
| C> DIR | $ 1s -1 | Insures success |

In effect, what we have done is rename the file kiwi_inc to aussie within the same directory. Note in Fig. 7-10 that the original (source) no longer exists. Files can be moved anywhere in the UNIX file system provided you have the correct permission. Under MS-DOS, the user is not so restricted.

## REDIRECTION COMMAND COMPARISON

Most commands take their input from the keyboard and send the resulting output back to the screen. A command normally reads its input from a place called the standard input, which happens to be your terminal/computer by default. Similarly, a command writes its output to the standard output, your terminal/computer by default. The UNIX and DOS operating systems provide a means of changing where the input and output is placed; this concept is known as *redirection*.

```
DOS
C)cd \usr\bill\proposal

C)dir

    Volume in drive C has no label
    Directory of  C:\usr\bill\proposal

    .               (DIR)       4-03-84    3:10p
    ..              (DIR)       4-03-84    3:10p
    XYZ_INC             8       4-03-84    3:18p
    KIWI_INC           45       5-24-85    3:44p
            4 File(s)     4075520 bytes free


C)ren kiwi_inc aussie

    After rename command


    Volume in drive C has no label
    Directory of  C:\usr\bill\proposal

    .               (DIR)       4-03-84    3:10p
    ..              (DIR)       4-03-84    3:10p
    XYZ_INC             8       4-03-84    3:18p
    AUSSIE             45       5-24-85    3:44p
            4 File(s)     4075520 bytes free

    C)
UNIX
$ cd /usr/bill/proposal
$ ls -al
total 4
drwxr-xr-x    2 root        root      80 Apr 10 22:10 .
drwxr-xr-x    3 root        root      48 Apr 10 21:52 ..
-rw-r--r--    1 root        root      43 Apr 10 22:01 kiwi_inc
-rw-r--r--    1 root        root       9 Apr 10 22:09 xyz_inc
$ mv kiwi_inc aussie
$ ls -al
total 4
drwxr-xr-x    2 root        root      80 Apr 10 22:10 .
drwxr-xr-x    3 root        root      48 Apr 10 21:52 ..
-rw-r--r--    1 root        root      43 Apr 10 22:01 aussie
-rw-r--r--    1 root        root       9 Apr 10 22:09 xyz_inc
$
```

**Figure 7-10** Before and after rename command

## Output Redirection Command Comparison

The standard input and output have operated in the default mode, taking data from the keyboard and displaying data on the screen in all examples up to this point.

Under the operating systems, the output from a command normally intended for the terminal/computer can be diverted to a file instead. This function is known as *output redirection.* If the notation > filename is appended to any command, the output of that command will be written to the specified file instead of your terminal. Let's begin by listing the contents of a file name:

| DOS | UNIX | Action |
| --- | --- | --- |
| C> TYPE names | $ cat names | Displays contents of names file |

There is nothing unusual about the results of this command. Input/output is to and from the terminal/computer. Now let's use output redirection > to place the output of the TYPE/cat command into a file called names.new.

| DOS | UNIX | Action |
| --- | --- | --- |
| C> TYPE names > names.new | $ cat names > names.new | Redirects output |
| C> TYPE names.new | $ cat names.new | Displays output |

The files are exactly the same. Our new file, names.new, was created as a result of the TYPE/cat command redirecting the output. If names.new already existed, then its contents will be overwritten. The use of the TYPE/cat command and > redirection in the above example causes TYPE/cat to place its output into a file instead of the standard output, the terminal. The TYPE/cat command coupled with output redirection can be used to create a file directly from the keyboard without the use of an editor. Simply key in the following:

| DOS | UNIX | Action |
| --- | --- | --- |
| C> COPY CON: tel_nos | $ cat > tel_nos | Redirects to file |
| john jones 677-1334 | john jones 677-1334 | data input |
| mary smith 798-9955 | mary smith 798-9955 | data input |
| paul nolan 555-8811 | paul nolan 555-8811 | data input |
| stan miller 455-1365 | stan miller 455-1365 | data input |
| ctrl-Z | ctrl-d | end of file |

Since no input filename was given, cat took its input directly from the standard input, your terminal or computer. With the > tel_nos specification we've indicated to write the results into a file called tel_nos. To end the input we must type a ctrl-d to indicate end of data entry. Under MS-DOS we indicate the end of a file by typing a Control Z. To verify that the data has been diverted to the proper place, we can TYPE/cat tel_nos.

## Append Command Comparison

| DOS | UNIX | Action |
| --- | --- | --- |
| copy names.new + tel_nos | cat tel_nos >> names.new | Appends tel_nos to names.new file |

The UNIX >> operators allow the user to add data to the end of a file. So to append the file tel_nos to our previous file, names.new, we would type

```
$ cat tel_nos >> names.new
```

The effect of the >> causes the output of the cat command to place its results at the end of the file names.new. Thus the file names.new contains the original data plus the contents of the file tel_nos.

Under DOS, we use the copy command to append files. To append tel_nos to the names.new file, we enter copy names.new + tel_nos. Names.new now contains the infomation previously contained in two files, names.new and tel_nos. Refer to Fig. 7-11 for sample sessions.

### Input Redirection Command Comparison

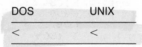

| DOS | UNIX |
|-----|------|
| < | < |

We can also redirect the input of a command as well as the output. The operator < is used to indicate redirection of input. The MS-DOS and UNIX command to sort the contents of a file is sort. Knowing that we can redirect input, we can use sort to sort our names.new file.

| DOS | UNIX | Action |
|-----|------|--------|
| C> SORT < NAMES.NEW | $ sort < names.new | Redirects input from file |

The output of the sort command goes to the terminal, as we did not indicate that it shouldbe otherwise. Therefore the standard output was used. We can of course redirect both input and outut to a command. Using our sort example, let's go one step further and redirect the output to a file called tel.sort.

| DOS | UNIX | Action |
|-----|------|--------|
| C> SORT < NAMES.NEW > TEL.SORT | $ sort < names.new > tel.sort | Sort and outputs to file instead of screen |
| C> TYPE TEL.SORT | $ cat tel.sort | Confirms sort was complete |

Although this command line does look rather cryptic at first, with a little practice it can be deciphered. Sort simply takes its input from a file called names.new. It performs the sorting function and then places the results in a file called tel.sort. See

```
DOS
C>type names.new
john jones
mary smith
paul nolan
stan miller

C>type tel_nos
john jones 677-1334
mary smith 798-9955
paul nolan 555-8811
stan miller 455-1365

C>copy names.new + tel_nos
NAMES.NEW
TEL_NOS
        1 File(s) copied

C>type names.new
john jones
mary smith
paul nolan
stan miller
john jones 677-1334
mary smith 798-9955
paul nolan 555-8811
stan miller 455-1365

C>

UNIX
$ cat names.new
john jones
mary smith
paul nolan
stan miller


$ cat tel_nos
john jones 677-1334
mary smith 798-9955
paul nolan 555-8811
stan miller 455-1365


$ cat tel_nos >> names.new
$ cat names.new
john jones
mary smith
paul nolan
stan miller
john jones 677-1334
mary smith 798-9955
paul nolan 555-8811
stan miller 455-1365
$
```

**Figure 7-11** Sample sessions for appending files

```
C> sort < names.new > tel.sort

C> type tel.sort
john jones
john jones 677-1334
mary smith
mary smith 798-9955
paul nolan
paul nolan 555-8811
stan miller
stan miller 455-1365

C>
$ sort < names.new > tel.sort
$ cat tel.sort
john jones
john jones 677-1334
mary smith
mary smith 798-9955
paul nolan
paul nolan 555-8811
stan miller
stan miller 455-1365
$
```

**Figure 7-12**  Sort with redirection

Fig. 7-12 for the session and results. There are, of course, many other uses of I/O redirection. We have only touched on a few examples; you should experiment with these concepts using test files to gain a better understanding of these powerful functions.

## SORT AND COMPARE COMMAND COMPARISON

| DOS | UNIX |
|------|------|
| SORT | sort |
| FC | diff |

Some very powerful tools are needed to sort and compare files. We have already seen an example of the sort command and how it can be used. On a larger scale, we could have a file containing 10,000 names and by issuing a single sort command we could produce an alphabetized list.

Sort has numerous options, such as sorting in reverse order, mapping lowercase to uppercase, and so on. For another example, we'll use sort in conjunction with the DIR and 1s commands to produce a file called test.txt containing the directory entries in reverse alphabetical order.

| DOS | UNIX | Action |
|---|---|---|
| C> DIR > temp.txt | $ 1s −1 > temp.txt | Stores directory in a temporary file |
| C> SORT /R < temp.txt > test. txt | | Sorts in reverse order |
| | $ sort −r < temp.txt > test.txt | |
| C> TYPE test.txt | $ cat test.txt | Confirms a successful operation |

The ability to combine redirection with UNIX utilities such as sort creates an extremely powerful environment for the user.

MS-DOS and UNIX systems provide tools to compare files as well, the FC(File Compare) and diff commands. The results of these commands are the character strings that are not common to two input files. Assume that file1 contains the words one, two, and three; file2 contains three, four, and five. To produce a list of the differences between the two files, one would do the following.

| DOS | UNIX | Action |
|---|---|---|
| C> FC file1 file2 | $ diff file1 file2 | Displays differences between file1 and file2 |

Another similar command is the UNIX compare command. The cmp command is used to compare two files and indicate the first place that they differ. It will not indicate how they differ nor any differences beyond the first.

## WHEN TO USE DIFF AND COMP

The file compare commands diff and cmp perform similar functions but return quite different results. Both commands have specific purposes, however, and can be used to your benefit. A general rule for cmp is to use this command when you expect the files to have the same contents. It's particularly useful when you want to verify that the files are identical. The cmp command will also work on any kind of file. The diff command should be used when you expect the files to be somewhat different and you want to know exactly which lines differ. The diff command, unlike cmp, only works with text files. Use cmp first and if the files differ, then use diff to print the lines that differ. MS-DOS does offer a COMP command for a quick determination if files are identical.

## FIND COMMAND COMPARISON

| DOS | UNIX |
|---|---|
| FIND | GREP |

Grep, although a very strange-sounding name, is actually one of the most-used UNIX commands. Grep is UNIX shorthand for "global regular expression and print." This, in addition, is derived from the editor sequence g/regular expression/p. This command is equivalent to MS-DOS's FIND command sequence.

| DOS | UNIX | Action |
|-----|------|--------|
| C> TYPE DENVER | $ cat denver | List file contents |

"Denver, Colorado, is called 'the mile high city' and is located at the base of the Rocky Mountains. Denver is also the home of the Broncos, a well known football team."

| DOS | UNIX | Action |
|-----|------|--------|
| C> FIND "football" DENVER | $ grep football denver | Displays all lines matching the pattern |

What the FIND/grep command does is search files for lines that match a pattern. Suppose you wish to search for the word "football" in the file denver: "known football team." is output as a result of the commands.

Grep can also be used to look for lines that don't match the pattern string. To obtain this "don't match" function, we use the -v option with grep, /V with FIND.

Suppose we would like to find all lines that do not contain the word "Denver."

| DOS | UNIX | Action |
|-----|------|--------|
| FIND V "Denver" DENVER | $ grep -v Denver denver | Locates all lines that don't contain the string Denver |

The above command yields the line, "known football team."

These examples are, of course, fairly simplistic and do not indicate the total power of FIND/grep. Consider a mailing list with several hundred entries. You would like to find all people living in Houston. You could use grep to search the file for the string Houston. Another example might be the termcap file in the UNIX system that contains terminal control sequences for several hundred terminals. You would like to find out if your vt100 terminal is defined, so you would grep termcap for vt100.

## MORE FILTER COMMAND COMPARISON

| DOS | UNIX |
|-----|------|
| MORE | pg |

Earlier we discussed the problem of listing very long files and having them scroll off the screen. UNIX System V Release 2 provides a very handy command, called pg, to solve this problem. The primary purpose of pg is to display a file a screen at a time. That is, the system displays enough text to fill one entire screen and then waits for you to hit a key before displaying the next page. The pg command is only included in System V Release 2. If your system is one of the Berkeley versions, you probably have a similar command known as "more." If you have neither, it is still possible to simulate this command using a shell script. More on this later in Chapter 8. Under MS-DOS, a filter called MORE is provided with the same functionality.

## DATE AND TIME COMMAND COMPARISON

| DOS | UNIX |
|------|------|
| DATE | DATE |
| TIME | DATE |

The user often needs to display or change the date and time of the system. MS-DOS offers two separate commands, DATE and TIME, for this purpose. By typing in DATE, the user is given the current setting and offered the option of entering the new DATE. TIME functions the same as DATE. Under UNIX a single command, date, is used for both. By entering the command date without any options, the current date and time are displayed. The syntax for changing them is as follows: date mmddhhmm[yy], where the options are month month, day day, hour hour, minute minute, and optional year.

## DISK USAGE COMMAND COMPARISON

| DOS | UNIX |
|--------|-------|
| CHKDSK | du -s |

If the user desires to know how much of the available disk space has been used, both operating systems allow for this. CHKDSK is entered followed by a drive name within DOS to yield the following output.

```
C> CHKDSK

Errors found, F parameter not specified
Corrections will not be written to disk.


3 lost clusters found in 3 chains.
Convert lost chains to files (Y/N)? y

10592256 bytes total disk space
  122880 bytes in 6 hidden files
   53248 bytes in 13 directories
 4382720 bytes in 203 user files
   12288 bytes would be in
         3 recovered files
 6021120 bytes available on disk

  262144 bytes total memory
  221952 bytes free
```

Under UNIX, the du -s sequence is entered. This yields the number of blocks occupied. A block is generally 512 or 1024 bytes in length. To obtain the amount used, multiply the output of the du command by the block size. It is important to note that the du command calculates blocks based on where in the tree structure the user is. To calculate a user's space, issue the command so that only the user's directories are included. Change directories to move to your own directory to accomplish this. If the total system usage is desired, issue the du sequence from the root directory.

## FILENAME COMPARISONS

UNIX filenames can be 14 characters long and can contain any character. DOS filenames are a little more restrictive in that all filenames are limited to eight characters, with a three-character extension. DOS filenames can contain alphanumeric characters as well as some special characters.

The listing indicates directories by <DIR> in the column where the actual size of the file in bytes is displayed. If the directory listed was not the root directory then two special directories would have been included. The first would be the dot (.) and the second dot-dot (. .) directory. These are the same as discussed under UNIX. The dot (.) directory is an alias for the current directory; the dot-dot (. .) directory always refers to the parent directory (one level up from the current directory).

You can also list files using the astersk (*) and question mark(?) for character substitution. The same rules apply as under UNIX.

DOS indicates the current drive (either floppy or hard) by the character preceding the > prompt. Typically, drive C refers to the hard disk and A and B to the floppy drives. Once a drive has been specified, all references to files that do not include a specific drive identifier will refer to the current active drive.

UNIX environments have no knowledge of drives and deal with all devices as files. Under the UNIX system, once a file system has been mounted, it can be referred to by it's full pathname and is treated the same as any other UNIX file.

## LINE ENDING SEQUENCE COMPARISON

A UNIX system ends each line of data with a linefeed character and stores the data in this format. When data is sent to the screen, UNIX Code then sends a carriage return-linefeed sequence. DOS, on the other hand, stores all files with the carriage return-linefeed sequence.

Is all this really important? If you transfer files between the two systems it becomes painfully important. All DOS files will not appear correctly under UNIX; conversely, all UNIX files will not appear correctly under DOS. The way to solve this problem is to filter out the carriage return before sending files to UNIX system from a DOS system and to include carriage returns in files sent to DOS from UNIX computers. This is exactly what is done with such products as PC INTERFACE from AT&T, which allows PCs to use UNIX systems as file servers. We will discuss products such as PC Interface in Chapter 8.

At this point it is important to realize that UNIX and DOS store data in slightly different formats. The user that transfers data to and from UNIX/DOS systems may need to be concerned about this difference. Refer to the section in Chapter 8 for a discussion of these differences and how to overcome them.

# 8

# bridging the gap between DOS and UNIX

## DOS TO UNIX SYSTEM—EASING THE TRANSITION

The merger of the DOS operating system and the UNIX operating system will eventually provide a common interface for the user. Until that time, DOS users moving to UNIX-like operating systems can do much to relieve the frustration and confusion that surround such a move. In this chapter we will discuss some ways to make UNIX systems more forgiving for the DOS user. In addition, we will explore some alternative approaches to ease this transition.

Moving from a DOS world to a UNIX operating system environment requires a basic knowledge of the differences that exist between the two systems. First, some of the command names are different yet perform similar actions. For example, in DOS you would use the type command to list a file on the screen. In UNIX system V the cat command performs a similar function. Another example is the DOS path separator. In DOS the path separator and root directory indicator is the backslash character \; in UNIX system V the slash / is used to separate path names in a command string. There are numerous subtle differences that can become irritating to the DOS user.

## CUSTOMIZING YOUR ENVIRONMENT

The good news is that the UNIX system is flexible enough to provide a way to customize your environment to suit your needs. By using the features of the built-in shell you can create small scripts that contain command strings. Once this collection of tools is created you can perform many powerful functions by issuing a single command.

In addition to the shell, UNIX operating system provides a special file for each user called **.profile** that auto-executes upon log-in. Within this file you can create customized prompts, execute applications, and control terminal attributes such as the backspace character.

This chapter will make extensive use of the UNIX programmable shell and the .profile file to aid you in customizing the environment to become more forgiving to a DOS user.

## WHAT IS THE SHELL?

The shell is a command interpreter that sits between the user and the operating system. When you log in to a UNIX computer, your commands are interpreted by the shell and translated into lower-level system code. The shell is programmable and allows you, the user, to create programs (called shell scripts in UNIX parlance) to carry out commands by executing this command file rather than typing in the commands repeatedly from the keyboard. With the shell we can create our own collection of personalized commands that mirror our existing knowledge of DOS commands. In essence, we can create alias commands. That is, we can create commands under the UNIX system that follow the syntax of DOS. For example, we can create our own personalized DIR command or our own TYPE command so that we can build safeguards against typing DOS commands when we are in the UNIX system.

## DOS COMMANDS

The following commands are the most commonly used and will become our starting point for writing shell scripts:

| DOS | Command | Function |
|-----|---------|----------|
| 1.  | DIR     | Used to list the names of all the files in a directory to the screen. |
| 2.  | ERASE   | Used to remove a file or files. |
| 3.  | FIND    | Used to search a file for a string. Find displays all lines that contain the search string. |
| 4.  | TYPE    | Used to list the contents of a file to the screen. |
| 5.  | COMP    | Used to compare the contents of two files and report the difference. |
| 6.  | REN     | Used to change the name of an existing file. |
| 7.  | PRINT   | Used to print the contents of a file to the attached printer; can also be used to check the status of the printer. |
| 8.  | COPY    | Used to create a copy of a file. |
| 9.  | TIME    | Displays date and time. |
| 10. | TREE    | Displays a pictorial view of the directory structure. |

## UNIX SYSTEM V SHELL COMMAND EQUIVALENTS

The following section illustrates the shell command scripts that come as close as possible to emulating the DOS equivalent.

Before we begin creating shell scripts, it's important to create a new directory to contain our new commands. To begin, log in to your home directory. In most cases this will be your /usr/your_id; create a new directory by typing:

```
$ mkdir bin
$ cd bin
$ pwd /usr/bill/bin
```

UNIX looks in a special place to search for commands. This place is called the PATH variable; it is normally set in .profile file in your log-in directory. A typical .profile contains the following information:

```
HOME=/usr/bill
PATH=:/bin:/usr/bin:
PS1="HI BILL"
stty -tabs echoe erase "^h"
TERM=5420
export TERM HOME PATH
date
```

The line we will modify is the second line:

```
PATH=:/bin:/usr/bin:
```

We can use the ed editor to add our new directory to the PATH search variable.

```
$ cd
$ ed .profile
2
PATH=:/bin:/usr/bin:
s/$/usr/bill/bin:

w
q
$
```

Now that we have our new directory included in the path string, we can begin to create our new commands. To begin, let's first change directory to /usr/your_id/bin.

```
$ cd /usr/your_id/bin
$ pwd
/usr/your_id/bin
$
```

The following section gives a step-by-step approach to create our ten new commands, then discusses how to use our newly created shell scripts.

1. dir—To create this shell script, type in the commands as follows:

```
$ cat > dir              # create the file
ls -p!pr -t -5 -w80      # ls command
<ctrl-d>                 # end input mode
$
```

To make our new dir command executable, type:

```
$ chmod +x dir    # make executable
```

**Use.**    This command string prints directory entries in a five-column format similar to the DOS DIR/W command. If you do not want the five-column output, leave out the 5 in the command string and it will default to single-column output.

**Example:**

```
$ cd /
$ dir
cd /
$ dir
OLDunix     core        icfs/         1p2        src/
bck/        demos       init/         mnt/       temp
bin/        dev/        install/      mon.out    temp00
boot/       emul.5410   junk.dbf      mplan      tmp/
cat/        etc/        lib/          save/      unix
choose      flop/       lookie        spl/       usr/
cmd         fls         lost+found/
$
$
```

2. erase—To create the shell script, type in:

```
$ cat > erase    # create the file
rm *             # remove the file(s)
<ctrl-d>         # end input mode
```

To make the file executable, type:

```
$ chmod +x erase
```

**Use.**    This command string will remove a file or files and will support the * wild-card function as it does under DOS. Note: Erase will remove multiple files by separating them with a space on the command line.

**Example:**

```
$ dir
cmds.inst      cx      list       nv     test99
column         dir     look.bk    rv     tree
cs             erase   new.echo   see
$
$ erase test99
$ dir
cmds.inst      cx      list       nv     see
column         dir     look.bk    rv     tree
cs             erase   new.echo
$
$
```

3. find—To create the shell script, type:

```
$ cat > find       # create the file
grep $1 $2         # search using grep
<ctrl-d>           # end input
```

To make the file executable, type:

```
$ chmod +x find
```

**Use.**   This command string searches the a file $2 for string $1 and displays all lines that contain the search string.

**Example:**

find 'AT&T' file 1.
Note: find is also a valid UNIX command. To execute the normal UNIX find you should type /bin/find. This command searches file 1 for the string AT&T and displays all lines that contain the string AT&T.

```
$
$ cat file1
AT&T offers computers that are both MS=DOS and UNIX-based.
These computers cover the range from single-user to multi-user systems.
In addition, AT&T is providing full support for the UNIX operating system.
UNIX appears to be popular in the office automation arena.
As AT&T continues to promote UNIX its future growth looks bright.
$
$
$
$ find "AT&T" file1
AT&T offers computers that are both MS-DOS and UNIX-based.
In addition, AT&T is providing full support for the UNIX operating system.
As AT&T continues to promote UNIX System V its future growth looks bright.
```

Note: The ' ' quotes were required because the ampersand character has special meaning to the shell.

    4. type—To create the shell script, type:

```
$ cat > type          # create file
cat $1|pg             # list contents of file
<ctrl-d>              # end input
```

To make the file executable, type:

```
$ chmod +x type
```

    **Use.** The type command will list the contents of a file to the screen. If the file is longer than 24 lines, it will stop the display and allow you to page through the file a page at a time. To continue the display press the space bar. To exit press the <del> key.

**Example:**

```
$ type /etc/passwd
root:5a12eYJpd7uDQ:0:1:0000-Admin(0000):/:
daemon:NONE:1:1:0000-Admin(0000):/:
bin:NONE:2:2:0000-Admin(0000):/bin:
sys:NONE:3:3:0000-Admin(0000):/usr/src:
adm:NONE:4:4:0000-Admin(0000):/usr/adm:
uucp:NONE:5:5:0000-uucp(0000):/usr/lib/uucp:
nuucp:10:10:0000-uucp(0000):/usr/spool/uucppublic:/usr/lib/uucp/uucico
rje:NONE:18:18:0000-rje(0000):/usr/rje:
sync:20:1:0000-Admin(0000):/:bin/sync
uname:20:1:0000-Admin(0000):/:/bin/uname
trouble:NONE:70:1:trouble(0000):/usr/lib/trouble:
```

    5. comp—To create our compare file command, type in:

```
$ cat > comp          # create the file
diff $1 $2
<ctrl-d>
```

To make the file executable, type:

```
$ chmod +x comp
```

    **Use.** The comp command can be used to compare the contents of two files. If the files are identical, the $ prompt will return. If the files differ, the first line of the file that shows a difference will be displayed.

**Example:**

```
$ cp file1 file2      copies file1 to file2
```

Both files are now identical. Let's run comp to check.

```
$ comp file1 file2
$
```

The UNIX system responds with a $, indicating that both files are identical, now let's modify file2.

```
$
$ cat >file2
this will make file2 different than file1
$
```

Let's check again by running comp.

```
$
$ comp file1 file2
1,5c1
< AT&T offers computers that are both MS-DOS and UNIX-based.
< These computers cover the range from single-user to multi-user
systems.
< In addition, AT&T is providing full support for the UNIX operating
system.
< UNIX appears to be popular in the office automation arena.
< As AT&T continues to promote UNIX its future growth looks bright.
---
$ > this will make file2 different than file1
```

The lines that are in file1 and not in file2 are indicated by the <. The lines in file2 that are not in file1 are indicated by the > character.

6. ren—To create our rename command, type:

```
$ cat > ren
mv $1 $2
<ctrl-d>
```

To make the file executable, type:

```
$ chmod +x ren
```

**Use.** The ren command will in effect rename a file to another name. The filename(s) can be a full path name and the wildcard * is supported.

**Example:**

```
$
$ dir
cmds.inst    cx      list        prompt    tree
column       dir     look.bk     ren       tree2
comp         erase   new.echo    rv        tree3
copy         file1   nv          see       type
cs           find    print
$
$
$
$
$
$ ren file1 file7
$
$
$ dir
cmds.inst    cx      list        prompt    tree
comp         erase   new.bk      rv        tree3
column       dir     look.bk     ren       tree2
copy         file7   nv          see       type
cs           find    print
```

Let's make sure the old file is gone:

```
$ type file1
cat: cannot open file1
$
$
$
$
```

Now let's look at the new file name:

```
$ type file7
AT&T offers computers that are both MS-DOS and UNIX-based.
These computers cover the range from single-user to multi-user
systems. In addition, AT&T is providing full support for the UNIX
operating system.
UNIX appears to be popular in the office automation arena.
As AT&T continues to promote UNIX its future growth looks bright.
```

7. print—To create the print command, type:

```
$ cat > print
case $# in
0> (lpstat -t;;
*> (lp $*;;
esac
```

To make the file executable, type:

```
$ chmod +x print
```

**Use.** The print command will print a file or files on the line printer. The printing takes place in the background so you can continue working. If no filename(s) is given, then just like the DOS command the status of the print queue will be displayed.

**Example:**

```
$ print file1
request id is pr1-S (1 file)    N / p = output of Lp Spooler
$ print
scheduler is running
system default destination: pr1
device for pr1: /dev/tty15
pr1 accepting requests since Apr 6 12:12
printer pr1 is idle. enabled since Apr 9 14:08
```

8. copy—To create the copy command, type the following:

```
$ cat > copy
cp $1 $2
<ctrl-d>
```

**Use.** The copy command will copy one or more files to the destination name. If the destination does not exist it is created. If the destination is a directory name, the file or files are copied into that directory with the same name.

**Example:**

```
$ copy work* /usr/bill/backup
$
```

9. time—To create the prompt command, type:

```
$ cat > time
date
<ctrl-d>
```

To make the file executable, type:

```
$ chmod +x time
```

**Use.**   The prompt command allows you to change the $ prompt to something else, like YOUR COMMAND. The prompt will appear after every line of input. The UNIX operating system does support another secondary prompt, called PS2, and that also could be included in a prompt2 command. See the UNIX users manual for a more detailed discussion of PS1 and PS2.

**Example:**

```
$ time
Tue Apr 9 14:26:30 Mst 1985
```

10. tree—The tree shell script is more complicated than the prior shell programs; care should be taken to enter the listing exactly as shown.

To create the tree program, type:

```
$ cat tree
BIN=/usr/mills/bin
if [ "0$1" != "0" ]
then
        cd $1
        dir=""$1''
else
        dir=`pwd`
fi
prefix="$2"
echo $dir
file .* * | (
        while read name type
        do
                name=`expr "$name" : "\(.*\):"`
                if [ "0$name" = "0." -o "0$name" = "0.." ]
                then
                        continue
                fi
                if [ "$type" = "directory" ]
                then
```

```
                                    echo "$prefix!"
                                    echo "$prefix+---\c"
                                    $BIN/tree $dir/$name "$prefix!"
                      else
                                    echo "$prefix! $name ($type)"
                      fi
            done
  )
  echo "$prefix----\n$prefix"
  $
```

Note: Replace the word mills with your log-in id.
To make tree executable, type:

$ chmod +x tree

**Use.**   The tree command can be used to display a pictorial view of directories. In addition, the tree command displays the type of file text, executable code, data, and so on. Tree will also tell you if a file is empty. The tree program is one of the authors' most-used commands and should be used by all system administrators for file maintenance.

Tree will accept a pathname such as /usr/mills and will list all the files from that point in the directory hierarchy down. If you type tree with no parameters (filenames), the tree will be displayed from the current directory down the tree.

**Example:**

```
  $
  $ tree /usr/mills
  /usr/mills
  !    .demo (ascii text)
  !    .news_time (empty)
  !    .profile (ascii text)
  !    a.out (3b2/3b5 executable not stripped)
  !
  +---/usr/mills/benchmarks
  !    !    chicago.c (c program text)
  !    !    sieve.c (c program text)
  !    !    sieve.0 (3b2/3b5 executable not stripped)
  !    !    sieve2.c (c program text)
  !    ----
  !
  !
  +---/usr/mills/bin
  !    !    cmds.inst (English text)
  !    !    column (commands text)
```

```
|    |    comp (commands text)
|    |    copy (commands text)
|    |    cs (commands text)
|    |    cx (commands text)
|    |    dir (commands text)
|    |    erase (commands text)
|    |    file1 (English text)
|    |    file7 (English text)
|    |    find (commands text)
|    |    list (commands text)
|    |    look.bk (commands text)
|    |    new.echo (commands text)
|    |    nv (commands text)
|    |    print (commands text)
|    |    print1 (commands text)
|    |    prompt (commands text)
|    |    ren (commands text)
|    |    rv (commands text)
|    |    see (commands text)
|    |    tree (commands text)
|    |    tree2 (commands text)
|    |    tree3 (commands text)
|    |    type (commands text)
|    ----
|
|    celsius (commands text)
|    contacts (ascii text)
|    dbase (3b2/3b5 executable not stripped)
|    dead.letter (ascii text)
|    degree (3b2/3b5 executable not stripped)
|    degrees.c (c program text)
|
+---/usr/mills/demos
|    |    gary.demo (commands text)
|    |
|    +---user/mills/demos/shell.demo
|    |    ' ,    count (commands text)
|    |    ' ,    counti (commands text)
|    |    ' ,    da (commands text)
|    |    ' ,    dai (commands text)
```

## SHELL SUMMARY

These ten shell scripts are intended to ease the transition to a UNIX system and help
prevent you from being frustrated by the differences in command syntax. We have
capitalized on the ability to customize UNIX to your individual requirements. If

your intention is to learn the UNIX command syntax, these shell scripts should serve as an example.

If you do implement these shell scripts in your system, you will be able to use a syntax similar to DOS while learning to use UNIX commands. We find ourselves working at home on DOS and at work on the UNIX system. These commands have proved invaluable, as they act as safeguards for our frequent mental lapses to DOS commands. Think of this set of commands as a DOS safety net.

Once these shell scripts are implemented you can still use the UNIX commands and are not impeded in any way by the presence of these shell scripts. Flexibility yet power: exactly what UNIX was designed to provide.

## MAKING DOS MORE UNIXLIKE

One of the most annoying features of DOS is that the backslash (\) is used as a delimiter to separate directory entries, while the UNIX system uses the slash (/) character. As you move from the DOS operating system to the UNIX operating system this can be very confusing, the source of undue anxiety. It is nearly impossible for the casual user to modify the UNIX system to use the backslash. However, it is fairly easy to modify DOS to support the /.

If you have a config.sys file in the root directory, add the following line using edlin:

```
switchar = -
```

If you do not have a config.sys file you can create one with edlin by:

```
C>edlin config.sys
New file
*i1
1:*switchar = -
2:* (press F6)
1:*switchar = - (press return)
*e
C>
```

Once this change is made you can use the / character to separate files in pathnames as in /word/doc1/intro. If you are accustomed to the \ you can also use that as in \word\doc1\intro. Both will work simultaneously.

## AT&T PC INTERFACE

Do you want to have the ability to share files with other PC users without swapping floppy disks? How about having the ability to share a hard disk, printers, and modem among multiple users? What about having the power of UNIX utilities

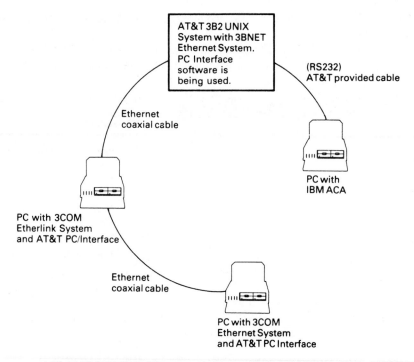

**Figure 8-1** Multiple PCs connected to an AT&T 3B2 UNIX system

available but yet take advantage of the multitude of DOS software that is available at the local computer store? AT&T's PC Interface is for you!

PC Interface allows multiple MS-DOS-based PCs to share the services of an attached 3B2 computer. The 3B2 becomes transparent to the PCs and becomes a logical drive to the PC users. PC Interface allows up 13 PCs to be connected to a single 3B2.

### Transparency

The PCs can upload and download files to the 3B2 by referencing the system as drive d:. To copy a file from floppy disk drive a: you would type:

```
A>diskcopy a: d:
```

After issuing this command, any files on the floppy disk would be transferred to the 3B2's hard disk. For example, you could copy a spreadsheet program to 3B2 and execute it by making drive d: the current drive and running the program.

```
A>d:
D>run spreadsheet
```

Transparency is the key to PC Interface. The users need not know that they are even connected to a UNIX computer, because the PC Interface software provides total transparency. You can still have a common printer connected to the 3B2 and still use the <shift>-<prtsc> function. The PC Interface converts the DOS commands into UNIX file commands and compatible file formats.

## Backup

Another use for PC Interface is to provide a common disk service from the 3B2 with all files resident on the 3B2's hard disk(s) and use the optional high-speed tape on the 3B2 XM for backup.

## Disk Server

By using the PC Interface you could eliminate the need to provide a hard disk at each PC or eliminate the need for a second floppy drive. The 3B2 can share its disks and hold programs as well as data files.

## Print Server

The 3B2 can also be set up to share printers with all the connected PCs. You can use both the DOS PRINT command and use <shift>-<prtsc> to print files using the 3B2's print spooler. No more do you need to provide a printer at each PC user's desk.

## The Bridge to the UNIX System

PC Interface allows the user to access the UNIX operating system in terminal emulation mode. The user can execute a function called CONTEXT SWITCH, which puts the current MS-DOS application on hold and allows the user to access UNIX. By depressing a couple of keys you are able to switch to and from both MS-DOS and UNIX operating systems. This suspend/resume capability allows full access to the UNIX system and the MS-DOS system. For example, you can put your database program on hold and access UNIX commands to check your mail (UNIX has built-in mail) and drop back into your database program exactly where you left off.

The PC Interface software runs in both the 3B2 and the PCs and will work with Ethernet, Omninet, or RS232. You can also connect a modem to the 3B2 and access the PC Interface remotely.

The PC Interface converts all DOS files to UNIX file format and takes care of such things as filename limitations and line ending sequences. The user could, for example, copy MS-DOS-based Multiplan files to the 3B2 and then use another application that is UNIX-based to access this data. You can also go the other way: take UNIX-based data files and use them in an MS-DOS application.

PC Interface provides an intermediate step in an evolution to the UNIX system. Users do not have to give up their wealth of DOS-based software for a ''bare'' UNIX system, but yet can take advantage of some of the features to which UNIX is so well suited, such as electronic mail and multi-user communication.

## XENIX 3.0 ON THE AT&T PC 6300

AT&T's MS-DOS computer—the PC 6300, based on the Intel 8086 chip—can run XENIX 3.0 and support up to two users. The XENIX operating system is based on an earlier version of the UNIX operating system called System III; it provides a subset of the features found in System V.

It is possible to have both XENIX 3.0 an MS-DOS coresident on the same hard disk, providing the ability to run either operating system. XENIX 3.0 does require a hard disk and 512K of memory on the PC 6300.

Coresident operating systems may prove to be a valuable alternative to a total system change to the UNIX system and could aid the user in the transition to a full-blown multi-user operating system. In addition, this environment provides a compromise by providing the opportunity to become familiar with the UNIX system without the loss of DOS.

Microsoft, the creator of XENIX 3.0, has indicated in public announcements that future releases of XENIX will be compatible with UNIX System V, in an endeavor to reduce end-user confusion.

ASCII chart

| | | | | | | | BITS | COLUMN | | | | | | | |
|---|---|---|---|---|---|---|---|---|---|---|---|---|---|---|---|

| B7 | | | | 0 | | 0 | | 0 | | 0 | | 1 | | 1 | | 1 | | 1 |
|---|---|---|---|---|---|---|---|---|---|---|---|---|---|---|---|---|

Bit header:
- B7: 0 0 0 0 1 1 1 1
- B6: 0 0 1 1 0 0 1 1
- B5: 0 1 0 1 0 1 0 1

| B4 B3 B2 B1 | ROW | 0 | | 1 | | 2 | | 3 | | 4 | | 5 | | 6 | | 7 | |
|---|---|---|---|---|---|---|---|---|---|---|---|---|---|---|---|---|---|
| 0 0 0 0 | 0 | NUL<br>CTRL @<br> | 0<br>0<br>0 | DLE<br>CTRL p<br> | 20<br>16<br>10 | SP<br>CTRL<br>(sp) | 40<br>32<br>20 | 0<br> | 60<br>48<br>30 | @<br> | 100<br>64<br>40 | P<br> | 120<br>80<br>50 | <br> | 140<br>96<br>60 | p<br> | 160<br>112<br>70 |
| 0 0 0 1 | 1 | SOH<br>CTRL a<br> | 1<br>1<br>1 | DC1<br>(XON)<br>CTRL q | 21<br>17<br>11 | !<br> | 41<br>33<br>21 | 1<br> | 61<br>49<br>31 | A<br> | 101<br>65<br>41 | Q<br> | 121<br>81<br>51 | a<br> | 141<br>97<br>61 | q<br> | 161<br>113<br>71 |
| 0 0 1 0 | 2 | STX<br>CTRL b<br> | 2<br>2<br>2 | DC2<br>CTRL r<br> | 22<br>18<br>12 | "<br> | 42<br>34<br>22 | 2<br> | 62<br>50<br>32 | B<br> | 102<br>66<br>42 | R<br> | 122<br>82<br>52 | b<br> | 142<br>98<br>62 | r<br> | 162<br>114<br>72 |
| 0 0 1 1 | 3 | ETX<br>CTRL c<br> | 3<br>3<br>3 | DC3<br>(XOFF)<br>CTRL s | 23<br>19<br>13 | #<br> | 43<br>35<br>23 | 3<br> | 63<br>51<br>33 | C<br> | 103<br>67<br>43 | S<br> | 123<br>83<br>53 | c<br> | 143<br>99<br>63 | s<br> | 163<br>115<br>73 |
| 0 1 0 0 | 4 | EOT<br>CTRL d<br> | 4<br>4<br>4 | DC4<br>CTRL t<br> | 24<br>20<br>14 | $<br> | 44<br>36<br>24 | 4<br> | 64<br>52<br>34 | D<br> | 104<br>68<br>44 | T<br> | 124<br>84<br>54 | d<br> | 144<br>100<br>64 | t<br> | 164<br>116<br>74 |
| 0 1 0 1 | 5 | ENQ<br>CTRL e<br> | 5<br>5<br>5 | NAK<br>CTRL u<br> | 25<br>21<br>15 | %<br> | 45<br>37<br>25 | 5<br> | 65<br>53<br>35 | E<br> | 105<br>69<br>45 | U<br> | 125<br>85<br>55 | e<br> | 145<br>101<br>65 | u<br> | 165<br>117<br>75 |
| 0 1 1 0 | 6 | ACK<br>CTRL f<br> | 6<br>6<br>6 | SYN<br>CTRL v<br> | 26<br>22<br>16 | &<br> | 46<br>38<br>26 | 6<br> | 66<br>54<br>36 | F<br> | 106<br>70<br>46 | V<br> | 126<br>86<br>56 | f<br> | 146<br>102<br>66 | v<br> | 166<br>118<br>76 |
| 0 1 1 1 | 7 | BEL<br>CTRL g<br> | 7<br>7<br>7 | ETB<br>CTRL w<br> | 27<br>23<br>17 | '<br> | 47<br>39<br>27 | 7<br> | 67<br>55<br>37 | G<br> | 107<br>71<br>47 | W<br> | 127<br>87<br>57 | g<br> | 147<br>103<br>67 | w<br> | 167<br>119<br>77 |
| 1 0 0 0 | 8 | BS<br>CTRL h<br> | 10<br>8<br>8 | CAN<br>CTRL x<br> | 30<br>24<br>18 | (<br> | 50<br>40<br>28 | 8<br> | 70<br>56<br>38 | H<br> | 110<br>72<br>48 | X<br> | 130<br>88<br>58 | h<br> | 150<br>104<br>68 | x<br> | 170<br>120<br>78 |
| 1 0 0 1 | 9 | HT<br>CTRL i<br> | 11<br>9<br>9 | EM<br>CTRL y<br> | 31<br>25<br>19 | )<br> | 51<br>41<br>29 | 9<br> | 71<br>57<br>39 | I<br> | 111<br>73<br>49 | Y<br> | 131<br>89<br>59 | i<br> | 151<br>105<br>69 | y<br> | 171<br>121<br>79 |
| 1 0 1 0 | 10 | LF<br>CTRL j<br> | 12<br>10<br>A | SUB<br>CTRL z<br> | 32<br>26<br>1A | *<br> | 52<br>42<br>2A | :<br> | 72<br>58<br>3A | J<br> | 112<br>74<br>4A | Z<br> | 132<br>90<br>5A | j<br> | 152<br>106<br>6A | z<br> | 172<br>122<br>7A |
| 1 0 1 1 | 11 | VT<br>CTRL k<br> | 13<br>11<br>B | ESC<br>CTRL [<br> | 33<br>27<br>1B | +<br> | 53<br>43<br>2B | ;<br> | 73<br>59<br>3B | K<br> | 113<br>75<br>4B | [<br> | 133<br>91<br>5B | k<br> | 153<br>107<br>6B | {<br> | 173<br>123<br>7B |
| 1 1 0 0 | 12 | FF<br>CTRL l<br> | 14<br>12<br>C | FS<br>CTRL \<br> | 34<br>28<br>1C | ,<br> | 54<br>44<br>2C | <<br> | 74<br>60<br>3C | L<br> | 114<br>76<br>4C | \<br> | 134<br>92<br>5C | l<br> | 154<br>108<br>6C | :<br> | 174<br>124<br>7C |
| 1 1 0 1 | 13 | CR<br>CTRL m<br> | 15<br>13<br>D | GS<br>CTRL ]<br> | 35<br>29<br>1D | -<br> | 55<br>45<br>2D | =<br> | 75<br>61<br>3D | M<br> | 115<br>77<br>4D | ]<br> | 135<br>93<br>5D | m<br> | 155<br>109<br>6D | }<br> | 175<br>125<br>7D |
| 1 1 1 0 | 14 | SO<br>CTRL n<br> | 16<br>14<br>E | RS<br>CTRL<br> | 36<br>30<br>1E | .<br> | 56<br>46<br>2E | ><br> | 76<br>62<br>3E | N<br> | 116<br>78<br>4E | ^<br> | 136<br>94<br>5E | n<br> | 156<br>110<br>6E | ~<br> | 176<br>126<br>7E |
| 1 1 1 1 | 15 | SI<br>CTRL o<br> | 17<br>15<br>F | US<br>CTRL -<br> | 37<br>31<br>1F | /<br> | 57<br>47<br>2F | ?<br> | 77<br>63<br>3F | O<br> | 117<br>79<br>4F | _<br> | 137<br>95<br>5F | o<br> | 157<br>111<br>6F | DEL<br>CTRL (bs) | 177<br>127<br>7F |

---

Legend

| | | |
|---|---|---|
| A | C | A = ASCII character |
| B | D | B = Keyboard generation of character |
| E | C | C = Octal representation |

D = Decimal representation
E = Hexadecimal representation

198

# B

## escape sequences for controlling popular terminals

When writing application programs for the PC6300 running a terminal emulation package, or UNIX systems, the programmer must know the specific terminal escape sequence for items such as homing the cursor, erasing the screen, and cursor positioning. The specific terminal user's manual should be consulted for such sequences but is not always available. The following charts may be used for this purpose, recognizing that most terminals offer more capabilities than listed.

Note: These sequences are also important to device dependent applications. For example, TERMCAP is a UNIX feature that capitalizes on terminal screen capabilities. Consequently, a PC emulating a given terminal can use device-dependent applications because UNIX will capitalize on features such as those in these charts.

| Feature | ADDS Regent 25 | ADDS Regent 30 | ADDS Viewpoint 60 |
|---------|------------|------------|--------------|
| READ CURSOR POSITION | ESC ? | ESC ENQ | ESC ENQ |
| CURSOR UP | CTRL Z | CTRL Z | CTRL Z |
| CURSOR DOWN | CTRL J | CTRL J | CTRL J |
| CURSOR RIGHT | CTRL F | CTRL F | CTRL F |
| CURSOR LEFT | CTRL U | CTRL U | CTRL U |
| HOME CURSOR | CTRL A | CTRL A | CTRL A |
| CLEAR TO END OF PAGE | ESC y | ESC k | ESC k |
| CLEAR TO END OF LINE | ESC t | ESC K | ESC K |
| LINE INSERT | ESC M | ESC M | ESC M |
| LINE DELETE | ESC 1 | ESC 1 | ESC 1 |
| CHARACTER INSERT | ESC F | ESC F | ESC F |
| CHARACTER DELETE | ESC E | ESC E | ESC E |
| POSITION CURSOR | ESC Y nn | ESC Y r c | ESC Y r c |
| CLEAR ALL | ESC * | CTRL L | CTRL F |
| UNDERSCORE | N/A | ESC n ' | ESC O ' |
| BLINK | N/A | ESC n B | ESC O B |
| REVERSE VIDEO | N/A | ESC n P | ESC O P |
| BLANK VIDEO | N/A | N/A | ESC O D |
| 132 COLUMN MODE | N/A | N/A | N/A |
| 80 COLUMN MODE | N/A | N/A | N/A |
| HORIZONTAL TAB SET | ESC 1 | N/A | N/A |
| LOCK KEYBOARD | ESC 5 | ESC 5 | ESC 5 |
| UNLOCK KEYBOARD | ESC 6 | ESC 6 | ESC 6 |
| NEXT PAGE | N/A | DC1 | N/A |
| PREVIOUS PAGE | N/A | SOH | N/A |
| PROTECT ON | ESC ) | ESC P | ESC O H |
| PROTECT OFF | ESC ( | ESC p | ESC O @ |
| RESET DEVICE | N/A | N/A | N/A |

Notes: (a) N/A indicates not available. (b) The letters nn, r, c, pn, and Pn should be substituted with an appropriate number to represent a row, column, or the number of times to perform a sequence. (c) These sequences are important to device dependent applications. For example, TERMCAP is a UNIX feature that capitalizes on terminal screen capabilities. Consequently a PC/XT emulating a given terminal can use device dependent applications because UNIX will capitalize on features such as those in these charts..

| Feature | AT&T4410 | AT&T4415 | DEC VT52 | DEC VT100 |
|---|---|---|---|---|
| READ CURSOR POSITION | ESC [6 n | ESC [6 n | N/A | ESC [6n |
| CURSOR UP | ESC [pn A | ESC [pn A | ESC A | ESC[Pn A |
| CURSOR DOWN | ESC [pn B | ESC [pn B | ESC B | ESC[Pn B |
| CURSOR RIGHT | ESC [pn C | ESC [pn C | ESC C | ESC[Pn C |
| CURSOR LEFT | ESC [pn D | ESC [pn D | ESC D | ESC[Pn D |
| HOME CURSOR | ESC [H | ESC [H | ESC H | ESC[H |
| CLEAR TO END OF PAGE | ESC J | ESC [OJ | ESC J | ESC[O J |
| CLEAR TO END OF LINE | ESC K | ESC [OK | ESC K | ESC[O K |
| LINE INSERT | ESC L | ESC [pn L | N/A | N/A |
| LINE DELETE | ESC M | ESC [pn M | N/A | N/A |
| CHARACTER INSERT | ESC [@ | ESC [pn @ | N/A | N/A |
| CHARACTER DELETE | ESC P | ESC [pn P | N/A | N/A |
| POSITION CURSOR | ESC[;n;pnH | ESC [y;x f | ESCY $r+31$ $c+31$ | ESC[Pn; Pn H |
| CLEAR ALL | ESC [2J | ESC [2J | N/A | ESC[2 J |
| UNDERSCORE | ESC [4m | ESC [?31;4 o | N/A | ESC[4m |
| BLINK | ESC [5m | ESC [?31;5 o | N/A | ESC[5m |
| REVERSE VIDEO | ESC [7m | ESC [?31;7 o | N/A | ESC[7m |
| BLANK VIDEO | N/A | ESC [?31;30o | N/A | N/A |
| 132 COLUMN MODE | ESC [?3h | ESC [?3; h | N/A | ESC[?3h |
| 80 COLUMN MODE | ESC [?3l | ESC [?3; 1 | N/A | ESC[?31 |
| HORIZONTAL TAB SET | N/A | ESC H | N/A | ESC H |
| LOCK KEYBOARD | N/A | ESC ` | N/A | N/A |
| UNLOCK KEYBOARD | N/A | ESC b | N/A | N/A |
| NEXT PAGE | N/A | ESC [pn U | N/A | N/A |
| PREVIOUS PAGE | N/A | ESC [pn V | N/A | N/A |
| PROTECT ON | N/A | ESC V | N/A | N/A |
| PROTECT OFF | N/A | ESC W | N/A | N/A |
| RESET DEVICE | N/A | ESC c | N/A | ESC c |

Notes: (a) N/A indicates not available. (b) The letters nn, r, c, pn, and Pn should be substituted with an appropriate number to represent a row, column, or the number of times to perform a sequence.

| Feature | Hazeltine 1420 |
| --- | --- |
| READ CURSOR POSITION | ESC CTRL E |
| CURSOR UP | ESC CTRL L |
| CURSOR DOWN | ESC CTRL K |
| CURSOR RIGHT | CTRL P |
| CURSOR LEFT | CTRL H |
| HOME CURSOR | ESC CTRL R |
| CLEAR TO END OF PAGE | ESC y |
| CLEAR TO END OF LINE | ESC t |
| LINE INSERT | ESC CTRL Z |
| LINE DELETE | ESC CTRL S |
| CHARACTER INSERT | ESC Q |
| CHARACTER DELETE | ESC W |
| POSITION CURSOR | N/A |
| CLEAR ALL | ESC CTRL L |
| UNDERSCORE | N/A |
| BLINK | N/A |
| REVERSE VIDEO | N/A |
| BLANK VIDEO | N/A |
| 132 COLUMN MODE | N/A |
| 80 COLUMN MODE | N/A |
| HORIZONTAL TAB SET | ESC 1 |
| LOCK KEYBOARD | ESC CTRL U |
| UNLOCK KEYBOARD | ESC CTRL F |
| NEXT PAGE | N/A |
| PREVIOUS PAGE | N/A |
| PROTECT ON | ESC CTRL Y |
| PROTECT OFF | ESC CTRL _ |
| RESET DEVICE | N/A |

Notes: (a) N/A indicates not available. (b) The letters nn, r, c, pn, and Pn should be substituted with an appropriate number to represent a row, column, or the number of times to perform a sequence.

| Feature | HP 2624 | HP 2648 | IBM 3101 |
|---------|---------|---------|----------|
| READ CURSOR POSITION | ESC ` DC1 | ESC ` DC1 | ESC 5 |
| CURSOR UP | ESC A | ESC A | ESC A |
| CURSOR DOWN | ESC B | ESC B | ESC B |
| CURSOR RIGHT | ESC C | ESC C | ESC C |
| CURSOR LEFT | ESC D | ESC D | ESC D |
| HOME CURSOR | ESC H | ESC H | ESC H |
| CLEAR TO END OF PAGE | ESC J | ESC J | ESC J |
| CLEAR TO END OF LINE | ESC K | ESC K | ESC I |
| LINE INSERT | ESC L | ESC L | ESC N |
| LINE DELETE | ESC M | ESC M | ESC O |
| CHARACTER INSERT | ESC Q | ESC Q | ESC P |
| CHARACTER DELETE | ESC P | ESC P | ESC Q |
| POSITION CURSOR | ESC&a #r#c | ESC&a #r#c | ESC Y xy |
| CLEAR ALL | ESC g | ESC g | ESC ; |
| UNDERSCORE | ESC &d D | ESC &d D | N/A |
| BLINK | ESC &d A | ESC &d A | ESC 3 I |
| REVERSE VIDEO | ESC &d B | ESC &d B | ESC 3 E |
| BLINK VIDEO | ESC &d S | ESC &d S | ESC 3 M |
| 132 COLUMN MODE | N/A | N/A | N/A |
| 80 COLUMN MODE | N/A | N/A | N/A |
| HORIZONTAL TAB SET | N/A | N/A | ESC 0 |
| LOCK KEYBOARD | N/A | N/A | ESC : |
| UNLOCK KEYBOARD | N/A | N/A | ESC ; |
| NEXT PAGE | ESC V | ESC V | N/A |
| PREVIOUS PAGE | ESC U | ESC U | N/A |
| PROTECT ON | ESC ] | ESC &dJ | ESC 3C |
| PROTECT OFF | ESC [ | ESC &d@ | ESC 3B |
| RESET DEVICE | ESC E | ESC E | N/A |

Notes: (a) N/A indicates not available. (b) The letters nn, r, c, pn, and Pn should be substituted with an appropriate number to represent a row, column, or the number of times to perform a sequence.

| Feature | Lear-Siegler ADM3/5 | Teletype 5410 | Teletype 5420 |
|---|---|---|---|
| READ CURSOR POSITION | ESC ? | N/A | ESC [6 n |
| CURSOR UP | CTRL K | ESC [A | ESC [pn A |
| CURSOR DOWN | CTRL J | ESC [B | ESC [pn B |
| CURSOR RIGHT | CTRL L | ESC [C | ESC [pn C |
| CURSOR LEFT | CTRL H | ESC [D | ESC [pn D |
| HOME CURSOR | CTRL | ESC [H | ESC [H |
| CLEAR TO END OF PAGE | ESC y | ESC [J | ESC [OJ |
| CLEAR TO END OF LINE | ESC t | ESC [K | ESC [OK |
| LINE INSERT | ESC E | ESC [L | ESC [pn L |
| LINE DELETE | ESC R | ESC [M | ESC [pn M |
| CHARACTER INSERT | ESC Q | ESC [@ | ESC [pn @ |
| CHARACTER DELETE | ESC M | ESC [P | ESC [pn P |
| POSITION CURSOR | ESC = r c | ESC[pn;pnH | ESC[y;x f |
| CLEAR ALL | ESC * | ESC [2J | ESC [2J |
| UNDERSCORE | N/A | ESC [4m | ESC[?31;4 o |
| BLINK | N/A | ESC [5m | ESC[?31;5 o |
| REVERSE VIDEO | N/A | ESC [7m | ESC[?31;7 o |
| BLANK VIDEO | N/A | ESC [8m | ESC[?31;30o |
| 132 COLUMN MODE | N/A | ESC [?3h | ESC[?3; h |
| 80 COLUMN MODE | N/A | ESC [?31 | ESC[?3; l |
| HORIZONTAL TAB SET | ESC 1 | N/A | ESC H |
| LOCK KEYBOARD | ESC # | N/A | ESC ' |
| UNLOCK KEYBOARD | ESC " | N/A | ESC b |
| NEXT PAGE | N/A | N/A | ESC [pn U |
| PREVIOUS PAGE | N/A | N/A | ESC [pn V |
| PROTECT ON | ESC ) | N/A | ESC V |
| PROTECT OFF | ESC ( | N/A | ESC W |
| RESET DEVICE | N/A | N/A | ESC c |

Notes: (a) N/A indicates not available. (b) The letters nn, r, c, pn, and Pn should be substituted with an appropriate number to represent a row, column, or the number of times to perform a sequence.

| Feature | Televideo 910 | Televideo 925 |
|---|---|---|
| READ CURSOR POSITION | ESC ? | ESC ? |
| CURSOR UP | CTRL K | CTRL K |
| CURSOR DOWN | CTRL V | CTRL V |
| CURSOR RIGHT | CTRL L | CTRL L |
| CURSOR LEFT | CTRL H | CTRL H |
| HOME CURSOR | CTRL ^ | CTRL ^ |
| CLEAR TO END OF PAGE | ESC y | ESC y |
| CLEAR TO END OF LINE | ESC T | ESC T |
| LINE INSERT | ESC E | ESC E |
| LINE DELETE | ESC R | ESC R |
| CHARACTER INSERT | ESC Q | ESC Q |
| CHARACTER DELETE | ESC W | ESC W |
| POSITION CURSOR | ESC = r c | ESC = r c |
| CLEAR ALL | ESC * | ESC * |
| UNDERSCORE | ESC G8 | ESC G8 |
| BLINK | ESC G2 | ESC G2 |
| REVERSE VIDEO | ESC G4 | ESC G4 |
| BLANK VIDEO | ESC G1 | ESC G1 |
| 132 COLUMN MODE | N/A | N/A |
| 80 COLUMN MODE | N/A | N/A |
| HORIZONTAL TAB SET | ESC 1 | ESC 1 |
| LOCK KEYBOARD | ESC # | ESC # |
| UNLOCK KEYBOARD | ESC " | ESC " |
| NEXT PAGE | N/A | ESC K |
| PREVIOUS PAGE | N/A | ESC J |
| PROTECT ON | ESC& ESC) | ESC& ESC) |
| PROTECT OFF | ESC' ESC( | ESC' ESC( |
| RESET DEVICE | N/A | N/A |

Notes: (a) N/A indicates not available. (b) The letters nn, r, c, pn, and Pn should be substituted with an appropriate number to represent a row, column, or the number of times to perform a sequence.

# C

## escape sequences for controlling popular printers

Often, the user of a PC/XT with a printer must set up the hard-copy device for print control. For example, when using a spreadsheet or word processor, a control sequence must be entered to compress the print to 17 characters per inch. The printer user's manual should be consulted for this but is not always available. The following charts serve as a quick reference for such printer control sequences, recognizing that most printers offer more capabilities than listed.

| Feature | Anadex<br>DP-6500 | Anadex<br>DP-9000/9500B | Anadex<br>DP-9001/9501B |
|---|---|---|---|
| 10 CHARACTERS/INCH | ESC Q | ESC Q | ESC Q |
| 12 CHARACTERS/INCH | ESC T | ESC R | ESC T |
| 17 CHARACTERS/INCH | ESC R | N/A | ESC R |
| ITALICS ON | ESC t | N/A | N/A |
| ITALICS OFF | ESC u | N/A | N/A |
| 6 LINES/INCH | ESC H | ESC H | ESC H |
| 8 LINES/INCH | ESC I | ESC I | ESC I |
| 10 LINES/INCH | N/A | N/A | N/A |
| 12 LINES/INCH | N/A | N/A | N/A |
| LETTER QUALITY | ESC r | N/A | N/A |
| DP QUALITY | N/A | N/A | N/A |
| DRAFT QUALITY | N/A | N/A | N/A |
| EXPANDED PRINT ON | ESC 5 | SO | SO |
| EXPANDED PRINT OFF | ESC 6 | SI | SI |
| SUBSCRIPT ON | ESC ⟨ | N/A | N/A |
| SUBSCRIPT OFF | ESC : | N/A | N/A |
| SUPERSCRIPT ON | ESC ⟩ | N/A | N/A |
| SUPERSCRIPT OFF | ESC : | N/A | N/A |
| UNDERLINE ON | ESC 8 | RS | RS |
| UNDERLINE OFF | ESC 9 | US | US |
| EXPANDED PRINT-ONE LINE ONLY | N/A | N/A | N/A |
| EMPHASIZED ON | ESC p | N/A | N/A |
| EMPHASIZED OFF | ESC q | N/A | N/A |
| DOUBLESTRIKE ON | ESC x | N/A | N/A |
| DOUBLESTRIKE OFF | ESC Q | N/A | N/A |
| RESET | N/A | N/A | N/A |

Notes: (a) N/A indicates not available. In some cases special fonts or upgrades can be used for these capabilities. (b) From a BASIC program, the CHAR$ function should be used to generate these escape sequences [e.g., CHAR$(14) should be used for the SO sequence]. (c) LETTER QUALITY on dot matrix printers refers to near-letter quality or correspondence-quality print. (d) Consult the ASCII chart in Appendix A for decimal equivalents to these sequences.

| Feature | Anadex DP-9625B | Anadex WP-6000 | Apple Dot Matrix |
|---|---|---|---|
| 10 CHARACTERS/INCH | ESC Q | ESC J0 | ESC N |
| 12 CHARACTERS/INCH | ESC T | ESC J2 | ESC E |
| 17 CHARACTERS/INCH | ESC R | ESC J7 | ESC Q |
| ITALICS ON | N/A | ESC X | N/A |
| ITALICS OFF | N/A | ESC Y | N/A |
| 6 LINES/INCH | ESC H | ESC E | ESC A |
| 8 LINES/INCH | ESC I | ESC F | ESC B |
| 10 LINES/INCH | N/A | N/A | N/A |
| 12 LINES/INCH | N/A | ESC ! | ESC T12 |
| LETTER QUALITY | ESC r | ESC I5 | N/A |
| DP QUALITY | N/A | ESC I6 | N/A |
| DRAFT QUALITY | N/A | N/A | N/A |
| EXPANDED PRINT ON | ESC 5 | ESC N | SO |
| EXPANDED PRINT OFF | ESC 6 | ESC O | SI |
| SUBSCRIPT ON | ESC ⟨ | ESC I4 | N/A |
| SUBSCRIPT OFF | ESC : | ? | N/A |
| SUPERSCRIPT ON | ESC ⟩ | ESC I3 | N/A |
| SUPERSCRIPT OFF | ESC : | ? | N/A |
| UNDERLINE ON | ESC 8 | ESC : | ESC X |
| UNDERLINE OFF | ESC 9 | ESC ; | ESC Y |
| EXPANDED PRINT-ONE LINE ONLY | N/A | N/A | N/A |
| EMPHASIZED ON | ESC p | N/A | ESC ! |
| EMPHASIZED OFF | ESC q | N/A | ESC " |
| DOUBLESTRIKE ON | ESC x | N/A | N/A |
| DOUBLESTRIKE OFF | ESC Q | N/A | N/A |
| RESET | N/A | N/A | N/A |

Notes: (a) N/A indicates not available. In some cases special fonts or upgrades can be used for these capabilities. (b) From a BASIC program, the CHAR$ function should be used to generate these escape sequences [e.g., CHAR$(14) should be used for the SO sequence]. (c) LETTER QUALITY on dot matrix printers refers to near-letter quality or correspondence-quality print. (d) Consult the ASCII chart in Appendix A for decimal equivalents to these sequences.

| Feature | Axiom IMP | Centronics 351 | C. Itoh Prowriter |
|---|---|---|---|
| 10 CHARACTERS/INCH | ESC 6 | ESC[1w | ESC N |
| 12 CHARACTERS/INCH | ESC ⟨ | ESC[2w | ESC E |
| 17 CHARACTERS/INCH | ESC 7 | ESC[4w | ESC Q |
| ITALICS ON | N/A | N/A | N/A |
| ITALICS OFF | N/A | N/A | N/A |
| 6 LINES/INCH | ESC 4 | ESC[1z | ESC A |
| 8 LINES/INCH | N/A | ESC[2z | ESC B |
| 10 LINES/INCH | N/A | N/A | ESC T nn |
| 12 LINES/INCH | ESC 5 | N/A | ESC T nn |
| LETTER QUALITY | N/A | N/A | N/A |
| DP QUALITY | N/A | N/A | N/A |
| DRAFT QUALITY | N/A | N/A | N/A |
| EXPANDED PRINT ON | ESC SO | ESC[5w | SO |
| EXPANDED PRINT OFF | ESC SI | ESC[1w | SI |
| SUBSCRIPT ON | N/A | ESC K | N/A |
| SUBSCRIPT OFF | N/A | ESC L | N/A |
| SUPERSCRIPT ON | N/A | ESC L | N/A |
| SUPERSCRIPT OFF | N/A | ESC K | N/A |
| UNDERLINE ON | N/A | ESC[4m | ESC X |
| UNDERLINE OFF | N/A | ESC[0m | ESC Y |
| EXPANDED PRINT-ONE LINE ONLY | N/A | N/A | N/A |
| EMPHASIZED ON | N/A | N/A | ESC ! |
| EMPHASIZED OFF | N/A | N/A | ESC " |
| DOUBLESTRIKE ON | N/A | N/A | N/A |
| DOUBLESTRIKE OFF | N/A | N/A | N/A |
| RESET | N/A | N/A | N/A |

Notes: (a) N/A indicates not available. In some cases special fonts or upgrades can be used for these capabilities. (b) From a BASIC program, the CHAR$ function should be used to generate these escape sequences [e.g., CHAR$(14) should be used for the SO sequence]. (c) LETTER QUALITY on dot matrix printers refers to near-letter quality or correspondence-quality print. (d) Consult the ASCII chart in Appendix A for decimal equivalents to these sequences.

| Feature | DATASOUTH 180 | DATASOUTH 220 | DEC LA 100 |
|---|---|---|---|
| 10 CHARACTERS/INCH | ESC [1w | ESC $10M | ESC [0w |
| 12 CHARACTERS/INCH | ESC [2w | ESC $12M | ESC [2w |
| 17 CHARACTERS/ INCH | ESC [4w | ESC $16M | ESC [4w |
| ITALICS ON | N/A | N/A | N/A |
| ITALICS OFF | N/A | N/A | N/A |
| 6 LINES/INCH | ESC [1z | ESC [1z | ESC [0z |
| 8 LINES/INCH | ESC [2z | ESC [2z | ESC [2z |
| 10 LINES/INCH | N/A | N/A | N/A |
| 12 LINES/INCH | N/A | N/A | ESC [3z |
| LETTER QUALITY | N/A | ESC $1M | ESC [3"z |
| DP QUALITY | N/A | ESC $10M | ESC [1"z |
| DRAFT QUALITY | N/A | ESC $13M | ESC [2"z |
| EXPANDED PRINT ON | ESC $5 | ESC $5 | ESC [5w |
| EXPANDED PRINT OFF | ESC $6 | ESC $6 | ESC [0w |
| SUBSCRIPT ON | N/A | N/A | N/A |
| SUBSCRIPT OFF | N/A | N/A | N/A |
| SUPERSCRIPT ON | N/A | N/A | N/A |
| SUPERSCRIPT OFF | N/A | N/A | N/A |
| UNDERLINE ON | N/A | N/A | ESC [4m |
| UNDERLINE OFF | N/A | N/A | ESC [0m |
| EXPANDED PRINT-ONE LINE ONLY | N/A | ESC $5 | N/A |
| EMPHASIZED ON | N/A | N/A | N/A |
| EMPHASIZED OFF | N/A | N/A | N/A |
| DOUBLESTRIKE ON | N/A | N/A | N/A |
| DOUBLESTRIKE OFF | N/A | N/A | N/A |
| RESET | N/A | N/A | N/A |

Notes: (a) N/A indicates not available. In some cases special fonts or upgrades can be used for these capabilities. (b) From a BASIC program, the CHAR$ function should be used to generate these escape sequences [e.g., CHAR$(14) should be used for the SO sequence]. (c) LETTER QUALITY on dot matrix printers refers to near-letter quality or correspondence-quality print. (d) Consult the ASCII chart in Appendix A for decimal equivalents to these sequences.

| Feature | Epson FX-80 | Epson Graphtrax 80 | Epson MX-80 |
|---|---|---|---|
| 10 CHARACTERS/INCH | DC2 | ESC Q | DC2 |
| 12 CHARACTERS/INCH | ESC M | N/A | N/A |
| 17 CHARACTERS/INCH | SI | ESC P | SI |
| ITALICS ON | ESC 4 | ESC 4 | N/A |
| ITALICS OFF | ESC 5 | ESC 5 | N/A |
| 6 LINES/INCH | ESC 2 | ESC 2 | ESC 2 |
| 8 LINES/INCH | ESC 0 | ESC 0 | ESC 0 |
| 10 LINES/INCH | ESC 1 | ESC 1 | ESC 1 |
| 12 LINES/INCH | N/A | N/A | N/A |
| LETTER QUALITY | N/A | N/A | N/A |
| DP QUALITY | N/A | N/A | N/A |
| DRAFT QUALITY | N/A | N/A | N/A |
| EXPANDED PRINT ON | ESC W | ESC S | SO |
| EXPANDED PRINT OFF | DC4 | ESC T | DC4 |
| SUBSCRIPT ON | ESC S1 | N/A | N/A |
| SUBSCRIPT OFF | ESC T | N/A | N/A |
| SUPERSCRIPT ON | ESC SO | N/A | N/A |
| SUPERSCRIPT OFF | ESC T | N/A | N/A |
| UNDERLINE ON | ESC-1 | N/A | N/A |
| UNDERLINE OFF | ESC-0 | N/A | N/A |
| EXPANDED PRINT-ONE LINE ONLY | SO | CHR$(14) | SO |
| EMPHASIZED ON | ESC E | ESC E | ESC E |
| EMPHASIZED OFF | ESC F | ESC F | ESC F |
| DOUBLESTRIKE ON | ESC G | ESC G | ESC G |
| DOUBLESTRIKE OFF | ESC H | ESC H | ESC H |
| RESET | ESC @ | ESC @ | N/A |

Notes: (a) N/A indicates not available. In some cases special fonts or upgrades can be used for these capabilities. (b) From a BASIC program, the CHAR$ function should be used to generate these escape sequences [e.g., CHAR$(14) should be used for the SO sequence]. (c) LETTER QUALITY on dot matrix printers refers to near-letter quality or correspondence-quality print. (d) Consult the ASCII chart in Appendix A for decimal equivalents to these sequences.

| Feature | Florida Data OSP-130 | GE 2030 | GE 2120 |
|---|---|---|---|
| 10 CHARACTERS/INCH | ESC US 13 | ESC N | ESC N |
| 12 CHARACTERS/INCH | ESC US 11 | ESC M | ESC M |
| 17 CHARACTERS/INCH | ESC US 8 | ESC C | ESC C |
| ITALICS ON | N/A | N/A | N/A |
| ITALICS OFF | N/A | N/A | N/A |
| 6 LINES/INCH | ESC RS 9 | ESC 6 | ESC 6 |
| 8 LINES/INCH | ESC RS 7 | ESC 8 | ESC 8 |
| 10 LINES/INCH | ESC RS 6 | N/A | N/A |
| 12 LINES/INCH | ESC RS 5 | ESC G | ESC G |
| LETTER QUALITY | ESC W | N/A | N/A |
| DP QUALITY | N/A | N/A | N/A |
| DRAFT QUALTITY | ESC & | N/A | N/A |
| EXPANDED PRINT ON | SO | N/A | N/A |
| EXPANDED PRINT OFF | SI | N/A | N/A |
| SUBSCRIPT ON | ESC D | N/A | N/A |
| SUBSCRIPT OFF | ESC U | N/A | N/A |
| SUPERSCRIPT ON | ESC U | N/A | N/A |
| SUPERSCRIPT OFF | ESC D | N/A | N/A |
| UNDERLINE ON | ESC E | N/A | N/A |
| UNDERLINE OFF | ESC R | N/A | N/A |
| EXPANDED PRINT-ONE LINE ONLY | SO | N/A | N/A |
| EMPHASIZED ON | ESC O | N/A | N/A |
| EMPHASIZED OFF | ESC & | N/A | N/A |
| DOUBLESTRIKE ON | ESC #2 | N/A | N/A |
| DOUBLESTRIKE OFF | ESC #1 | N/A | N/A |
| RESET | ESC ⟨cr⟩ P | N/A | N/A |

Notes: (a) N/A indicates not available. In some cases special fonts or upgrades can be used for these capabilities. (b) From a BASIC program, the CHAR$ function should be used to generate these escape sequences [e.g., CHAR$(14) should be used for the SO sequence]. (c) LETTER QUALITY on dot matrix printers refers to near-letter quality or correspondence-quality print. (d) Consult the ASCII chart in Appendix A for decimal equivalents to these sequences.

| Feature | IBM 80 CPS Graphics | IBM 80 CPS Matrix | IDS P80 & P132 |
|---|---|---|---|
| 10 CHARACTERS/INCH | DC2 | DC2 | CTRL ] |
| 12 CHARACTERS/INCH | N/A | N/A | CTRL |
| 17 CHARACTERS/INCH | SI | SI | CTRL — |
| ITALICS ON | N/A | N/A | N/A |
| ITALICS OFF | N/A | N/A | N/A |
| 6 LINES/INCH | ESC 2 | ESC 2 | ESC B,8,$ |
| 8 LINES/INCH | ESC 8 | ESC 0 | ESC B,6,$ |
| 10 LINES/INCH | ESC 1 | ESC 1 | N/A |
| 12 LINES/INCH | N/A | N/A | ESC B,4,$ |
| LETTER QUALITY | N/A | N/A | ESC R,1,$ |
| DP QUALITY | N/A | N/A | N/A |
| DRAFT QUALITY | N/A | N/A | ESC R,2,$ |
| EXPANDED PRINT ON | ESC 1 | SO | CTRL A |
| EXPANDED PRINT OFF | ESC 0 | DC4 | CTRL B |
| SUBSCRIPT ON | ESC 1 | N/A | CTRL T |
| SUBSCRIPT OFF | ESC T | N/A | CTRL Y |
| SUPERSCRIPT ON | ESC O | N/A | CTRL Y |
| SUPERSCRIPT OFF | ESC T | N/A | CTRL T |
| UNDERLINE ON | ESC-1 | ESC-1 | N/A |
| UNDERLINE OFF | ESC-0 | ESC-0 | N/A |
| EXPANDED PRINT-ONE LINE ONLY | SO | SO | N/A |
| EMPHASIZED ON | ESC E | ESC E | N/A |
| EMPHASIZED OFF | ESC F | ESC F | N/A |
| DOUBLESTRIKE ON | ESC G | ESC G | N/A |
| DOUBLESTRIKE OFF | ESC H | ESC H | N/A |
| RESET | N/A | N/A | N/A |

Notes: (a) N/A indicates not available. In some cases special fonts or upgrades can be used for these capabilities. (b) From a BASIC program, the CHAR$ function should be used to generate these escape sequences [e.g., CHAR$(14) should be used for the SO sequence]. (c) LETTER QUALITY on dot matrix printers refers to near-letter quality or correspondence-quality print. (d) Consult the ASCII chart in Appendix A for decimal equivalents to these sequences.

| Feature | Infoscribe 1100 | Infoscribe 500 | Malibu 200 |
|---|---|---|---|
| 10 CHARACTERS/INCH | ESC 6 | ESC 6 | ESC E12 |
| 12 CHARACTERS/INCH | ESC 8 | ESC 8 | ESC E10 |
| 17 CHARACTERS/INCH | ESC 7 | ESC 7 | ESC E07 |
| ITALICS ON | ESC A | N/A | N/A |
| ITALICS OFF | ESC @ | N/A | N/A |
| 6 LINES/INCH | ESC 4 | ESC 4 | ESC LO8 |
| 8 LINES/INCH | ESC 5 | ESC 5 | ESC LO6 |
| 10 LINES/INCH | N/A | N/A | N/A |
| 12 LINES/INCH | N/A | N/A | ESC LO4 |
| LETTER QUALITY | ESC 9 | ESC 9 | ESC @SL |
| DP QUALITY | ESC 6 | N/A | N/A |
| DRAFT QUALITY | ESC : | N/A | ESC @SD |
| EXPANDED PRINT ON | CTRL N | SO | ESC @W1 |
| EXPANDED PRINT OFF | CTRL O | SI | ESC @W0 |
| SUBSCRIPT ON | ESC C | ESC C | ESC U |
| SUBSCRIPT OFF | C-RETURN | ESC R | ESC D |
| SUPERSCRIPT ON | ESC B | ESC B | ESC D |
| SUPERSCRIPT OFF | C-RETURN | ESC R | ESC U |
| UNDERLINE ON | N/A | N/A | N/A |
| UNDERLINE OFF | N/A | N/A | N/A |
| EXPANDED PRINT-ONE LINE ONLY | N/A | N/A | N/A |
| EMPHASIZED ON | N/A | N/A | N/A |
| EMPHASIZED OFF | N/A 9 | N/A | N/A |
| DOUBLESTRIKE ON | ESC 9 | N/A | N/A |
| DOUBLESTRIKE OFF | ESC 6 | N/A | N/A |
| RESET | ESC R | ESC @ | ESC SUB I |

Notes: (a) N/A indicates not available. In some cases special fonts or upgrades can be used for these capabilities. (b) From a BASIC program, the CHAR$ function should be used to generate these escape sequences [e.g., CHAR$(14) should be used for the SO sequence]. (c) LETTER QUALITY on dot matrix printers refers to near-letter quality or correspondence-quality print. (d) Consult the ASCII chart in Appendix A for decimal equivalents to these sequences. C-Return is shorthand for carriage return or end of line character.

| Feature | Mannesmann Spirit80 | MT-160 | NEC PC-8023A |
|---|---|---|---|
| 10 CHARACTERS/INCH | DC2 | ESC [4w | ESC N |
| 12 CHARACTERS/INCH | N/A | ESC [5w | ESC E |
| 17 CHARACTERS/INCH | SI | ESC [6w | ESC Q |
| ITALICS ON | ESC 4 | N/A | N/A |
| ITALICS OFF | ESC 5 | N/A | N/A |
| 6 LINES/INCH | ESC 2 | ESC [3z | ESC A |
| 8 LINES/INCH | ESC 0 | ESC [4z | ESC B |
| 10 LINES/INCH | ESC 1 | N/A | ESCT(1)(5) |
| 12 LINES/INCH | ESC 3 18 | N/A | ESCT(1)(2) |
| LETTER QUALITY | N/A | ESC [1y | N/A |
| DP QUALITY | N/A | N/A | N/A |
| DRAFT QUALITY | N/A | ESC [0y | N/A |
| EXPANDED PRINT ON | ESC W 1 | ESC W1 | DC2 |
| EXPANDED PRINT OFF | ESC W0 | ESC W0 | DC4 |
| SUBSCRIPT ON | ESC S 1 | ESC [1z | N/A |
| SUBSCRIPT OFF | ESC T | ESC [2z | N/A |
| SUPERSCRIPT ON | ESC S 0 | ESC [0z | N/A |
| SUPERSCRIPT OFF | ESC T | ESC [2z | N/A |
| UNDERLINE ON | ESC −1 | ESC [4m | ESC X |
| UNDERLINE OFF | ESC −0 | ESC [0m | ESX Y |
| EXPANDED PRINT-ONE LINE ONLY | SO | SO | N/A |
| EMPHASIZED ON | ESC E | ESC [ =z | ESC ! |
| EMPHASIZED OFF | ESC F | ESC [)z | ESC " |
| DOUBLESTRIKE ON | ESC G | N/A | N/A |
| DOUBLESTRIKE OFF | ESC H | N/A | N/A |
| RESET | ESC @ | ESC [6~ | N/A |

Notes: (a) N/A indicates not available. In some cases special fonts or upgrades can be used for these capabilities. (b) From a BASIC program, the CHAR$ function should be used to generate these escape sequences [e.g., CHAR$(14) should be used for the SO sequence]. (c) LETTER QUALITY on dot matrix printers refers to near-letter quality or correspondence-quality print. (d) Consult the ASCII chart in Appendix A for decimal equivalents to these sequences.

| Feature | Okidata 2410 | Okidata 83A | Panasonic KX-P1090 |
|---|---|---|---|
| 10 CHARACTERS/INCH | ESC 6 | RS | ESC + P + (01) |
| 12 CHARACTERS/INCH | ESC A | N/A | ESC + P + (00) |
| 17 CHARACTERS/INCH | ESC B | GS | N/A |
| ITALICS ON | N/A | N/A | ESC + 4 |
| ITALICS OFF | N/A | N/A | ESC + 5 |
| 6 LINES/INCH | ESC 4 | ESC 6 | ESC + 2 |
| 8 LINES/INCH | ESC 5 | ESC 8 | ESC + 0 |
| 10 LINES/INCH | N/A | N/A | ESC + 1 |
| 12 LINES/INCH | N/A | N/A | ESC + A + 6 |
| LETTER QUALITY | ESC 7 | N/A | N/A |
| DP QUALITY | ESC 8 | N/A | N/A |
| DRAFT QUALITY | ESC 9 | N/A | N/A |
| EXPANDED PRINT ON | ESC C | US | ESC + W + (01) |
| EXPANDED PRINT OFF | ESC Z | RS | ESC + W + (00) |
| SUBSCRIPT ON | ESC D | N/A | ESC + S + (01) |
| SUBSCRIPT OFF | ESC E | N/A | ESC + T |
| SUPERSCRIPT ON | ESC F | N/A | ESC + S + (00) |
| SUPERSCRIPT OFF | ESC E | N/A | ESC + T |
| UNDERLINE ON | ESC U | N/A | ESC + − + (01) |
| UNDERLINE OFF | ESC V | N/A | ESC + − + (00) |
| EXPANDED PRINT-ONE LINE ONLY | N/A | N/A | N/A |
| EMPHASIZED ON | N/A | N/A | ESC + E |
| EMPHASIZED OFF | N/A | N/A | ESC + F |
| DOUBLESTRIKE ON | N/A | N/A | ESC + G |
| DOUBLESTRIKE OFF | N/A | N/A | ESC + H |
| RESET | SI | N/A | ESC + |

Notes: (a) N/A indicates not available. In some cases special fonts or upgrades can be used for these capabilities. (b) From a BASIC program, the CHAR$ function should be used to generate these escape sequences [e.g., CHAR$(14) should be used for the SO sequence]. (c) LETTER QUALITY on dot matrix printers refers to near-letter quality or correspondence-quality print. (d) Consult the ASCII chart in Appendix A for decimal equivalents to these sequences.

| Feature | Printek 920 | Printronix MVP 150B | Star Gemini 10 |
|---|---|---|---|
| 10 CHARACTERS/INCH | ESC [1w | DC2 | DC2 |
| 12 CHARACTERS/INCH | ESC [2w | ESC V | ESC B2 |
| 17 CHARACTERS/INCH | ESC [4w | SI | SI |
| ITALICS ON | N/A | N/A | ESC 4 |
| ITALICS OFF | N/A | N/A | ESC 5 |
| 6 LINES/INCH | ESC [1x | ESC 2 | ESC 2 |
| 8 LINES/INCH | ESC [2x | ESC 0 | ESC 0 |
| 10 LINES/INCH | N/A | ESC 1 | ESC 1 |
| 12 LINES/INCH | ESC [4x | N/A | N/A |
| LETTER QUALITY | N/A | ESC P | N/A |
| DP QUALITY | N/A | ESC R | N/A |
| DRAFT QUALITY | N/A | N/A | N/A |
| EXPANDED PRINT ON | SO | SO | ESC W1 |
| EXPANDED PRINT OFF | SI | DC4 | ESC W0 |
| SUBSCRIPT ON | ESC [3x | N/A | ESC S1 |
| SUBSCRIPT OFF | ESC [1x | N/A | ESC T |
| SUPERSCRIPT ON | ESC [3x | N/A | ESC SO |
| SUPERSCRIPT OFF | ESC [1x | N/A | ESC T |
| UNDERLINE ON | ESC [4m | ESC-1 | ESC-1 |
| UNDERLINE OFF | ESC [m | ESC-0 | ESC-0 |
| EXPANDED PRINT-ONE LINE ONLY | N/A | N/A | SO |
| EMPHASIZED ON | N/A | ESC E | ESC E |
| EMPHASIZED OFF | N/A | ESC F | ESC F |
| DOUBLISTRIKE ON | N/A | ESC G | ESC G |
| DOUBLESTRIKE OFF | N/A | ESC H | ESC H |
| RESET | ESC c | ESC @ | ESC @ |

Notes: (a) N/A indicates not available. In some cases special fonts or upgrades can be used for these capabilities. (b) From a BASIC program, the CHAR$ function should be used to generate these escape sequences [e.g., CHAR$(14) should be used for the SO sequence]. (c) LETTER QUALITY on dot matrix printers refers to near-letter quality or correspondence-quality print. (d) Consult the ASCII chart in Appendix A for decimal equivalents to these sequences.

| Feature | Toshiba P1350 |
|---|---|
| 10 CHARACTERS/INCH | ESC E 12 |
| 12 CHARACTERS/INCH | ESC E 10 |
| 17 CHARACTERS/INCH | ESC E 07 |
| ITALICS ON | N/A |
| ITALICS OFF | N/A |
| 6 LINES/INCH | ESC L 08 |
| 8 LINES/INCH | ESC L 06 |
| 10 LINES/INCH | N/A |
| 12 LINES/INCH | ESC L 04 |
| LETTER QUALITY | ESC*2 |
| DP QUALITY | ESC*0 |
| DRAFT QUALITY | ESC*1 |
| EXPANDED PRINT ON | ESC ! |
| EXPANDED PRINT OFF | ESC " |
| SUBSCRIPT ON | ESC U |
| SUBSCRIPT OFF | ESC D |
| SUPERSCRIPT ON | ESC D |
| SUPERSCRIPT OFF | ESC U |
| UNDERLINE ON | ESC I |
| UNDERLINE OFF | ESC J |
| EXPANDED PRINT-ONE LINE ONLY | N/A |
| EMPHASIZED ON | N/A |
| EMPHASIZED OFF | N/A |
| DOUBLESTRIKE ON | N/A |
| DOUBLESTRIKE OFF | N/A |
| RESET | ESC SUB I |

Notes: (a) N/A indicates not available. In some cases special fonts or upgrades can be used for these capabilities. (b) From a BASIC program, the CHAR$ function should be used to generate these escape sequences [e.g., CHAR$(14) should be used for the SO sequence]. (c) LETTER QUALITY on dot matrix printers refers to near-letter quality or correspondence-quality print. (d) Consult the ASCII chart in Appendix A for decimal equivalents to these sequences.

**Escape Sequences for Controlling Popular Printers**

| Feature | AT&T 455/457/458 | AT&T 470/475 | AT&T 473 |
|---|---|---|---|
| CPI:10 | N/A | ESC N | DC2 |
| CPI:12 | N/A | ESC E | N/A |
| CPI:17 | N/A | ESC Q | SI |
| ITALICS:ON | N/A | N/A | N/A |
| ITALIC:OFF | N/A | N/A | N/A |
| LPI:6 | ESC L 08 | ESC A | ESC 2 |
| LPI:8 | ESC L 06 | ESC B | ESC 0 |
| LPI:10 | ESC L 04 | ESC T 14 | ESC 1 |
| LPI:12 | N/A | ESC T 11 | ESC 3 11 |
| CORR:QLTY | N/A (STD) | N/A (ST) | N/A |
| DP:QLTY | N/A | N/A | N/A |
| DRAFT:QLTY | N/A | N/A | N/A |
| EXPAND:ON | N/A | SO H | ESC W0 |
| EXPAND:OFF | N/A | SI H | ESC W1 |
| SUBSCR:ON | ESC U | N/A | ESC S1 |
| SUBSCR:OFF | ESC D | N/A | ESC T |
| SUPSCR:ON | ESC D | N/A | ESC S0 |
| SUPSCR:OFF | ESC U | N/A | ESC T |
| UNDLNE:ON | ESC I | ESC X | ESC_0 |
| UNDLNE:OFF | ESC J | ESC Y | ESC_1 |
| EXP:1LN | N/A | N/A | SO |
| EMPH:ON | ESC Q | ESC I | ESC E |
| EMPH:OFF | ESC R | ESC '' | ESC F |
| DBL:STRK | ESC K 2 | N/A | ESC G |
| DSTRK:OF | ESC M | N/A | ESC H |
| NORMAL | | ESC c 1 | N/A |

N/A INDICATES NOT AVAILABLE

# D

## DOS / UNIX
## command comparison

The following represents a summary of prominent DOS commands and their UNIX counterparts. For examples of their use, consult Chapters 7 and 8.

| DOS | UNIX | Action |
|-----|------|--------|
| CD | pwd | Displays current directory |
| CD \ | cd / | Moves to root directory |
| CD .. | cd .. | Moves up one level in the hierarchy |
| CD path | cd path | Changes current directory |
| CHKDSK | du | Calculates disk usage |
| COMP | cmp | Compares files for equality and lists first location of difference |
| Control Num Lock any key | Control s<br>Control q | Hold/stop<br>Continue |
| Control Break/C | Delete key | Interrupts current operation |
| COPY | cp | Copies files |
| COPY FILE + FILE | >> | Appends file to existing file |
| DATE | date | Date is displayed |
| DEL or ERASE | rm | Deletes a file |
| DIR | ls -l | Lists directory entires |
| ESC key | @ | Kills a line |
| FC | diff | Displays differences between files |
| FIND | grep | Displays all lines matching a pattern |
| MD or MKDIR | mkdir | Creates a directory |
| MORE | pg | Displays a single page at a time |
| PRINT | lp | Outputs data on system printer |
| PROMPT | shell in chapter 8 | Changes operating system prompt |
| RD or RMDIR | rmdir | Removes a directory |
| REN | mv | Renames a file |
| SORT | sort | Sorts data |
| TIME | date | Time is displayed |
| TREE | shell in chapter 8 | Lists structure of directories |
| TYPE | cat | Lists contents of filename |
| > | > | Redirect output |
| < | < | Redirect input |
| ¦ | I | Pipe symbol |

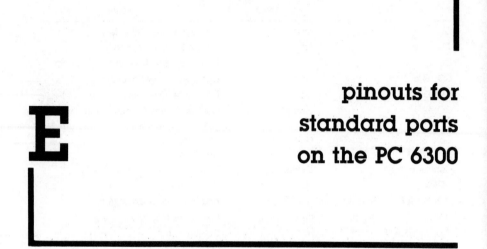

# E

## pinouts for standard ports on the PC 6300

This displays the back of the PC 6300 system unit. This is given as a reference for the location of all parts listed in this appendix.

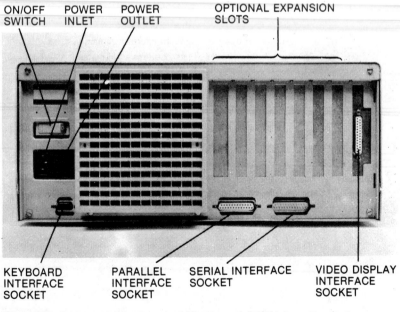

ON/OFF SWITCH    POWER INLET    POWER OUTLET      OPTIONAL EXPANSION SLOTS

KEYBOARD INTERFACE SOCKET     PARALLEL INTERFACE SOCKET    SERIAL INTERFACE SOCKET     VIDEO DISPLAY INTERFACE SOCKET

**Figure E-1** *System module rear panel* (Courtesy of AT&T Information Systems, Inc.)

**Serial Port Pinouts**

| Pin No. | Signal | Cct | I/O | Description |
|---------|--------|-----|-----|-------------|
| 1 | PRGND | AA | — | Protective Ground—Connected to basic module frame. |
| 2 | T×D | BA | O | Transmitted Data, to DCE—Generated by data terminal equipment and transferred to local modem or data set for transmission over the communication channel to the remote data terminal equipment. |
| 3 | R×D | BB | I | Received Data, from DCE—Generated by local modem or data set in response to data signals received over the communication channel from remote data teminal equipment. |
| 4 | RTS | CA | O | Request to Send, to DCE—Used to condition the local modem or data set for data transmission. |
| 5 | CTS | CB | I | Clear to Send, from DCE—Used to indicate whether or not the modem or data set is ready to transmit data. |
| 6 | DSR | CC | I | Data Set Ready, from DCE—Used to indicate the status of the local modem or data set. |
| 7 | GND | AB | — | Signal Ground/Common Return—Common ground reference for interchange circuits, except Protective Ground. |
| 8 | DCD | CF | I | Receive Line Signal Detect (Data Carrier Detected), from DCE—Used to indicate that the data carrier has been detected by the modem or data set. |
| 20 | DTR | CD | O | Data Terminal Ready, to DCE—Used to control the switching of modem or data set to the communication channel. |
| 22 | RI | CdE | I | Ring Indicator, from DCE—Indicates that a ringing signal is being received on the communication channel. |

**Parallel Port Pinouts**

| Pin Nos. | Signal | I/O | Description |
|---|---|---|---|
| 1 | -STROBE | I/O | Strobe—A low-level pulse used to transfer character data from the interface to the printer. |
| 2–9 | PTD0 to PTD7 | I/O | Data lines—Used to carry the character data from the interface to the printer. |
| 10 | -ACK | I | Acknowledge—A low level indicates that the current data has been accepted by the printer and the printer is ready to receive new data. |
| 11 | BUSY | I | Busy—A high level indicates that the printer cannot accept new data. |
| 12 | PE | I | Paper End—A high level indicates that the printer is out of paper. |
| 13 | SLCTI | I | Select—Indicates that the printer is in the selected condition. |
| 14 | -AUTOFDX | I/O | Auto Feed—A low level instructs the printer to feed one line of paper after printing. |
| 15 | -ERROR | I | Error—A low level indicates that the printer is in the error condition. |
| 16 | -INT | I/O | Initialize Printer—A low-level pulse that resets the printer to its initial state and clears the printer buffer. |
| 17 | -SLCTIN | I/O | Select Input—A low level enables the printer to accept new data. |
| 18–25 | GND | — | Ground—On eight contacts. |

**Keyboard Interface Pinouts**

| Pin | TTL Signals | Signal Level |
|---|---|---|
| 1 | Keyboard Data | +5 V dc |
| 2 | Keyboard Clock | +5 V dc |
| 3 | Ground | 0 |
| 4 | Ground | 0 |
| 5 | +12 Volts | +12 V dc |

**Mouse Interface Pinouts Found on the Back of the Keyboard**

| Pin | Function | Pin | Function |
|---|---|---|---|
| Pin 1 | +5 V | Pin 6 | GND |
| Pin 2 | Ya | Pin 7 | Middle Switch |
| Pin 3 | Yb | Pin 8 | Right Switch |
| Pin 4 | Xa | Pin 9 | Left Switch |
| Pin 5 | Xb | | |

# F

# pinouts for ports on the UNIX PC

## UNIX PC PINOUTS

This appendix contains the actual pin assignments for the UNIX PC's RS232 Serial and Centronics Parallel ports.

**RS232 Signals**

| Pin | Name | Direction |
|-----|------|-----------|
| 1 | Ground | Bidirectional |
| 2 | Transmit Data | Output |
| 3 | Receive Data | Input |
| 4 | Request to send | Output |
| 5 | Clear to send | Input |
| 6 | Data set ready | Input |
| 7 | Ground | Bidirectional |
| 8 | Carrier detect | Input |
| 15 | Transmit clock | Input |
| 17 | Receive clock | Input |
| 20 | Data teminal ready | Output |
| 22 | Ring indicator | Input |
| 24 | DTE transmit clock | Output |

**UNIX PC to Terminal Cable Connections**

---

**UNIX PC**

**Terminal**

---

| 1 | ------------------------------------------------------------------------ | 1 |
| 2 | ------------------------------------------------------------------ > | 3 |
| 3 | < ---------------------------------------------------------------- | 2 |
| 4 | ------------------------------------------------------------------------ | 4 |
| 5 | < ------------------------------------------------------------ > | 5 |
| 6 | < ------------------------------------------------------------ > | 6 |
| 7 | ------------------------------------------------------------------------ | 7 |
| 8 | ------------------------------------------------------------------------ | 20 |
| 20 | ------------------------------------------------------------------------ | 8 |

---

**UNIX PC**

**Printer**

| 1 | ------------------------------------------------------------------------ | 1 |
| 2 | ------------------------------------------------------------------ > | 3 |
| 3 | < ---------------------------------------------------------------- | 2 |
| 4 | ------------------------------------------------------------------------ | 4 |
| 5 | < ---------------------------------------------------------------- | 5 |
| 6 | < ------------------------------------------------------------ > | 6 |
| 8 | < ------------------------------------------------------------ > | 8 |
| 20 | ------------------------------------------------------------------------ | 20 |

---

These are for reference only. Each printer and terminal may have unique cabling requirements. Consult "RS-232 Made Easy" by Martin D. Seyer for exact cables.

**The Parallel Interface**

| Signal Pin | Return Pin[1] | Signal | Direction[2] |
|---|---|---|---|
| 1 | 19 | STROBE | OUT |
| 2 | 20 | DATA 1 | OUT |
| 3 | 21 | DATA 2 | OUT |
| 4 | 22 | DATA 3 | OUT |
| 5 | 23 | DATA 4 | OUT |
| 6 | 24 | DATA 5 | OUT |
| 7 | 25 | DATA 6 | OUT |
| 8 | 26 | DATA 7 | OUT |
| 9 | 27 | DATA 8 | OUT |
| 10 | 28 | ACKNLG | IN |
| 11 | 29 | BUSY | IN |
| 12 | 30 | PE | IN |
| 13 | -- | LP SELECT | -- |
| 14 | -- | AUTO FEED XT | -- |
| 15 | -- | NC | -- |
| 16 | -- | OV | -- |
| 17 | -- | CHASSIS GND | -- |
| 18 | -- | NC | -- |
| 19–30 | -- | GND | -- |
| 31 | -- | INIT | OUT |
| 32 | -- | ERROR | IN |
| 33 | -- | GND | -- |
| 34 | -- | NC | -- |
| 35 | -- | -- | -- |
| 38 | -- | SLCT IN | OUT |

[1]Ground lead
[2]Indicates direction relative to UNIX PC

# G

# pinouts for ports on the 3B2 super micro

**Specifications - Serial**

| 8-Pin<br>Modular<br>Jack or Plug | 25-Pin<br>RS-232-C Jack or Plug<br>Printer or Terminal | 25-Pin<br>RS-232-C PLug<br>Automatic Dial Modem |
|---|---|---|
| 1 Prot Grd | 1 Frame ground | 1 Frame ground |
| 2 Reserved | 4 Reserved | 5 Reserved |
| 3 TXD0 | 2 Transmit data | 2 Transmit data |
| 4 DTR0 | 20 Data terminal ready | 20 Data terminal ready |
| 5 RXD0 | 3 Receive data | 3 Receive data |
| 6 DCD0 | 8 Data carrier detect | 8 Data carrier detect |
| 7 Sig Grd | 7 Signal ground | 7 Signal ground |
| 8 Reserved | 5 Reserved | 4 Reserved |

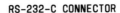

RS-232-C CONNECTOR

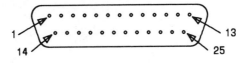

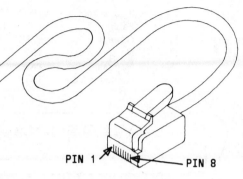

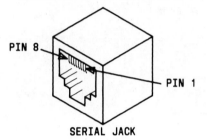

PLUG WHICH GOES
INTO SERIAL PORT

SERIAL JACK

**Specifications - Parallel**

| Pin | Description | Designation |
|-----|-------------|-------------|
| 1 | Data strobe | PRSTB0 |
| 2 | Data bit 1 | PRPA01 |
| 3 | Data bit 2 | PRPA02 |
| 4 | Data bit 3 | PRPA03 |
| 5 | Data bit 4 | PRPA04 |
| 6 | Data bit 5 | PRPA05 |
| 7 | Data bit 6 | PRPA06 |
| 8 | Data bit 7 | PRPA07 |
| 9 | Data bit 8 | PRPA08 |
| 10 | No connection | NC |
| 11 | Busy | PRBUSY1 |
| 12 | Printer Error | PRPE1 |
| 13 | Select | PRSEL1 |
| 14 | $\pm 0$ volts | GRD |
| 15 | No connection | NC |
| 16 | Ground | GRD |
| 17 | Frame ground | Frame ground |
| 18 | No connection | NC |
| 19–29 | Ground | GRD |
| 30 | Ground | GRD |

| 31 | Input prime   | PRREST0 |
|----|---------------|---------|
| 32 | Fault         | PRFALT0 |
| 33 | Ground        | GRD     |
| 34 | No connection | NC      |
| 35 | No connection | NC      |
| 36 | No connection | NC      |

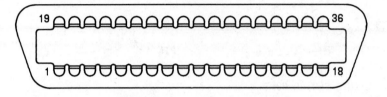

Pinouts for Parallel Ports

# H

## editor command comparison (EDLIN, ED, VI)

The following table can be used for referencing commands available to perform a particular edit function. This table by no means covers all the options of each command nor every command available. This appendix is intended to serve as an aid to the DOS user who may already be familiar with EDLIN.

| Action | EDLIN | ED | VI |
|---|---|---|---|
| Edits line no. | <line> | <line> | arrow keys |
| Append | A | a | a |
| Copy | C | (#, #) t # | :#, #co# |
| Delete | D | d | #dd |
| Ends editing | E | wq | :wq |
| Insert | I | i | i |
| End insert mode | <ctrl-Z> | . | <esc> |
| List text | L | 1, $n | arrow keys |
| Move text | M | (#, #) m# | :#, #m# |
| Pages text one page | P | | <ctrl-f> |
| Quit without save | Q | q | :!q |
| Replace | R | g | r |
| Searches | S | s | /string |
| Transfer (read in) a file | T | r | :r |

Note: The # designates line numbers that an action is to be performed on. For example, move lines X through Y and place after Z.

# I

## centronics parallel
## interface standard

| Signal Name | Pin(s) | Source | Category | Description |
|---|---|---|---|---|
| Data strobe | 1, 19 | IBM | Timing | A 1-microsecond pulse used to clock data from the IBM to the printer. |
| Data 1 | 2, 20 | IBM | Data | Each one of these leads provides for a single bit of a data character. A |
| Data 2 | 3, 21 | IBM | Data | high represents a 1; a low represents a 0. |
| Data 3 | 4, 22 | IBM | Data | |
| Data 4 | 5, 23 | IBM | Data | |
| Data 5 | 6, 24 | IBM | Data | |
| Data 6 | 7, 25 | IBM | Data | |
| Data 7 | 8, 26 | IBM | Data | |
| Data 8 | 9, 27 | IBM | Data | |
| Acknowledge | 10, 28 | Ptr | Control | This pulse indicates either the reception of a character or the end of a functional operation. |
| Busy | 11, 29 | Ptr | Control | A signal level indicating that the printer cannot receive any more data. This is caused by a paper-out or other fault condition. Consult the manual for a list of the conditions affecting this control lead. |
| PE | 12 | Ptr | Control | A control lead indicating that the printer is out of paper. |
| Select | 13 | Ptr | Control | A control lead indicating that the printer is selected by the IBM. |
| 0 volts | 14 | Ptr | Ground | A signal ground reference for other signals. |
| OSCXT | 15 | Ptr | — | A 100/200-kHz signal, varying among printers. |
| 0 volts | 16 | N/A | Ground | A signal ground reference. |
| Chassis ground | 17 | Ptr | Ground | A frame ground for electrical protection. |
| + 5 volts | 18 | Ptr | — | Positive voltage. |
| Input prime | 31, 30 | IBM | Control | A signal that clears the printer buffer and reinitializes the control logic. |
| Fault | 32 | Ptr | Control | A signal that indicates a printer fault condition. |

**Notes:** (a) The second pin number indicates the twisted-pair return or signal reference lead. The IBM interface uses pins 18 to 25 on the DB25 connector for this purpose. See the following table for crossovers between the two types of connectors. (b) Pins 1, 10, 31, and 32 are active or on when they are low. All others are high to indicate an on condition.

### Typical Pin Crossovers between the PC and the Centronics Parallel Connectors

| IBM DB25S | | Amphenol |
|---|---|---|
| 1 | ←——————→ | 1 |
| 2 | ←——————→ | 2 |
| 3 | ←——————→ | 3 |
| 4 | ←——————→ | 4 |
| 5 | ←——————→ | 5 |
| 6 | ←——————→ | 6 |
| 7 | ←——————→ | 7 |
| 8 | ←——————→ | 8 |
| 9 | ←——————→ | 9 |
| 10 | ←——————→ | 10 |
| 11 | ←——————→ | 11 |
| 12 | ←——————→ | 12 |
| 13 | ←——————→ | 13 |
| 14 | ←——————→ | 14 |
| 15 | ←——————→ | 32 |
| 16 | ←——————→ | 31 |
| 17 | ←——————→ | 36 |
| 18 | ←——————→ | 33 |
| 19 | ←——————→ | 19 |
| 20 | ←——————→ | 21 |
| 21 | ←——————→ | 23 |
| 22 | ←——————→ | 25 |
| 23 | ←——————→ | 27 |
| 24 | ←——————→ | 29 |
| 25 | ←——————→ | 30 |

# J

## RS-232 circuit summary with CCITT equivalents

Figure J-1 is a summary of the RS-232 interface pin assignments. For ease of reference, each signal is grouped into one of the categories of ground, data, control, or timing. For explanations of each, refer to the text. Both the EIA and CCITT nomenclatures are given for cross-reference between the U.S. and international versions of the standard.

| Pin | Interchange Circuit | CCITT Equivalent | Description | Gnd | Data | | Control | | Timing | |
|---|---|---|---|---|---|---|---|---|---|---|
| | | | | | From DCE | To DCE | From DCE | To DCE | From DCE | To DCE |
| 1 | AA | 101 | Protective ground | X | | | | | | |
| 7 | AB | 102 | Signal ground/common return | X | | | | | | |
| 2 | BA | 103 | Transmitted data | | | X | | | | |
| 3 | BB | 104 | Received data | | X | | | | | |
| 4 | CA | 105 | Request to send | | | | | X | | |
| 5 | CB | 106 | Clear to send | | | | X | | | |
| 6 | CC | 107 | Data set ready | | | | X | | | |
| 20 | CD | 108.2 | Data terminal ready | | | | | X | | |
| 22 | CE | 125 | Ring indicator | | | | X | | | |
| 8 | CF | 109 | Received line signal detector | | | | X | | | |
| 21 | CG | 110 | Signal quality detector | | | | X | | | |
| 23 | CH | 111 | Data signal rate selector (DTE) | | | | | X | | |
| 23 | CI | 112 | Data signal rate selector (DCE) | | | | X | | | |
| 24 | DA | 113 | Transmitter signal element timing (DTE) | | | | | | | X |
| 15 | DB | 114 | Transmitter signal element timing (DCE) | | | | | | X | |
| 17 | DD | 115 | Receiver signal element timing (DCE) | | | | | | X | |
| 14 | SBA | 118 | Secondary transmitted data | | | X | | | | |
| 16 | SBB | 119 | Secondary received data | | X | | | | | |
| 19 | SCA | 120 | Secondary request to send | | | | | X | | |
| 13 | SCB | 121 | Secondary clear to send | | | | X | | | |
| 12 | SCF | 122 | Secondary received line signal detector | | | | X | | | |

Figure J-1   **RS-232 Circuit Summary with CCITT Equivalents**

# K

## AT&T PC 6300 PLUS

Courtesy of AT&T Information Systems Inc.

The AT&T PC 6300 PLUS is a dual purpose computer, having the capability to run MS DOS and UNIX System V concurrently. The PC 6300 PLUS can be configured as a system with concurrent MS DOS and UNIX System V, a pure UNIX System V computer or a pure super MS DOS computer. This computer includes a unique feature called **OS Merge.** The OS MERGE function allows MS DOS to run as a task under UNIX System V and provides the ability to switch between MS DOS and UNIX System V at the touch of a single key.

The AT&T PC 6300 PLUS can support 3 active users running under the UNIX operating system while MS DOS is accessible only from the main keyboard in a single user mode.

## MICROPROCESSOR

Like the IBM PC AT and most AT compatibles, the 6300 PLUS uses the Intel 80286 chip. This chip runs at 6 MHZ in the 6300 Plus and provides both the horsepower to run a multi-user/multitasking operating system, such as the UNIX system, while maintaining the ability to run existing MS DOS software. The 6300 PLUS runs the latest version of MS DOS called version 3.1.

## MEMORY

The 6300 PLUS comes standard with 512K bytes of memory on the motherboard and can be upgraded to provide 1MB of memory with the addition of the memory upgrade kit. More memory can be added using plug-in memory cards. These memory cards provide up to 2MB of memory in 512K increments and the system can support up to three of these cards for a total memory capacity of 7MB. All memory utilizes 256K chips.

The memory limitation of MS DOS 3.1 is 640K bytes while the UNIX system can utilize memory in the 16MB range. The memory beyond 640K is usable by some DOS applications that support the LOTUS/INTEL Expanded Memory Specification (EMS) also known as the LOTUS/INTEL Above Board Specification. The memory of the PC 6300 PLUS supports both *real mode* (contiguous) used by standard MS DOS applications and *paged mode* (non-contiguous) used by LOTUS/INTEL EMS applications.

The memory scheme used in the 6300 Plus is called **no wait state** memory. In layman's terms this means that the cpu does not have to wait one cpu cycle for the memory to respond to a request. This scheme is different than the IBM PC AT which requires ''one wait state'' for a memory request. It should be noted however, that when accessing memory provided by plug-in slots the 6300 PLUS will incur one wait state.

What does all this mean to the user? **Speed** !! In early benchmarks utilizing MS DOS applications such as LOTUS 1-2-3, WORDSTAR, MICROSOFT WORD and DBASE II the PC 6300 PLUS ran about 25% faster than the IBM PC AT in a DOS only mode and 15% faster in an UNIX + DOS merged mode.

### Math Co-processor

The PC 6300 PLUS has a socket that will support an 80287 math co-processor that can greatly enhance floating point operations. Most graphics and statistical packages will take advantage of this chip if it is installed.

### Bus Expansion Slots

The PC 6300 is very much like the AT&T PC 6300 in that the same bus architecture is employed. The 6300 PLUS provides seven plug-in slots (one of which is taken up by the hard disk controller if you have the hard disk model). Just like the 6300 the 6300 PLUS has three slots that can use AT&T's 16 bit boards.

### Bus Compatibility

The PC 6300 PLUS eight bit bus is compatible with most IBM PC/XT boards and thus is compatible with any eight bit boards that currently work with the PC 6300, IBM PC/XT, and IBM PC clones. The PC 6300 PLUS 16 bit bus is compatible with the PC 6300's 16 bit bus and therefore any 16 bit boards that work in the PC 6300 will work in the PC 6300 PLUS. This 16 bit bus however, is *not* compatible with the IBM AT's 16 bit bus. How do you determine what is an eight bit board versus a 16 bit board? All eight bit boards have a single connector that mates with a single socket on the bus while 16 bit boards have two connectors that mate with two sockets on the bus. Along with some electrical differences it is the position of the sockets on the motherboard that present the biggest physical differences between IBM PC AT's 16 bit bus and the PC 6300 PLUS 16 bit bus.

### Floppy Disks

The PC 6300 PLUS can be equipped with either a single or a dual 5.25 inch floppy disk drive. Like the AT and it's clones the disks are available in either 360 KB (48 TPI) or 1.2MB (96 TPI) capacities. The 1.2MB drives provide higher density and will take less diskettes to backup a system. On the other hand the 360 KB drives provide a higher degree of compatibility with existing IBM PC's and look-alikes.

### Hard Disk

The PC 6300 PLUS can be equipped with a single internal 20 MB half-height hard disk. The hard disk is a requirement for any system that will run the UNIX system and is advisable in many MS DOS situations where high performance is desired.

### Keyboard and Mouse

The 6300 PLUS can use the same keyboard (model 301) as the PC 6300 or can use a new keyboard called the model 302 keyboard. The model 302 keyboard is slightly different than the standard PC keyboard in that the function keys are layed out across the top of the keyboard rather than the left side. In addition the model 302 keyboard includes an additional key designated as **MSG WNDW.** This is the key that allows the user to switch between MS DOS and UNIX. The standard keyboard uses the CTRL-ALT-BACKSPACE key sequence to perform the same function.

The model 302 keyboard is modeled after the IBM Selectric Typewriter keyboard and may be preferred by some touch typists used to this layout. Many MS DOS users may be very familiar with the standard PC keyboard layout and could find the location of the function keys difficult to adapt to.

Either keyboard uses the PC 6300 compatible two-button mouse that plugs in to a socket provided in the keyboard.

### Monitor and Graphics

The PC 6300 PLUS uses the same monitor as the PC 6300 and comes standard with high resolution capability (640 X 400). The optional color monitor is also the same one that is used with the 6300.

### Serial/Parallel Ports

The PC 6300 PLUS comes standard with both a serial and IBM Parallel port built in.

### Multi-User Ports

One of the benefits of the UNIX System is it's ability to support more than one concurrent user. To add more users to the 6300 PLUS you can install the optional ports board. This board provides four RS232 ports. The official number of supported active busy users is three while less busy user support is five users. This limitation is based on overall response time rather than a limitation imposed by either system hardware or software. The application environment typically will dictate the *actual* number of supported users.

## OS MERGE

OS MERGE is a term that is used to describe the technology that is used in the PC 6300 PLUS to allow MS DOS to run as task under UNIX System V. Developed by AT&T Information System Laboratories, the technology includes proprietary VLSI (very large scale integrated circuitry) chips on the motherboard and software installed at boot time. The design criteria called for the system to provide operating system concurrency while maintaining a very high degree of compatibility with existing IBM PC software.

The 6300 PLUS will in fact run LOTUS 1-2-3 including the graphics, FLIGHT SIMULATOR and most other MS DOS software. What OS MERGE provides is the ability to run LOTUS 1-2-3, for example and to switch to UNIX System V without suspending the MS DOS application.

OS MERGE is clearly a technological breakthrough when you consider the following: If you were running XENIX on an IBM AT and you had multiple users connected to your system and you wish to run an MS DOS program you would have to shut the system down and reboot MS DOS, run your application and then reboot XENIX. It should be obvious that the XENIX users are not going to tolerate this activity without complaining.

With OS MERGE you could run your MS DOS application without interfering with the other users and also flip back and forth between MS DOS and UNIX System V.

Because OS MERGE is unique AT&T Information Systems Laboratories has applied for a patent for the OS MERGE technology used in the PC 6300 PLUS.

In addition to providing the ability to support MS DOS as a task under UNIX System V OS MERGE also allows DOS and UNIX files to share the same directories. OS MERGE will respond to either MS DOS commands or UNIX commands. For example to list files on a UNIX system you would type *ls -l* on a DOS system you would type *DIR* with OS MERGE installed you could type either command and it would be executed. MS DOS applications can be invoked directly from the UNIX system and will cause DOS to start up and the program executed. This is just one example many other commands can be accessed from the UNIX system prompt.

## INSTALLATION

To install a *pure* MS DOS PC 6300 PLUS you would follow the same steps as you would to install any other PC look-alike. The built-in RS232 becomes COM1: and the parallel port COM2:. See Chapter 4 for more information on this subject.

The more typical configuration of the PC 6300 Plus is the MS DOS plus UNIX System V configuration commonly known as the "merge" option. This provides the operating system switch capability discussed in the OS MERGE section.

You could also install the PC 6300 PLUS as a "pure" MS DOS system and later install UNIX System V to take advantage of OS MERGE. The following section assumes that you are installing both MS DOS and UNIX System V and utilizing OS MERGE.

### Installing UNIX System V

This process requires that you first bring up the system in UNIX mode then partition the hard disk, format the hard disk and load the UNIX System from floppy disks. The UNIX system plus OS MERGE comes on seven floppy disks.

By powering the system up with Disk 1 of the Foundation set in the floppy disk drive you will be allowed to partition the hard disk drive.

### Hard Disk Partitioning

Once the power up sequence has taken place you'll have some options available to partition the disk. You can either partition for d (DOS only) or u (UNIX + DOS merged). The recommendations suggest that you partition 85% of the disk for UNIX + DOS merged and 15% for MS DOS only. The reason for the 15% MS DOS only partition is that some MS DOS applications may not run under merge and should be run in DOS only mode.

After the hard disk is partitioned repartitioning the disk will erase any data on the disk requiring that you first perform a backup.

## SYSTEM ADMINISTRATION

The PC 6300 PLUS configured as UNIX + DOS merged provides a "window" like environment very similar to the AT&T UNIX PC Model 7300 for such things as installing new software, installing logins, changing passwords etc. To access the sysadmin function; login as root and at the UNIX System superuser prompt # type in sysadmin.

```
                              # sysadmin

     Administration

       -Changing Password
        Date and Time
        Disk Backup
        Disk Restore
        Floppy Disk Diagnostics
        Floppy Disk Operations
        Hardware Setup
        Mail Setup
        Printer Information
        Software Setup
        User Logins



     Highlight selection and press Return. Press F9 to exit.
                              PREV WIN NEXT WIN
        F1      F2      F3      F4      F5      F6      F7      F8
```

From this menu you can select items by either typing the first character(s) of any item or using the arrow keys to highlight the desired item. Note: if you have logged in as another user you will be denied access to sysadmin. To gain access you can either logout and log back in as root or type **su root** followed by the root password if one was installed.

The sysadmin functions allow you to setup the printer and modem as well as user logins, floppy disk operations, system backup, change system date and time, show installed software and also run diagnostics.

The sysadmin functions mirror the AT&T UNIX PC Model 7300 Office interface and with the exception of keyboard differences performs exactly the same. For a more detailed account of this interface please refer to chapter 5 The AT&T UNIX PC.

## BENEFITS - AN APPLICATIONS VIEW

The PC 6300 PLUS combines the "best of both worlds". This includes the multitude of MS DOS based software that is available at the local computer store and also the power of the UNIX system that is just now coming of age. With all the computer jargon that abounds the industry today let's not cast off this statement as sales hype without a closer look.

Consider the following scenario:

Like most MS DOS users you have your favorite spreadsheet and word processor and that you use this software on a daily basis. You arrive at your office/home and boot up LOTUS 1-2-3 bring up a large spreadsheet that contains your income tax data as you make some changes that require a recalc of your 100 X 100 cell spreadsheet you decide to send some mail to your boss in Chicago. So you press the (MSG WNDW) key and switch to UNIX while allowing your spreadsheet to continue doing it's recalc. Once in the UNIX system you invoke the mail utility and send a short message to your boss. While creating your message you become impatient and switch back to DOS to check to see that your spreadsheet is done. Finding it not done yet you switch back to UNIX and continue to send mail to your boss. Having completed the mail command you switch back to DOS and your spreadsheet. Meanwhile concurrent with your MS DOS activity the UNIX mail utility takes over and makes a call to your boss's computer and sends the mail to the remote system and also a confirmation message to you that the mail has been sent.

Is this scenario far fetched? No! We actually performed this test and others to test UNIX System V and MS DOS concurrency.

Because OS MERGE allows a level of transparency between UNIX System V and MS DOS files you can combine features of both systems. For example feed your word processing documents to the UNIX spell check utility, or the UNIX encryption utilities or even to the UNIX C compiler.

Technically this means that you can build command lines that include such things as the redirection of an MS DOS programs output into the input of a UNIX command or filter. This combination of UNIX commands and DOS commands is available to all MS DOS programs that use standard ROM BIOS system calls (most MS DOS programs). Programs that do not use standard ROM BIOS calls but rather write directly to the system hardware can still run under merge but the redirection of I/O is not possible.

## MS DOS | UNIX SYSTEM V - BRIDGING THE GAP

Starting MS DOS from the UNIX System:

The PC 6300 PLUS configured as a DOS and UNIX system with OS MERGE installed allows the user access to DOS in a couple of ways. One way is to startup DOS as a background UNIX process. This is done by typing the following:

$$\$ \text{ dos } \&$$

followed by a carriage return. The & (ampersand) char indicates that the process is to be started in the background. Once this command line is executed MS DOS will be started up and you will receive the MS DOS initial message followed by the MS DOS prompt.

$$c>$$

To switch back to UNIX you would either press the MSG WNDW key (model 302 keyboard) or CTRL-ALT-BACKSPACE (model 301 keyboard). By using this sequence you can switch back and forth between both environments.

Another way to start up DOS is to bring it up without the & (ampersand) char at the end of the command line. This will still execute MS DOS but will not allow you to switch back and forth between environments. Once you exit MS DOS by typing "exit" you will be back in the UNIX system.

Finally you could type the following at the UNIX prompt:

.    $ dos program-name

with or without the & followed by a carriage return. This would cause the MS DOS program (program-name) to be executed under MS DOS. The ampersand char & would be necessary if you wanted the capability to switch back and forth between DOS and the UNIX system. If you execute the command without the trailing & ampersand char then when you exit the MS DOS program you will be placed back in the UNIX system.

## MS DOS AND UNIX FILE DIFFERENCES

### Filenames

UNIX System V allows filenames to be up to 14 characters long and is case (upper/lower) sensitive. In addition UNIX has a list of characters known as "metacharacters" that have a special meaning to the shell. MS DOS allows filenames to be 8 characters long with a three character extension, is not case sensitive and knows nothing about the UNIX system metacharacters.

If you were to type the MS DOS dir command in a UNIX directory you would expect that filenames that do not conform to the MS DOS naming conventions would cause problems. OS MERGE resolves this problem by truncating the filename to between three and five characters and adding a unique index of one to three characters enclosed in braces at the end of the filename. This scheme allows the user to either type dir or 'ls -l' and receive output that conforms to the environment specified implied by the command type.

### Pathname Separator

The UNIX system uses the slash character / to separate pathname entries while DOS uses the backslash \ character to perform the same function. OS MERGE requires that you conform to the rules of the active environment.

### Line Ending Sequence

The UNIX system and DOS have different line ending sequences. UNIX System V uses a new line character while DOS uses a carriage return + new line character to delimit the end of a line. If you use the UNIX system to work with a text file created under DOS then you would have superfluous carriage returns in the file. The PC 6300 Plus provides two commands DOS2UNIX and UNIX2DOS to convert files to either system format.

To convert an MS DOS text file to UNIX file format you would type the following:

```
$ dos2unix oldfile newfile
```

This would create a copy of oldfile but with the correct line ending sequence to work with UNIX System V.

To convert an UNIX System V file to MS DOS format you would type:

```
$ unix2dos oldfile newfile
```

Where "newfile" would be a copy of an oldfile that is compatible with MS DOS line ending sequence.


## HELPFUL HINTS

### Commands

The UNIX system and MS DOS have some commands that have the same names. An example would be the command "type". These commands would have different meaning to either system. You can refer specifically to the MS DOS commands by using a full path name reference. All MS DOS commands exist in a UNIX directory /osm/bin. So to refer to the MS DOS type command you would type:

$ /osm/bin/type

By fully qualifying the command you are sure to execute the desired command.

## PATH Variable

The UNIX system will search the directory structure for commands according to the contents of the shell variable PATH. In order for MS DOS commands to be executed without full qualification (those that are not common to both systems such as DIR) you should modify your .profile to include /osm/bin in the path variable. The following is a sample .profile that includes this addition:

```
$ cat .profile
PS1= "UNIX > "
PATH=: /$HOME/bin: /osm/bin: /bin: /usr/bin
export PATH
```

This would cause the osm/bin directory to be searched when you issue a command. In this case once this change has been made you could type in DIR at the UNIX system prompt and receive appropriate output.

When issuing the command *dos program name* & at the UNIX system prompt it is necessary to include the extension. For example to execute a binary file called wp.exe in the directory /u/mills/word/ you would have to type:

$ dos /u/mills/word/wp.exe &

Without the .exe extension the UNIX system would not find the file to execute.

# DOS-73 system

## FEATURES

In October of 1985, AT&T announced the availability of a system that gives the owner of the UNIX PC the best of both computer worlds—UNIX operating system and MS-DOS. This product, manufactured for AT&T by Alloy Computer Products, is a board that plugs into one of the slots of the UNIX PC and gives the user another computer capable of running thousands of MS-DOS based programs. This includes programs that can be run on the AT&T PC 6300 and other IBM PC compatibles.

### DOS-73 Hardware

The hardware for the DOS-73 system consists of a board equipped with an 8 Mhz 8086 CPU and 512 KBytes of RAM. An optional 8087 Co-processor is also available. The system emulates an IBM PC with a Hercules graphics board. It also offers a choice of thin or wide fonts to improve the screen presentation of information from programs that use highlighting.

The DOS-73 system is capable of supporting the peripherals associated with the UNIX PC itself. These include the printers, built-in intelligent modem, and clock-calendar. Consult Chapter 5 for a discussion of the specific items available on the UNIX PC.

In addition to the UNIX PC peripherals, the DOS computer can support its own serial I/O port. An RS-232 compatible port is included with the DOS-73 system. This is configured as COM2 and can be used to connect a serial printer, an external modem, or any serial device that can be connected to a standard IBM PC or compatible.

## DOS-73 Software

The software includes the MS-DOS 3.1 operating system and utilities. In addition to the operating system, diagnostics and system files are included.

The UNIX PC supports the DOS-73 computer and software as a task under the standard UNIX operating system. Because of this feature, a remote user can actually access the DOS system and have full MS-DOS functionality with the exception of graphics. The reason for this is that the remote terminal will not support the same bit-mapped graphics as an IBM PC compatible would. However, this is a feature not normally experienced with a standard MS-DOS computer.

The DOS-73 system also offers very flexible disk capabilities. Because the board utilizes the standard UNIX PC disk system, both floppy and hard drives are supported. The floppy drive can be addressed as either A: or B:, while the hard disk can be referenced as C:, D:, E:, etc. The DOS-73 can format, read, and write PC-DOS compatible diskettes. Whereas, without the DOS board, the UNIX PC is only capable of reading an MS-DOS file.

The user can create up to 256 virtual disks. These virtual disks are contained within the hard disks of the UNIX PC. Up to 12 disks per user can be assigned to DOS volumes. If one of the volumes is set up as a UNIX disk, data may be exchanged between DOS and UNIX. Refer to the text for examples of why this is important.

## DOS-73 On-line Help

The UNIX PC offers the standard feature of on-line help allowing the user to easily reach for assistance anywhere in the applications. The DOS-73 system is no exception as it offers the same style of help facility. The help screens can be accessed from any DOS-73 window. A HELP Table of Contents is also available from which to choose the appropriate topic. Figure L-1 shows the window that contains the Table of Contents. The mouse, cursor keys, or keyboard may be used to access the different topics.

## Keyboard

Because of the differences between the PC compatibles and the UNIX PC keyboard, templates are provided. These are included with the User's Guide and identify the commonly used MS-DOS keys and commands, such as the print screen keys and function key mapping. In addition there is a key for accessing UNIX commands from the MS-DOS screen. If this is not enough, a help facility is provided to aid the user with the keyboard differences.

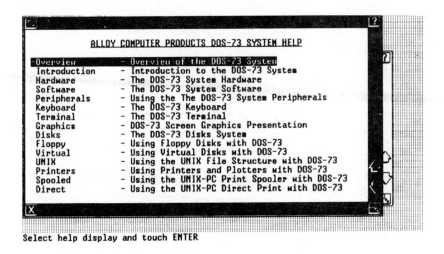

Select help display and touch ENTER

## MS-DOS Window

A feature is included with the DOS-73 system allowing the MS-DOS environment to be treated as another window in the overall UNIX PC window environment. By hitting a function key, a window border is placed automatically around the MS-DOS session. This allows the DOS screen to be sized. It can be shrunk or expanded and moved anywhere on the UNIX PC's screen. The user then can access any other window on the screen by pointing to it with the mouse. To return to the full MS-DOS session, merely hit the function key again.

## Spooled Printing

The default printer for the DOS-73 user can be set up through the User Agent as the UNIX PC parallel printer. This includes the UNIX capability of spooling print jobs. Should direct printing (non-spooled) or different printer be required, a Printer Management (PM) utility is provided.

## Modem

The UNIX PC built-in modem behaves like a Hayes Smartmodem with a COM1: address. Software used to operate with a Hayes modem should work without modification. The DOS-73 board, COM2:, can be used to connect a standalone modem.

## Mouse

The UNIX PC mouse behaves like a MS-DOS compatible Microsoft mouse. The two leftmost buttons equate to the two buttons found on a Microsoft mouse, leaving the third UNIX PC mouse button unused.

### Installation

The DOS-73 system comes complete with all hardware and software necessary to implement an MS-DOS computer inside of your UNIX computer. The user only needs to provide a phillips head screwdriver. The actual installation is documented in the User's Guide. Basically the user merely removes a faceplate on the back of the UNIX PC and inserts the board into one of the 3 expansion slots. Because the board will only go in one way, the user needn't worry about how to insert it. After insertion, the only step left is fasten the plate on the board to the UNIX PC.

## HOW TO USE

### Setting Up Disks

After the DOS-73 software is installed, a step completed totally with the mouse, the installation is complete. This installation step automatically creates a 250 KByte virtual disk containing all of the MS-DOS programs and utilities. Should the user desire to set up other disks to store applications, the Volume Management windows are used. By merely pointing to various items, the user opens a "Create Virtual Disk" window. See Figure L-2 for a sample session. The creation is as simple as naming the disk and entering how large the disk should be. Accessing the "Session Configuration" window allows the user to assign a DOS volume (D:, E:, etc.) to the created volume. Depending on the total storage available within the UNIX PC, the user can have megabytes of storage available to them.

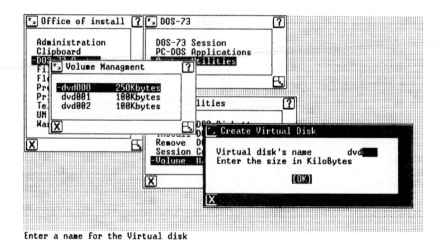

Enter a name for the Virtual disk

## Modem

Hayes Microcomputer Products' Smartcom will work with the UNIX PC built-in modem to access other computer systems. The communication software should be loaded to hard disk then executed in the same fashion as it would have been in a pure IBM PC compatible. It is important to note that the modem has an address of COM1 (not COM2).

The communication user should be aware that the features of UNIX offer advantages over the MS-DOS environment with regard to multi-tasking activities. In particular, the user can use the UNIX PC's terminal emulation capabilities to access another computer, while running LOTUS or dBASE in the MS-DOS window. This allows the MS-DOS application to remain active while the user jumps to other activities under UNIX.

A remote terminal, or PC emulating a terminal, can dial into the modem within the UNIX PC and access the MS-DOS environment. Although only one user can run the DOS-73 system at a time, many users can be logged into the UNIX operating system of the UNIX PC. This allows the local UNIX PC operator to be in the middle of a UNIX application simultaneously with a terminal in a distant city running a DOS program.

## Printers

The default print option is for the DOS-73 user to be routed to the parallel printer using the spooler. If a different printer is desired, the Printer Management (PM) utility is invoked. The format is as follows:

```
PM dev: [d/s], [baud, parity, data, stop]
```

where:

```
dev = printer device:LPT1:, LPT2:, or COM2:
d = direct mode (LPT1: and LPT2: only)
s = spooled mode (LPT1: and LPT2: only)
baud = baud rate (COM2: port only)
parity = parity (COM2: port only)
data = number of data bits (COM2: port only)
stop = number of stop bits (COM2: port only)
```

The UNIX serial printer is configured as LPT1: If the user desires to select the serial printer in a direct mode, the format of the above command is "PM LPT1:D".

The DOS-73 serial printer is configured for COM2: and is selected with the command, "PM COM2:". The default setup is 9600 bps, no parity, 8 data bits, and 1 stop bit. These values are altered with PM utility using the above syntax.

## Key Reassignment

Different keys on the UNIX PC keyboard may be reassigned for user ease. This allows the keyboard to be changed to match the user's needs. Shorthand notation for frequently used commands may be setup. For example, since the "dir" command is frequently used, a function key can be assigned this action. The sequence, "ESC [ 0;68;"dir";13p" can be entered to accomplish this. The user documentation outlines how to perform others like this.

## Benefits - An Application View

The benefit of the DOS-73 board is that of not having to give up access to thousands of MS-DOS programs. For example, LOTUS 1-2-3 is not available under UNIX at the time of publication. Because of its popularity, users may be hesitant to convert to the more powerful UNIX system. This board allows the transition to a system with expandibility without giving up the benefits associated with today's software. This feature alone may be enough justification for the dual processor machine.

As the user's sophistication increases, the demands placed on their computer increases. UNIX operating system is a full-feature system supporting multi-user and multi-tasking operations. With the addition of MS-DOS, the sophisticated user can enhance their use of a computer.

An example of the sophisticated combination of MS-DOS and UNIX system includes the case where an executive and secretary share information. The UNIX PC could be located on the executive's desk with a terminal used by the secretary. The executive could be in the middle of a LOTUS 1-2-3 spreadsheet, while the secretary was using a word processing system under UNIX, such as Crystal Writer. If the secretary needed a section of the spreadsheet to be included in the document, the executive could store information in a file that is transferred from DOS to UNIX. The secretary merely inserts the information in this file into the document being prepared. All of this is accomplished without a paper shuffle. The UNIX PC could just as easily have been located on the secretary's desk with the executive using a terminal.

A second example is that of an employee who runs a dBASE III program under MS-DOS, yet desires communications with either remote computers or remote people to occur simultaneously. Assume that a sort is initiated within dBASE III. While this is running, the user could call up the telephone directory of the UNIX PC and select a number to dial. A session could be automatically set up to retrieve mail from a remote computer or service (such as AT&T Mail). Also, a phone conversation with another individual is possible while the other activities are occurring.

If a remote user is operating a PC 6300 and desires to print a document on the laser printer attached to the UNIX PC at the office . . . no problem. The PC user would run communication software and dial into the UNIX PC. By logging into the DOS-73 system and uploading the file into the UNIX PC's disk system, the file could be printed on the laser printer. Also the user could send mail to the UNIX PC operator indicating that the information should be given to a member of the staff. The status of the job being printed could also be monitored through the standard UNIX PC capabilities.

### Bridging the DOS I UNIX Gap

The user of the UNIX and DOS-73 systems will have occasions when they desire to share information between MS-DOS and UNIX as outlined in some of the previous sections. To allow for the interchange of information between the two file systems the DOS-73 System allows for importing and exporting files. Please consult the text chapters for the differences between the two operating systems.

## HELPFUL HINTS

1. When accessing UNIX files, the filenames must contain only uppercase letters, be no longer than 8 characters with a single dot, followed by no more than 3 characters. This is the format of the MS-DOS filenames.
2. The user should enter the standard DOS backslash (\) as the pathname separator, not the UNIX slash.
3. Removal of a virtual disk is irreversible.
4. The MS-DOS commands, MD, CD, RD, and TYPE, differentiate between upper and lower case.
5. Some commands, such as EDLIN, automatically convert the filename into uppercase. If the user creates a file named, 'nathan', EDLIN would convert it to NATHAN, forcing the user to access it in caps. Issue a DIR command to list the correct filenames.